Artificial Intelligence in Forensic Science

Artificial Intelligence in Forensic Science addresses the current and emerging opportunities being utilized to apply modern Artificial Intelligence (AI) technologies to current forensic and investigation practices. The book also showcases the increasing benefits of AI where and when it can be applied to various techniques and forensic disciplines. The increasing rate of sophisticated crimes has increased the opportunity and need for the forensic field to explore a variety of emerging technologies to counter criminals—and AI is no exception. There are many current investigative challenges that, with ingenuity and application, can be helped with the application of AI, especially in the digital forensic and cyber-crime arena. The book also explains many practical studies that have been carried out to test AI technologies in crime detection, uncovering evidence, and identifying perpetrators. In the last decade, the use of AI has become common in many fields and now is an ideal time to look at the various ways AI can be integrated into judicial, forensic, and criminal cases to better collect and analyze evidence, thereby improving outcomes.

T0384840

Artificial Intelligence in Forensic Science

An Emerging Technology in Criminal Investigation Systems

Edited by
Kavita Saini, Swaroop S. Sonone,
Mahipal Singh Sankhla, and
Naveen Kumar

CRC Press
Taylor & Francis Group
Boca Raton London New York

CRC Press is an imprint of the
Taylor & Francis Group, an **informa** business

Designed cover image: © Golden Dayz, Shutterstock Images

First edition published 2024
by CRC Press
2385 NW Executive Center Drive, Suite 320, Boca Raton FL 33431

and by CRC Press
4 Park Square, Milton Park, Abingdon, Oxon, OX14 4RN

CRC Press is an imprint of Taylor & Francis Group, LLC

© 2024 selection and editorial matter, Kavita Saini, Swaroop S. Sonone, Mahipal Singh Sankhla, and Naveen Kumar; individual chapters, the contributors

Reasonable efforts have been made to publish reliable data and information, but the author and publisher cannot assume responsibility for the validity of all materials or the consequences of their use. The authors and publishers have attempted to trace the copyright holders of all material reproduced in this publication and apologize to copyright holders if permission to publish in this form has not been obtained. If any copyright material has not been acknowledged please write and let us know so we may rectify in any future reprint.

Except as permitted under U.S. Copyright Law, no part of this book may be reprinted, reproduced, transmitted, or utilized in any form by any electronic, mechanical, or other means, now known or hereafter invented, including photocopying, microfilming, and recording, or in any information storage or retrieval system, without written permission from the publishers.

For permission to photocopy or use material electronically from this work, access www. copyright.com or contact the Copyright Clearance Center, Inc. (CCC), 222 Rosewood Drive, Danvers, MA 01923, 978-750-8400. For works that are not available on CCC please contact mpkbookspermissions@tandf.co.uk

Trademark notice: Product or corporate names may be trademarks or registered trademarks and are used only for identification and explanation without intent to infringe.

ISBN: 978-1-032-26337-3 (hbk)
ISBN: 978-1-032-26336-6 (pbk)
ISBN: 978-1-003-28781-0 (ebk)

DOI: 10.4324/9781003287810

Typeset in Palatino
by KnowledgeWorks Global Ltd.

CONTENTS

v

FIGURES

FIGURES

TABLES

TABLES

CONTRIBUTORS

Palak Aneja, Doctoral Research Fellow, Rashtriya Raksha University, Gandhinagar, Gujarat, India

Ankita, PhD Scholar, Department of Anthropology, Panjab University, Chandigarh, India

Vinay Aseri, Department of Forensic Science, Vivekananda Global University, Jaipur, Rajasthan, India

Kumud Kant Awasthi, Department of Life Sciences, Vivekananda Global University, Jaipur, Rajasthan, India

Sumit Kumar Choudhary, Sr. Assistant Professor, Rashtriya Raksha University, Gujarat, India

Surya Shekhar Daga, Department of Forensic Science, Vivekananda Global University, Jaipur, Rajasthan, India

Priyanshi Garg, Department of Biochemistry and Forensic Science, Gujarat University, Ahmedabad, India

Neha Gupta, Assistant Professor, Guru Ghasidas University, Bilaspur, Chhattisgarh, 495009, India

Mohammed Irfan, Department of Forensic Dentistry, Federal University of Pelotas, Brazil

Divyansh Jain, Department of Forensic Science, Vivekananda Global University, Jaipur, Rajasthan, India

Abraham Johnson, School of Medico-Legal Studies, National Forensic Sciences University, Gujarat, India

Ananta Joshi, Department of Forensic Science, School of Life Science, Christ Deemed-to-be University, Bangalore, Karnataka

Navjot Kaur, PhD Scholar, Department of Forensic Science, University Institute of Allied Health Sciences, Chandigarh University, Punjab, India

Rajesh Kumar, Assistant Director, DNA Division, State Forensic Science Laboratory, Rajasthan, Jaipur 302016, India

Poonam Kumari, Department of Forensic Science, Vivekananda Global University, Jaipur, Rajasthan, India

Sneha Lohar, Department of Forensic Science, Vivekananda Global University, Jaipur, Rajasthan, India

Dipak Kumar Mahida, Department of Biochemistry and Forensic Science, Gujarat University, Ahmedabad, Gujarat, India

Surbhi Mathur, Sr. Assistant Professor, National Forensic Sciences University, Gandhinagar, Gandhinagar, Gujarat, India

Badal Mavry, Department of Forensic Science, Vivekananda Global University, Jaipur, Rajasthan, India

Vernika Mehta, Doctoral Research Fellow, National Forensic Sciences University, Gandhinagar, Gujarat, India

Muskan, PhD Scholar, Department of Forensic Science, School of Bio-engineering and Bio-sciences, Lovely Professional University, Punjab, India

Varad Nagar, Department of Forensic Science, Vivekananda Global University, Jaipur, Rajasthan, India

Arpit Nirvan, Department of Computer Science and Engineering, I.T.S Engineering College, Greater Noida, Uttar Pradesh, India

Kapil Parihar, Department of Forensic Science, Vivekananda Global University, Jaipur, Rajasthan, India

Abhishek R. Rai, Department of Forensic Science, Vivekananda Global University, Jaipur, Rajasthan, India

Sukanya Sachdeva, Division of Pesticides, ICMR- National Institute of Occupational Health, Ahmedabad, India

Kavita Saini, Professor and Division Chair (DIP), School of Computing Science & Engineering (SCSE), Galgotias University, Delhi NCR, India

Shubham Saini, PhD Scholar, Department of Forensic Science, School of Bio-engineering and Bio-sciences, Lovely Professional University, Punjab, India

Mahipal Singh Sankhla, Department of Forensic Science, University Center for Research and Development (UCRD), Chandigarh University, Mohali, Punjab, India

Anuj Sharma, Department of Forensic Science, Vivekananda Global University, Jaipur, Rajasthan, India

Navneet Sharma, IMS Engineering College, Dr. APJ Abdul Kalam Technical University, Ghaziabad, India

Parvesh Sharma, Faculty, Department of Biochemistry & Forensic Science, Gujarat University, Gandhinagar, Gujarat, India

Vaibhav Sharma, Department of Forensic Science, Vivekananda Global University, Jaipur, Rajasthan, India

Saurabh Shukla, Assistant Professor, Department of Forensic Science, School of Bio-engineering and Bio-Sciences, Lovely Professional University, Punjab, India

Anubhav Singh, School of Forensic Science and Risk Management, Rashtriya Raksha University, Gujarat

Apoorva Singh, Department of Forensic Science, Vivekananda Global University, Jaipur, Rajasthan, India

Gaurav Kumar Singh, Department of Forensic Science, University Institute of Allied Health Sciences, Chandigarh University, Punjab, India

Perumal Sivaperumal, Department of Textile and Fibre Engineering, Indian Institute of Technology, New Delhi, India

Kalpesh Solanki, Assistant Professor, Rashtriya Raksha University, Gujarat, India

Swaroop S. Sonone, School of Forensic Sciences, JSPM University Pune, Maharashtra, India

Krittika Sood, Research Assistant, National Forensic Sciences University, Gandhinagar, Gandhinagar, Gujarat, India

Kunwar Veer Vikram Srivastav, Forensic Scientific Assistant, DNA Division, State Forensic Science Laboratory, Rajasthan, Jaipur 302016, India

Chandra Shekhar Yadav, School of Forensic Sciences, National Forensic Science, Gandhinagar, Gujrat, India

ABOUT THE EDITORS

Kavita Saini is Professor in the School of Computing Science and Engineering, Galgotias University, India. She received her PhD degree from Banasthali Vidyapeeth, Banasthali. She has 20 years of teaching and research experience supervising Master's and PhD scholars in emerging technologies. She has published more than 90 research papers in national and international journals and conferences. She has written and published 18 authored books for undergraduate and postgraduate courses for a number of universities including MD University, Rothak, and Punjab Technical University, Jallandhar with National Publishers. She has also served as editor for a number of books published internationally. She has also delivered technical talks on Blockchain: An Emerging Technology, Web to Deep Web and other emerging Areas and Handled many Special Sessions in International Conferences and Special Issues in international journals. Her research interests include smart and sustainable agricultural, Blockchain technology, Industry 5.0, and cloud and edge computing, digital twin and Web-Based Instructional Systems (WBIS).

Swaroop S. Sonone is Assistant Professor in the School of Forensic Sciences, at JSPM University Pune, India. He completed his Master's degree in Forensic Science, specializing in Digital & Cyber Forensics. He advocates for raising awareness about the critical role of Forensic Science in society, and has given talks at various forums highlighting the importance of forensic techniques in unraveling complex cases and ensuring justice. He has participated in national and international conferences and workshops, contributing innovative research and insights. He has published a number of papers in Scopus Indexed Journals. His research area includes Forensic Science, Digital Forensics and Cyberpsychology.

Mahipal Singh Sankhla is Assistant Professor in the Department of Forensic Science, University Centre for Research and Development (UCRD), Chandigarh University, India. He was nominated by the Govt. of India to mentor the "Atal Innovation Mission" of Niti Aayog to set up ATL Labs across Indian schools. He earned a Bachelor of Science (Hons) degree in Forensic Science and a Master of Science degree in Forensic Science. He has submitted a PhD thesis in Forensic Science to Galgotias University in

Greater Noida, U.P. He has received training from laboratories including the Forensic Science Laboratory (FSL) Lucknow, CBI (CFSL) New Delhi, Codon Institute of Biotechnology Noida, and Rajasthan State Mines and Minerals Limited (R&D Division) Udaipur. He has received several awards and accolades for his outstanding work, including a "Junior Research Fellowship—JRF" from the DST-Funded Project at "Malaviya National Institute of Technology—MNIT," Jaipur, a "Young Scientists Award," a "Young Researcher Award," and a "Forensic Researcher Award." He has also been credited with two Indian copyrights, one German patent, and has filed three Indian patents. He has edited eight books and published over 30 book chapters with various national and international publishers, and his research work has been published in more than 160 peer-reviewed national and international journals. He remains actively engaged in research activities, serving as a member of editorial boards and a reviewer for various scientific journals, as well as participating in organizing committees for many national and international conferences.

Naveen Kumar is a faculty member and Head at the Indian Institute of Information Technology Vadodara, India, in the Department of Computer Science and Engineering. He has over 23 years of teaching and research experience. His broad area of research is information security and privacy. His research interests are in data access control, cloud security, electric vehicles management, and transportation problems. He has a Master's degree in information technology from Guru Gobind Singh Indraprastha University and a PhD degree in Computer Science from DA-IICT Gandhinagar, India.

1

Introduction to Artificial Intelligence in Forensic Science

Arpit Nirvan, Swaroop S. Sonone, Kavita Saini,
and Mahipal Singh Sankhla

INTRODUCTION

Artificial intelligence (AI) technologies have made their way into forensics. Sophisticated algorithms are now used in forensic science for e-discovery, DNA sequencing, and forensics-related document reviews. Among the hot issues in the field of forensic investigations is crime scene restoration; as the principle of matter exchange by Locard says, "There are no spots without evidence, and there is no flawless cloak" [1]. It was commonly believed that, in the field of forensic science, the skills required to reconstruct crime scenes were so specialized that a team of specialists was required to construct the scene from the presented data. So, crime scene restoration was considered to be difficult and expensive. To overcome this situation, it would be preferential to have an AI system that is fast, efficient, accurate, and in comparison, cheaper to use. Crime scene restoration needs investigation technology to be more advanced, informalized, and intelligent. For this, computer-originated animations are preferred as they are regarded as an ideal AI technology to accurately conceptualize crime scenes and accident scenes to a team of forensic specialists to help them

DOI: 10.4324/9781003287810-1

to read the situation and hold on to complex structural information. One of the biggest advantages of computer-formulated animations using AI is that they can be used in court for manifest demonstration [2].

Forensic animations use four approaches to reconstruct criminal scenes: VR (virtual reality), AR (augmented reality), computer-generated 3D animation, and a combination of real and virtual imagery. Motion technology, such as that based on sensors, cameras, glove and haptic, is used in computer-formulated animations as virtual reality and augmented reality use motion technology in order to generate user gestures to study real-time interaction. And the sensor-based system is employed to collect precise data of crime scenes by using electromagnets, electrochemical, and ultrasound technologies. 3D point cloud and CarSim [3] are examples of AI computer-generated animations of crime scenes. CarSim is also called a converter as it converts the written texts of visualized reports into crime scenes or accident scenes of motor vehicles, and can accurately convert 35 percent of the written texts of visualized reports, whereas 3D point cloud technology can generate the projection of a pellet, and prototype it to determine the source of a sufferer gunfire injury [4]. 3D technology combines with photography sensing technology to form a 3D point machine that automatically moves around the room to obtain all-inclusive coverage of crime scenes.

Data mining is a fast-growing area where AI holds the ability to handle Big Data with many approaches. Big Data and AI are the same in some respects because aspects such as increasing volumes, velocities, and variety of data are common in both. AI uses different and difficult pattern recognition techniques—deep learning techniques to handle large volumes of data. AI even helps users to access the desired data from sets of Big Data over a minimal period. Variety in Big Data is alleviated by capturing and structuring the unstructured data using AI in data analytics tools. AI applications analyze unstructured data and somehow categorize and understand the data so that the resulting information can be used to instruct a processor to interact with other applications. Some of the data analytics tools which use AI and ML (machine learning) algorithms are Apache Hadoop, Tableau, KNIME, and Orange. Some of the known issues with AI in bulky Data is that Big Data includes filthy data with inaccuracy, imperfection, and distinctive perfection whereas the nature of some ML algorithmic programs can drive their service in a MapReduce habitat more effectively.

Affiliation of a character with oneself or an individual is called Personal Identification. To comprehend individual personality today is certifiably not a simple assignment, as the technological alteration of our character identities has continued progressively and undetectably. The start of the advanced period is the extraordinary separation point in human history. As shown by the research, every day new data is recorded or added to preexisting data. And such vast data cannot be recorded on paper as it has the chance of being lost or disposed of, so AI got to discover how to hold on to that amount of data safely. AI in Personal Identification or to manage one's identity is much more necessary for any criminal record, identification, lost, missing, family documents, etc. An average business network has hundreds or an even larger number of identities, every one of which has its scope of the issue that it should be managed consistently [5, 6]. AI in personal identification brought so many advantages to make identification more advanced and to speed up its work power to identify someone. On paper, when we record or save someone's identity information, it becomes risky as anyone can easily access it and even change it. AI, however, doesn't allow this as it has proper safeguarding and security so that it cannot be accessed easily. AI can fundamentally help with the execution of fruitful Identity and Access Management, easing a lot of dissatisfaction. An appropriately executed Identity and Access Management framework offers the benefits of hazard relief and better administration, as well as the advancement of "safe" Digital Enterprises [7]. By the means of AI, all personal identification matters are now interconnected to one another, as well as easy to find out. AI is the reason in this field to gain some privilege.

ARTIFICIAL INTELLIGENCE

AI has gained more than enough research significance in the area of multimedia investigation in forensic science. A large amount of audio/video and textual data is being collected from crime scenes during an investigation that requires well-organized deep learning algorithms in terms of precision and efficiency. Various AI-based methods and techniques are used to enhance preciseness and efficiency, minimizing the complexity and noise cancellation of various media that are gathered from crime scenes at the time of investigation. Convolutional neural networks are considered one of the best AI features for the renowned performance of the classification of images/audios and videos. Deep learning in AI is used for audio/video processing, denoising, and DE mosaicking of crime scene images, and overhead views of crime scenes. AI in the multimedia investigation is used for the following purposes:

1. Pack down representation of textual data using AI in deep learning.
2. Compact and precise algorithms for analysis of media using AI in deep learning.
3. Retrieval of various multimedias using AI.
4. Deep algorithms to recognize the voice from audio/videos.
5. AI is used in multimedia for data indexing and retrieval.

Deep learning in AI includes models, performance evaluation algorithms and improvement, and application development techniques for the media in the multimedia investigation.

DOMAINS OF AI IN FORENSIC SCIENCE

As we look at today's scenario, all the things that revolve around us are in a way digital forensic, defined as a tool or an implement to riddle out misdeeds used alongside computers (i.e., harassment, together with account scams) as well as for resolving felony, as opposed to human beings where authentication might inhabit a computer (i.e., funds concealment, teen persecution). AI in digital forensics is elucidated as the utilization of logical standards which are used in finding data or improving technology from a computerized gadget or medium. As we go further through digital forensics, we come to know about its six different domains, or kinds of distinct analysis, such as: AI in Data Forensics, AI in Cloud Forensics, AI in Android/Mobile Forensics, AI in Memory Forensics, AI in Network Forensics, AI in Drone Forensics. All these six domains have their standard tools, which are shown in Figure 1.1.

AI in Data Forensics

AI in Data Forensics is all about how to utilize the information or Metadata for examination and track down genuine proof or truth. It has standard tools such as Bulk Extraction, EVT Xtract, Scalpel. AI in cloud forensics is a kind of forensic that manages tremendous organizations and is identified with the examination of the episode that is finished by or over the cloud. In some cases, there are limits in cloud legal assessment and at that point where the cloud become communal, the actual admittance to the cloud is declined for the examination group on account

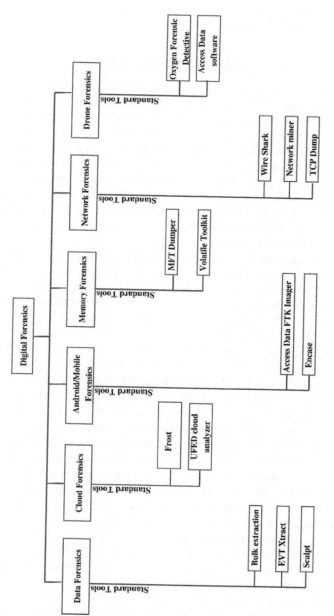

Figure 1.1 Domains of AI digital forensics.

of protection issues [8]. Some of the standard tools of cloud forensics are Frost, UFED Cloud Analyzer.

AI in Android/Mobile Forensics

AI in Android/Mobile Forensics is elucidated as the analyst investigating all sorts of ways identified with cell phones to observe metadata or data identified with the occurrence that has occurred. Some of its excellent gears of mobile/android/ios forensics are Encase as well as ADF (Access Data FTK) Imager. AI in memory forensics is the domain of digital forensics in which the analyst researches and examines the information that is erased, eliminated, or moved from the framework with the assistance of apparatuses and strategies, and tracks down the conceivable metadata to find absolute proof. Some standard gears pre-owned to analyze Memory recollection forensics are dumper of MFT as well as VT (Volatile Toolkit). In AI in Network Forensics, in this domain of digital forensics, investigators inspect and gather proof from the organization and organization layer. There is a circulated structure for network scientific investigation also, the significance of the appropriated framework [9]. Network tools or instruments can explain the occurrence and caution the client of the risk [10]. Some of the standard tools of network forensics are Wire Shark, Network Miner, and TCP Dump. Whereas AI in drone forensics is used to high-tech the technology and principles at which the drones are working, in terms of using and improving the methodology of these gadgets and talking about its tools it uses Oxygen Forensics Detective and Access Data Software. Digital forensics has been continuously expanding widely with its tools, as has its work towards the machinery and main gadgets like drones, which is such an excellent progression in its specific manner. Digital forensics faces many challenges and needs to be enhanced dramatically much more in terms of machinery as well as being systematic, stronger interrelated, and more greatly funded. Despite the extending difficulty, the tools of computer technologists should be in a state of preoccupation and should be accessible [11]. In terms of gadgets like drones, digital forensics is upgrading and providing many more ideas to enhance their work and uses in modern life with new techniques. And in the modern lifestyle or world, we are surrounded by all these machines and gadgets so we should know about them, their functions and all.

Mankind is rising to grasp the impression of AI in everyone's life by virtue of automated technology, which is openly obtainable to all.

In a criminological investigation, when a group of specialists examines the victim, an important job for them is to calculate the period that has rolled by between the demise of the victim and the finding of the body, and that period is called the post-mortem interval (PMI). Blood from a crime or accident scene can be analyzed by directly using AI-based devices for the prescription of alanine transaminase (AST), cholesterol, and lactate dehydrogenase (LDH). Also, the Ph level of the blood is measured and all the data get collected and combined, after which they are compared with a different database to estimate PMI. The idea of calculating the period of demise in the course of criminal investigations depends on the utilization of AI-headed devices that use deep learning ML to calculate different biomarkers of blood like protein biomarkers, lipid biomarkers, and the Ph level of the blood. MRI analysis in forensic post-mortem is also improved by methods, techniques, and algorithms of AI and ML.

AI in Forensic Anthropology

Anthropology is a discipline in which the skeletal remains of deceased people are collected after post-mortem to determine their biological profile. The main aim of AI in forensic anthropology is to estimate sex, age, and biological profile: the ancestry of the deceased from their skeletal remains. Previously, the most widely used AI statistical methods for classification in forensics were BLR (regression of binary logistics) and LDA (linear discriminant analysis). But in today's era, ML in AI is used to make precise predictions by using mathematical tools from training data without being explicitly programmed to do so. ML algorithms, DT, ANN, SVM, naïve Bayes classification (NBC), MARS, and XGB all are used in anatomical sex and family tree determination processes in contrast to the traditional categorization strategies, BLR and LDA. Forensic odontology, however, is a discipline that involves the inspection, appraisal, administration, and presentation of dental pieces of evidence in forensic science [12]. The relationship between the cause of death, the biological behavior of any disease, and patient outcome after treatment can be analyzed through AI in forensic odontology. Neural Network and deep learning in ML, Statistical and semantic Natural language Processing (NLP), robotic process, physical robots, and rule-based expert systems are the types of AI that are used in forensic odontology. AI is considered the best device to collect, store, and evaluate data collected from crime scenes for forensic evidence in legal cases.

The twenty-first century is now reaching, creating, and exploring new techniques, and still has so much to find. AI is one of these techniques: the capacity of advanced machines or machine-controlled robots to perform assignments ordinarily associated with smart creatures such as us, Humans. And with the connection of forensics biology, AI is getting more effective, powerful, and advanced. AI and forensic biology are creating methods and techniques cooperatively. The use of AI is a recent fad in criminological medication as well as a potential turning point for the entire criminological area [13–18]. If we look into today's conditions, for example, AI is currently used to assess lungs in Computed Tomography scans, as well as to see the weakening of patients of Covid-19 [19–21]. The time, utilization, and disappointment of an examination or investigation can be tackled by AI. As we connect AI and forensic biology, there are networks called ANNs (Artificial Neural Networks), which are data handling frameworks that emulate biological neural organization networks that structure pieces of the mind and its logical structure [22]. The fundamental motivation behind AI application is to comprehend and apply the human mentality and dynamic instrumentation of the psyche. In coming times, AI will be the controller of all machines and will be able to do all the work in forensic biology.

AI in Forensic Psychology

Psychology: whenever we read this term, a clear image of mind behavioral actions is formed and we define it as a logical investigation of the psyche and actions. Further moving onwards, for mind-reading or neuroimaging devices we use the combination of forensic psychology with AI. And with the utilization of AI strategies, we can attain advancement in brain reading by pursuing innovative techniques and numerous applications of ANN. In recent times, interest in the advancement of new instruments and procedures to develop hazard evaluation methods in the field of forensic psychiatry and criminal equity has been evolving. AI is being utilized to improve the prescient precision of risk estimation. With the help of AI, or the use of AI in forensic psychology, all the obstacles of human brain activity could be diagnosed at an early stage, which could then be solved at an early stage. There are so many machines that perform or play a major and different role in the field of forensic psychology, and AI seems very helpful in this. With emerging AI in forensic psychology we are gaining so many advantages, and will also gain more in the future as it is expanding more day by day.

AI in Wildlife Forensics

Wildlife forensics is an arising area of science, helpful in recognizing species and accomplishment of wildlife crimes and additionally in observing the well-being of natural variables on the prosperity of wildlife populations. Wildlife commerce frames the world's third biggest gathering of illicit occupation next to opiates and guns [23]. To maintain the wildlife in the ecosystem or to balance the ecosystem, it is important to learn its perspective, habitat, and existence, where AI and ML play a vital role. The use of new machines or tools such as microscopic perception gears like Scanning Electron Microscope and Energy Dispersive X-Ray Spectroscopy has been compelling in some cases, for example where deoxyribonucleic acid (DNA) was extricated from rigid biotic materials [24]. AI in wildlife forensics has been demonstrated to be a quick, exact, and dependable criminal examination process with all-inclusive analysis and easy availability. Humans and animals are so much connected and have certain similarities that, with the help of AI, we are able to know from which wild animal we evolved and over how many years. A technique such as the Molecular DNA technique, with the help of a proper populace reference data set, bioinformatics, and factual models, is in censorious progress with AI, which helps in wildlife forensic investigation [25–27]. It has moreover helped to settle issues over taxonomic argument, decisive spatiotemporal hereditary difference, transformative history, beginnings, and even endemism. Because of AI in wildlife forensics, we get to know all about the early life of existing animals by their footprints, their bones, hairs, tissue, etc. And we have categorized them into different classifications, kingdoms, class, species; from their physical appearance to their genetic engineering, all identified by the application of AI. AI has enabled us to keep a database of all the information on wildlife such as the animals which are now extinct to the animals which will become extinct in the future or that have a low ratio.

The subject area of forensic technology has to face multiple challenges accompanied by the emergence of cybercrime, the vast use of the Internet, and the immense increase of bulky information and data [28]. Forensic science needs more advanced and effective AI-based tools which allow us to identify relevant criminals from the huge volume of noisy data. As criminal data is collected from the majority of sources it is compared with previously collected data, analyzed, stored in particular sections, and after that stored for future reference. AI is used for batch processing concepts and to sift out relevant criminal data from the database.

AI in Fingerprinting

Fingerprint technology is the most widely used technology on a crime scene as fingerprints are the most common and important physical evidence on crime scenes. AI in fingerprinting is used in numerous ways such as fingerprint formation, DNA sequencing, drug recognition, detecting evidence analysis and spotting document credentials, etc. An AI program is used to handle fluorescence images of the developed latent fingerprints. An advanced mode of fingerprint identification program can be developed by image technology based on deep learning. This feature uses image features to replace traditional features, which changes the cognition of fingerprint detection in forensic science. This kind of technology uses 60 percent of fingerprint features, 13 percent of facial and iris features, 0.5 percent features of a keystroke, and 2.5 percent features of digital signatures [29]. The AI model uses ANN, which can be stated as a network that learns by examples. ANN is used for pattern recognition and data classification-like applications through the learning process. Such kinds of AI-based models for fingerprinting in forensic science help specialists to handle the fingerprint database by using Neural Networks. We can say that AI-automated fingerprint recognition (IAFR) is the most efficient method with which to identify human identity. Figure 1.2 shows the various uses of AI in forensic science.

AI is a crucial discipline in today's digital era as it is enriched with various algorithms, techniques, and ML methods to perform the strategic task of the collection of questioned documents and their organizations. As in questioned documentation of forensics, multiple methods/algorithms/techniques have been used through AI applications. In today's scenario, data analytics is the key area in which AI concepts are driving documentation activities, ensuring work is performed in an accurate and precise format. AI-based chatbots are being used for questioned documentation, as they use AI and ML to determine real-time information, recommendations, suggestions, etc. Nowadays, chatbot works on the phenomenon of Deep Learning Techniques (DLT) [30–31] such as DRL [23], DNN, DHNN, and computerized automation for questioned documentation in forensic science [32–34].

ANN applications will be able to define vast extents of forensic science like crime restoration, data acquisition and recovery processes, forensic ballistic divisions, narco-analysis and psychology divisions, and cyber forensics. AI has been in use with its great number of applications and techniques for less than 50 years. Still, specialists have to work harder for the well-being of society.

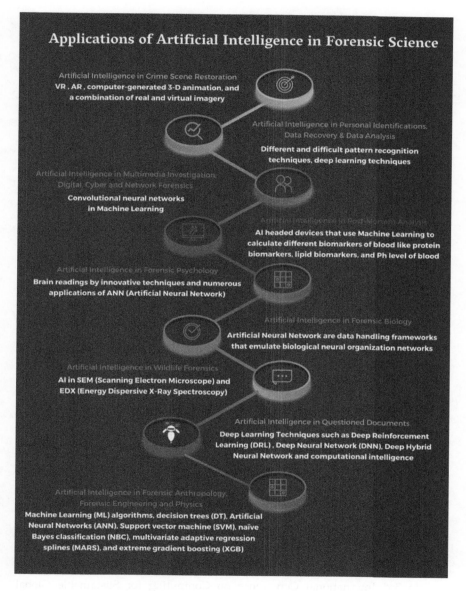

Figure 1.2 Various applications of AI in forensic science.

CONCLUSION

There are some problems that still need to be considered ahead of the coming future. One is that the takeover of privacy problems will stand out to the common people; another is that manual control will be restricted to far fewer areas as compared with the current situation. We can conclude, however, that AI can bring a marvellous, productive, and digital revolution (Intelligent system) into the area of forensic science.

REFERENCES

[1] Guo Kai and Liang Weihu (2016) The extraction and application of material evidence in spot investigation. *Law and Society*, 11: 256 (in Chinese).
[2] Burton, A.M., Schofield, D. and Goodwin, L.M. (2005) Gate of global perception: Forensic graphics for evidence presentation. Proceedings of the 13th Annual ACM International Conference on Multimedia; 2005 November 6–11; Singapore. New York, NY: Association for Computing Machinery; 103–11.
[3] Egges, A., Nijholt, A. and Nugues, P. (2001) Generating a 3D simulation of a car accident from a formal description: the CarSim System. In: Giagourta, V., Strintzis, M.G., editors. Proceedings of the International Conference on Augmented, Virtual Environments and Three-Dimensional Imaging; 2001 May 30–June 1; Mykonos, Greece. Thessaloniki, Greece: Informatic and Telematics Institute – CERTH; 220–3.
[4] Agosto, E., Ajmar, A., Boccardo, P., et al. (2008) Crime scene reconstruction using a fully geomantic approach. *Sensors*, 8(10): 6280–6302.
[5] Cole, D. (1991) Artificial intelligence and personal identity. *Synthese*, 88(3): 399–417. doi:10.1007/bf00413555.
[6] Sgouros, N. (1998) Interaction between physical and design knowledge in design from physical principles. *Engineering Applications of Artificial Intelligence*, 11(4): 449–59. doi:10.1016/s0952-1976(98)00037-2.
[7] Balmer, J. and Greyser, S. (2002) Managing the multiple identities of the corporation. *California Management Review*, 44(3): 72–86.
[8] Burney, A., Asif, M. and Abbas, Z. (2016) Forensics issues in cloud computing. *Journal of Computer and Communications*, 4: 63–69.
[9] Chhabra, G.S. and Singh, P. (2015). Distributed Network Forensics Framework: A systematic review. *International Journal of Computers and Applications*, 119(19): 31–5.
[10] Shrivastava, G. (2016). Network forensics: Methodical literature review. In 3rd International Conference on Computing for Sustainable Global Development (INDIACom) (pp. 2203–8). IEEE.
[11] Saltzer, J.H. and Frans Kaashoek, M. (2009) *Principles of computer system design: An introduction*. Morgan Kaufmann.

[12] Janardanan, R.P. and Logeswaran, R. (2018) Recent image processing techniques in forensic odontology: A systematic review. *Biomedical Journal of Scientific and Technical Research*, 2(5): 1–6.

[13] Ya-ting, F., Qiong, L., Tong, X., et al. (2020) New opportunities and challenges for forensic medicine in the era of artificial intelligence technology. *Journal of Forensic Medicine*, 36: 77–85. doi:10.12116/J.ISSN.1004-5619.2020.01.016.

[14] Khanagar, S.B., Vishwanathaiah, S., Naik, S., Al-Kheraif, A., Devang Divakar, D., Sarode, S.C., Bhandari, S. and Patil, S. (2021) Application and performance of artificial intelligence technology in forensic odontology – a systematic review. *Legal Medicine*, 48: 101826. doi:10.1016/J.LEGALMED.2020.101826.

[15] Lefèvre, T. (2018) Big data in forensic science and medicine. *Journal of Forensic and Legal Medicine*, 57: 1–6. doi:10.1016/J.JFLM.2017.08.001.

[16] Himanshi, N. (2021) Application of artificial intelligence in the field of forensic medicine. *Indian Journal of Forensic Medicine & Toxicology*, 15. doi:10.37506/IJFMT.V15I4.

[17] Franke, K. and Srihari, S.N. (2008) Computational forensics: An overview. Lecture notes in computer science (including subseries lecture notes in artificial intelligence and lecture notes in bioinformatics), 5158 LNCS, 1–10. doi:10.1007/978-3-540-85303-9_1.

[18] Cossellu, G., de Luca, S., Biagi, R., Farronato, G., Cingolani, M., Ferrante, L. and Cameriere, R. (2015) Reliability of frontal sinus by Cone Beam-Computed Tomography (CBCT) for individual identification. *Radiologia Medica*, 120: 1130–6. doi:10.1007/S11547-015-0552-Y.

[19] Li, L., Qin, L., Xu, Z., Yin, Y., Wang, X., Kong, B., Bai, J., Lu, Y., Fang, Z., Song, Q. et al. (2020) Using artificial intelligence to detect COVID-19 and community-acquired pneumonia based on pulmonary CT: Evaluation of the diagnostic accuracy. *Radiology*, 296(2): E65–E71, doi:10.1148/RADIOL.2020200905.

[20] Sessa, F., Bertozzi, G., Cipolloni, L., Baldari, B., Cantatore, S., D'Errico, S., Mizio, G. di, Asmundo, A., Castorina, S., Salerno, M. et al. (2020) Clinical-forensic autopsy findings to defeat COVID-19 disease: A literature review. *Journal of Clinical Medicine*, 9(7): 2026, doi:10.3390/JCM9072026.

[21] Shamout, F.E., Shen, Y., Wu, N., Kaku, A., Park, J., Makino, T., Jastrzębski, S., Witowski, J., Wang, D., Zhang, B. et al. (2021) An artificial intelligence system for predicting the deterioration of COVID-19 patients in the emergency department. npj *Digital Medicine*, 4(1): 1–11. doi:10.1038/s41746-021-00453-0.

[22] Lipmann, R.P. (1987) An introduction to computing with neural nets. *IEEE ASSP Magazine*, April 4(2): 4–22. doi:10.1109/MASSP.1987.1165576.

[23] Sahajpal, V., Goyal, S.P., Raza, R. and Jayapal, R. (2009) Identification of mongoose (Genus: *Herpestes*) species from hair through band pattern studies using discriminate functional analysis (DFA) and microscopic examination. *Science and Justice*, 49: 205–9.

[24] Verma, A.K., Khan, S., Joshi, P.C., Bahuguna, A. and Dev, K. (2016) Wildlife forensic techniques: DNA Extraction from hard Biological matter of Chital (Axis axis), molecular analysis, use of SEM and EDX in species identification. *Journal of Biotechnology and Biochemistry*, 2(7): 104–10.

[25] Ogden, R. (2011) SNP discovery: Next generation sequencing unlocking the potential of genomic technologies for wildlife forensics. *Molecular Ecology Resources*, 11(1): 109–16.

[26] Bertolino, S., Girardello, M. and Amori, G. (2014) Identifying conservation priorities when data are scanty: A case study with small mammals in Italy. *Mammalian Biology*, 79: 349–56.

[27] Iyengar, A. (2014) Forensic DNA analysis for animal protection and biodiversity conservation: A review. *Journal for Nature Conservation*, 22: 195–205.

[28] Hunton, P. (2009) The growing phenomenon of crime and the internet: A cybercrime execution and analysis model. *Computer Law and Security Review*, 25: s28 s35.

[29] Sonavane, R. and Sawant, B.S. (2007) Noisy fingerprint image enhancement technique for image analysis: A structure similarity measure approach. *IJCSNS*, 7(9).

[30] Bharati, P. and Pramanik, A. (2020) *Deep learning techniques—R-CNN to mask R-CNN A survey. Computational intelligence in pattern recognition*. Springer, Singapore, pp. 657–68.

[31] Gambhir, P. (2019) Review of Chatbot design and trends. In: Proceeding of artificial intelligence and speech technology, Indira Gandhi Delhi Technical University for Women, Delhi.

[32] Ali, A., Zhu, Y., Chen, Q., Yu, J. and Cai, H. (2019) Leveraging spatio-temporal patterns for predicting citywide traffic crowd flows using deep hybrid neural networks. In: 2019 IEEE 25th international conference on parallel and distributed systems (ICPADS), IEEE, December, pp. 125–32.

[33] Ali, B. and Ravi, V. (2021) Developing dialog manager in chatbots via hybrid deep learning architectures. In: Satapathy, S.C., Zang, Y.D., Bhateja, V. and Majhi, R. (eds), *Intelligent data engineering and analytics*. Springer, Singapore, pp. 301–10.

[34] Ali, A., Zhu, Y. and Zakarya, M. (2021) *A data aggregation based approach to exploit dynamic spatio-temporal correlations for citywide crowd flows prediction in fog computing. Multimedia tools and applications*. Springer, Singapore, pp. 1–33.

2

Artificial Intelligence in Crime Scene Reconstruction

Sukanya Sachdeva, Priyanshi Garg, Navneet Sharma,
and Perumal Sivaperumal

INTRODUCTION

A crime scene can be a physical place, spot, area, building, etc., where you can find evidence related to the crime that took place (UNODC, 2008). In the case of cybercrime, the device/instrument used to commit a crime can itself be considered a crime scene. After barricading the crime scene, the first step toward solving the crime begins with exploring and recognizing potential evidence. Once the potential evidence is recognized, it should be properly collected, transported to the laboratory, and analyzed to establish its role in the occurrence of crime. Validating the physical evidence present at the crime scene is the key to its reconstruction (Koen & Goetz, 2017).

"Forensic crime scene reconstruction is the process of determining the sequence of events about what occurred during and after a crime," as defined by the Department of Emergency Services and Public Protection of Connecticut, US (DESPP, 2022). Broadly, it can also be explained as creating the same scenario, series of events, containing similar pieces of evidence as they were in reality, to get a better understanding of the incident

DOI: 10.4324/9781003287810-2

and present the same in the court of law for the decision-making process irrespective of time and space.

The examination and reconstruction of a crime scene are based on two principles: one is that, when two things come into contact, there occurs an exchange of trace matter between them which is known as "Locard's principle of exchange," and the other is "facts do not lie." Both significantly impact the justice delivery system. Reconstruction of a crime scene can be done in two ways. One is reconstruction around evidence and the other is reconstruction around events. The former relies only on the evidence rather than the surroundings whereas the latter relies on a series of events (Houck et al., 2018b).

The mere presence of the evidence at a crime scene or the statements of eyewitnesses is not sufficient to point out the perpetrator unless the modus operandi is elucidated in a court of law. Modus operandi, which means a particular way of committing a crime by an individual, can only be established by using evidence/facts as building blocks for the reconstruction of the crime scene. It establishes the motive as to why the suspect behaved in that particular way or what circumstances led the perpetrator to commit a crime. Often the perpetrator tries to fabricate or tamper with the crime scene in order for the crime to be misinterpreted as an accident. One cannot conclude whether it is homicide, suicide, or an accident without hypothesizing the series of events that must have taken place to cause the crime to occur. Creating a dummy version of the events and the place helps the investigator to process the chain of thoughts and their respective consequences to answer the whys, what, and how of the crime scene. There was a famous movie, *Talvar*, based on a real-life case, where, in order to understand whether the noise of air conditioning in the parents' room was loud enough to shield the yelps of Aarushi Talwar coming from the next room, as told by the parents, the chief investigator had to reconstruct the whole scenario, in the same manner, in order to reach a conclusion.

No two crime scenes are ever the same. An investigator might use their past experiences but should not compare the crime scenes as each of them demands a different method/methodology to be adapted before reaching a conclusion. The choice of methods relies upon many factors like the area of the crime scene, the amount of evidence, the extent of damage, etc., and is generally decided on by the chief investigator. Even brilliant minds are capable of overlooking or ignoring the minute details under different circumstances, which is why the investigator must treat every crime scene as if it had never happened before. Though it is possible to visit the crime scene again under rare circumstances, provided one

16

seeks permission from the court to refer to the details that were missed at first, this does raise questions about the credibility of the investigator and the evidence found at the crime scene, and hence must be avoided at all costs. Furthermore, reconstructing a crime scene is not an easy task when conducted manually as searching for evidence is time consuming, and its simultaneous processing, as well as its analysis, are difficult. A cross-check, and revisiting of the facts along with data, are required. Hence, the intervention of artificial intelligence (AI) has become a necessity for the problem stated above.

AI, artificial neural networks (ANN), deep learning, and machine learning (ML) are part of digital forensics and have a history of their utilization in breaking cybercrimes. Now, slowly but effectively, they are pitching in with other techniques to solve crimes; for example, establishing blood pattern analysis, gunshot residues detection, etc. (Rigano, 2019). So far, we have been relying on a computational approach for carrying out tasks effectively due to its large storage capacity and easy access.

A story demonstrated through 3D visualization will always be better understood than a written one. Let's discuss some problem statements that caused AI to be involved with crime scene reconstruction. Two-dimensional photographs make it less convenient for authorities to imagine what could have happened, videography defines the position and relative position of evidence, but area mapping cannot be performed with ease.

In constructing a 3D crime scene, using individually clicked photos is another way of visualizing the whole crime scene at once. To do this, the expert will take photos from all angles, making a pan motion, and later connect them to create a single photo depicting the crime scene; this is referred to as the stitching method. It can be created from different angles and different ranges i.e., close, mid, and wide, to give a 360° view of the scene (Dass et al., 2020). But this technique has its limitations too. It's important to keep the same exposure of light, brightness, and contrast to create a uniform 3D picture. Sometimes a picture shows the size of the object more or less than the actual size of it, which should be kept in mind and accordingly should be demonstrated true to size in all the photographs. The quality of the photo is another key point one should focus on. The quality of the photos should be high and the same for all. Apart from this, even creating a 3D picturization using individual photos might take a significantly large number of them.

Without a proper postulation depicting modus operandi, mens rea, or corpus delicti, one might end up with erroneous judgment. AI provides one with the opportunity to peek into past events by creating a virtual simulation of the whole process, pixel by pixel, and how it might have proceeded gradually. All AI needs is to be fed the subjective data, the objective data, and information on the behavior of the criminals and victims to predict possible reactions. AI can make it look as if you are witnessing the whole scene yourself, and nothing could be more transparently revealing than that.

In the following sections, we will discuss how AI was introduced to get the better of human shortcomings. We will look at how virtual reality simulation (VRS) could be a tool for solving cases, how unmanned aerial vehicles (UAVs) and rovers could be a potential future replacement for crime scene experts, and how the Human Patient Simulator could uncomplicate the reactions of anatomy and medicine in court. All of these have proven useful in the reconstruction of the crime scene, and some emerging technologies might do the same.

ARTIFICIAL INTELLIGENCE IN CBRN FORENSICS

CBRN, sometimes referred to as CBRNe, stands for Chemical, Biological, Radiological, Nuclear explosives. It is majorly concerned with uncontrollable outbreaks of severe health impacts on humans when the matter falling into these categories is used. Even a very tiny amount is sometimes sufficient to cause damage that is difficult to handle and may have consequences in many years to come. Whether it is chlorine gas used by Germans, mustard gas used by Iraq, the black death pandemic of Europe, bubonic plague, or anthrax, the results have clearly forced authorities around the globe to come together and look for its management.

Another aspect of such a crime scene is that it seems to be contained in a particular spot, whereas there can be multiple crime scenes if the pathogen is carried over by soil or air. Unlike normal crime scenes, these demand prior operational and management training for all the personnel who are supposed to enter the crime scene. Here the most important thing is to collect information regarding the crime scene, such as: What happened? How? And to what extent? This is to prepare the response team with efficient equipment as they enter the scene. Then comes managing the scene and saving lives, and only once these are sorted is the focus shifted towards evidence collection (Houck et al., 2018a).

Even after all the preparedness and drills, one can only reduce the extent of destruction and not completely eliminate it, which should be the primary focus. Combining AI with CBRN forensics is the key to preventing it from happening; such mass-level disruptions are neither planned overnight nor are they part of routine work. Hence, such activities can be put under physical and digital surveillance so that relevant action can be taken on time. AI can help in planning, executing, and decision-making (Smyth et al., 2018).

Apart from the severity of these weapons, one more aspect that makes this field extremely important is the modifications within the unit. These weapons can be largely modified, producing different symptoms every time they are used, delaying the medical management process, and thereby creating havoc. Keeping that in mind, one can train in the medical management of such emergencies. The following sections will discuss how these situations can be smartly and effectively tackled.

Triage Management

The term "triage" comes from the French word *trier*, which means "to sort." This term was initially used in the medical field where, while attending multiple severely injured patients, doctors had to prioritize the ones with the highest survival chances in order to increase the number of survivors (Shiaeles et al., 2013). Hence, in a situation of mass destruction, where a large number of populations are affected, medical attention is given to those who need it the most and simultaneously have the most chance of survival.

Triage has entered the primary digital forensic examination zone using the same strategy as the sorting of evidence at a crime scene. There are some pieces of evidence that lose their integrity over time; for example, biological specimens, when not collected or preserved within their respective expiration, become less reliable. Although forensic experts are trained enough to properly collect and preserve evidence, ensuring its safe transport to the laboratory, crime scenes that cover a large area are chaotic and confusing, involve a lesser number of response forces, and require a smart investigation immediately. Not only is the reliability of the evidence preserved but, also, due to immediate processing of the evidence, the huge burden of data analysis is reduced to a great extent. Furthermore, the load on the justice delivery system over pending cases will consequently be minimized.

Triage managed by AI could revolutionize the process of crime scene reconstruction, provided it is fed with enough data to respond accordingly. As reconstruction is also based on evidence collection, through AI triaging, we can decide the sequence of relevant evidence to be collected and the best possible way of preservation. This reduces the time and errors to a great extent. The aim is to live-process and analyze all the evidence, but this is not feasible due to the high time consumption and non-portability of sophisticated, highly reliable instruments. Hence, we can divide the category of evidence collection into three parts: (1) triage evidence, (2) preliminary evidence, and (3) detailed evidence. Furthermore, the introduction of the concept of triage is still very new in the reconstruction of crime scenes.

Human Patient Simulator

A Human Patient Simulator is a human dummy, or mannequin, capable of producing symptoms similar to those of humans. The idea behind the product was to initiate a free-from-consequences, hands-on method of training for medical professionals. Since its development, this method of training hasn't just been limited to medical professionals but has also been used by military personnel, special forces, and quick response forces for instant management of disaster situations. CBRNe disaster preparedness and victims' management training has also been given using a Human Patient Simulator (Gautam et al., 2017; Smyth et al., 2018).

In India, almost 400,000 violent crimes were reported in the year 2020 as per the data of the National Crime Record Bureau (NCRB, 2022). The victims of such violent crimes often become casualties if not given proper medical attention on the spot. Generally, the first responders are police officers or investigators who are completely unaware of how to give basic treatment to the victims at the crime scene. Due to a low awareness of basic cardiopulmonary resuscitation (CPR), like life-saving techniques, among first responders, the chance of losing a life and a potential eyewitness increases. An eyewitness or victim can play a crucial role in the reconstruction of such crime scenes where data is insufficient to come to a conclusion, or a part of the whole chain of events is uncertain.

The Human Patient Simulator is connected to a computer system and is operated manually. In order to train the person, the operator is supposed to feed in a specific situation, say, arsenic poisoning, and the dummy starts to show the respective symptoms, similar to a human. These simulation studies have been successful in preparing professionals for managing difficult situations.

Unmanned Aerial Vehicles/Unmanned Ground Vehicles

Unmanned aerial vehicles (UAVs), sometimes referred to as unpiloted aerial vehicles, or "drones," are remotely operated aircraft along with their control station managed by a pilot on the ground, collectively known as Unmanned Aerial Systems (UAS). They came into existence around the eighteenth century, when the intention to develop was to use them for patrolling and combat in the military (Everaerts, 2008). Since then, UAVs have triumphed in all the fields they have been employed in, with little or complete modification to the system, for example to deliver goods, infrastructure surveillance, remote sensing, mapping, photogrammetry, agribusiness, spying, soil monitoring, crop monitoring, mining, monitoring archeological sites, in the conservation of wildlife by keeping an eye on poaching and even to record personal functions or events (Singhal et al., 2018).

Components of UAVs consist of four parts, mainly (a) the aircraft housing the rotors, motors, GPS, and accessories, (b) the Ground Control Station (GCS) from where the aircraft's movement is controlled, directed, and real-time data can be accessed, visualized, and interpreted in real-time, operated by a trained person, (c) the communication link between the two, and (Singhal et al., 2018) (d) optional parts, say high-resolution camera for surveillance, different electromagnetic radiations ranging from visible to thermal or sensors to fulfill specific requirements (Mendis, 2017).

Based on fixed and moving parts, as well as the number and positioning of rotors which are responsible for different aerodynamics, the drones are divided into different categories. Types of UAVs or drones, on the basis of their possible usage in crime scene reconstruction, are:

1. Drone photography: used for taking photos at angles under different lighting conditions with high-quality imaging. This can be used to keep a record of the amount of evidence present at a crime scene, with both close-range for details and mid-range for size comparison.
2. Drone surveillance: used for having an aerial view of the scene to ascertain the area to be covered for swiping, the extent of damage to the scene, and to maintain a timed record of the people entering and leaving the crime scene.
3. Drone mapping: equipped with laser scanners, this is employed in creating a blueprint of the infrastructure or area layout of the scene to ensure safe entrance and exit, used for minimum hindering of the evidence collection process and to rescue lives simultaneously.

Apart from the usage, the drones can also be classified as fixed-wing drones, multirotor (Hackney & Clayton, 2015), flapping-wing drones, and vertical take-off landing drones (VTOL), on the basis of their structure and the number of rotors, flight altitude, endurance, and varying aerodynamics (Singhal et al., 2018). Some examples of commercially available drones around the world are Blade BLH7480A, DJI Phantom4, Parrot ANAFI, and Quantum Nova.

We now know that UAVs are the new generation of machines capable of producing real-time data that can be managed and processed simultaneously (Everaerts, 2008). They are capable of delivering and picking up goods and taking aerial photographs, depending on the different accessories attached.

UAVs can overcome the errors that occur when investigating a crime scene in which the area to be covered is huge, and estimating the extent of casualty and damage is a challenging process. Consequently, they can prevent the overlooking of evidence associated with tiresome negligence or manual error. Crime scenes of mass destruction, for example bomb blasts, airplane crashes, or road accidents, where the crucial pieces of evidence could be found anywhere in the area to be investigated, are massive and fragile (Urbanová et al., 2017). Along with aerial photography, UAVs are capable of capturing fingerprints found at the crime scene and sending them directly to the bureau for further processing (Mendis, 2017).

Now, as UAVs are the eyes of the sky, unmanned ground vehicles (UGVs) or remotely operated vehicles (ROVs) are the eyes on the ground. They are designed to travel or climb on uneven terrains and carry heavy loads. DAKSH® is a remotely operated vehicle developed by Defence Research and Development Organisation (DRDO, India) that is used for short-distance monitoring and survey operations. It can recognize and handle Improvised Explosive Devices (IEDs) and is well equipped to keep a check for nuclear and chemical contamination levels. Also developed by DRDO, India are: UXOR (an unexploded ordnance handling robot), capable of handling and deactivating a huge number of missiles and bombs; and NETRA®, a UAV, employed for surveillance, equipped with high-quality lenses, zooming capabilities, and a thermal imager, and used for detailed night operations (DRDO, 2019).

UAV/UGV—AI in Crime Scene Reconstruction

Reconstructing a crime scene requires all the data, facts regarding persons and, most importantly, the environment that was part of the scene at the time of the incident. AI performs all tasks in the right order and in a correct and unbiased manner. It preserves the crime scene till it reaches the court of law or even after. This ensures the credibility of the evidence, thereby increasing the rate of conviction against crimes. With the use of AI, all the permutations and combinations of processing a crime scene are presented on the table to the investigator who then can choose the best fit for the situation.

Consider UAV as the body of the investigator and AI to be the mind, whereas the architect behind all of this will still be at the station controlling the game. UAVs will become the eyes to observe and store, and their robotic claws will become the hands of the crime scene investigators to pick and preserve the evidence. The role of AI here would be to process the data and smartly analyze it to provide the best possible routes for searching and collecting evidence for further necessary action.

AI is the primary key in analyzing and interpreting live data, whereas UAV is the primary key in quick-freezing all these details in order to reconstruct the crime scene (Mendis, 2017). UAV has the advantage of being equipped with accessories on board to accomplish various tasks, for example: lenses for covering different ranges, a GPS system for live location tracking of evidence, a laser for blueprint mapping and weapons detection, UV or IR lighting for detection of biological fluids, claws for holding and transporting evidence; all of this while still recording the crime scene in real time, thereby ensuring a chain of custody.

UAVs combined with AI can be used to decide what section of an area is to be covered. Once approved by the operating centre, this method can be used to transport the evidence collected to the station or nearby collection-preservation spot. It is capable enough to sweep the whole area without missing a spot, enter fragile and narrow spaces, and even collect delicate evidence with proper care and store it for further analysis. This enables the decision-makers sitting on the other side to take the imperative actions without delay and accelerate the justice delivery process. Aside from this, the embedded AI can simultaneously determine whether the object at the scene of the crime holds enough relevance to be considered as evidence or not. For cases where there is terrorist activity involved, UAV can provide the real-time situation in order to estimate the perpetrators and victims in the red zone, and AI can aid in the estimation of the type and number of weapons or artilleries carried by the terrorist group. This will help the first responders to make strategies and act on when and how to barge in and save lives.

ARTIFICIAL INTELLIGENCE AND VIRTUAL REALITY SIMULATION

Immersive technologies like augmented reality (AR) and virtual reality (VR) have become an indispensable part of education, entertainment, training, and defense (Interrante et al., 2018). Though they originated around the eighteenth century for military purposes, these advancements have been recognized in the sector of criminal investigation only recently. They have also been successfully employed in training astronauts and pilots by developing virtual cockpits (Greenwald et al., 2017). VRS, as the name goes, is an artificial reality, cutting off from the real world while still giving real experiences.

Experiments performed in the laboratories allow us to make mistakes often and learn from them, making one an expert in that field. On the other hand, there are some other areas where even one mistake can pose a serious life risk, whether it's performing surgery on a person or studying the effects of drugs on a body or training for combat or first aid purposes. Until the emergence of VRS, professionals had been trained through books and on rare occasions on human bodies, which creates more room for mistakes. Such simulations make it easier for the trainees to process a real-time reaction with an open mind, making room for circumstantial responses. They provide a safe, interactive, and equally immersive platform for training and investigation purposes, removing the shortcomings of manual errors (Greenwald et al., 2017).

Head-mounted displays were initially used by techies, and then later introduced to the general public as an attachment with mobile phones with which to have a novelty fictional 3D experience. The idea was purely on an entertainment basis (Interrante et al., 2018). Today, a major reason why certain cases don't reach their final destination in court is the lack of professional training in crime scene handling. For obvious reasons, training was limited to textbook learning. Consequently, the experts involved in the investigation or analysis were unable to produce or reconstruct the crime scene properly in court. This could only be solved by providing hands-on training to the professionals, which is possible through VRS (Mayne & Green, 2020).

VRS aids in producing a 3D presentation in front of the observer (person who is using the VRS system) of how things must have occurred and propagated at the crime scene. Initially, one needed a moderator or a supervisor to guide the observer through the crime scene, as in what they are looking at, what is coming ahead of them, which evidence is placed where, and its significance at the scene (Süncksen et al., 2019). But with the new advancement, the whole scene can be equipped with verbal and written annotations as one travels through the crime scene (Weiler et al., 2018). VRS also makes it more convenient to look at the crime scene from different angles where each of the angles could denote different perception points of the witnesses present (Süncksen et al., 2019).

An investigator rarely comes across a "clean" crime scene, i.e., a sorted one. It might be an arson case where the extent of damage was great, and the observer needs to be navigated through the scene, simultaneously understanding the relevance and positioning of some evidence. VRS allows temporary modifications to the whole scenario, hiding, highlighting, adding, or removing certain objects or events as per the observer's convenience for a better understanding of the incident. All the post calculations that are made while analyzing the crime scene in the lab could be achieved while taking a walk through the crime scene, whether it's taking measurements of the objects, inter distances, the possible trajectory of gunshot or blood spatters, or the probable positioning of the culprit or witnesses at the scene (Sieberth et al., 2019); not to mention that the biggest achievement would be using AI-VRS as a non-destructive technique for analysis. Impressions found at the scene are analyzed by casting them on a hard surface to ease the analysis, but soft impressions like footprints are susceptible to change after casting, so one must be careful while doing so. AI-VRS can scan the whole impression and propose the possible objects, using the measurements that might have caused them. Neural networks like "YOLO" (you only look once) allow us to identify various objects at the crime scene (Weiler et al., 2018). This reduces manual inspection of hours-long videos of the scene afterward and aids in a quick conclusion.

The other well-established fact regarding a crime scene is that it changes with time, and evidence is more likely to deteriorate if not collected and preserved properly and in a timely fashion. VRS holds the potential to bring experts across the globe to the crime scene without being physically present to give their skillful input on managing the complex crime scene with absolutely no delay. VRS inhibits the physical distinction between demonstrator and end-user.

Furthermore, one should not forget that a human mind suffers from fatigue and bias in processing large data, which is cumbersome in terms of quality over quantity, as well as the incapability of distinguishing beyond the limits of our senses. Hence, reconstructing a virtual 3D crime scene where you can act as a virtual witness is not enough to come to a conclusion. AI is not just about making decisions but also predicting other possible consequences for future measures.

Crime scene reconstruction is not limited to physical evidence. The other equally important factor is modus operandi, establishing the mental component to deduce a hypothesis. We have already discussed this. Brain mapping has been in use to ascertain the grounds of witness or perpetrator statements based on physical or chemical changes in their bodies.

Here, neural networks could be used in conjunction with VRS to project each visual of the incident, the chain of thoughts, and present it in front of the court. This is executed systematically and could act as major evidence for the basis of which decisions are made in court.

AI-VRS technology could become an indispensable part of mobile forensics and crime scene reconstruction for being robust, accessible, convenient to use, efficient, and cost effective. Clearly, the 3D virtual crime scene induces the cognitive approach more as compared with 2D photographs.

LIMITATIONS

Often in the process, we forget that this machine-driven intelligence is created by humans in order to overcome the shortcomings of humans, so sometimes there might be a glitch, an error, or a faulty program upon which we are relying. When the technology evolves, so evolves the mind of the perpetrator on how to hack the system and get away with the crime. Every program has a backdoor known only to the creator and the other expert minds working in that area, but not everyone takes benefits from it. The major reason for adapting AI over the human mind is the data holding capacity, but this is also one of the limitations as the data can be hacked, modified, or even deleted from the server. The physical files containing the details of a case are only accessible to the people who have access to the place, which automatically narrows the range of suspicion, whereas the data present on the server is accessible to anyone with adequate knowledge beyond the restrictions of time and geographical location. As the methods and technologies explained in the sections above are still evolving, their relative newness makes them more prone to attack without the perpetrators getting caught. Most of these technologies are cost effective and not regulated by the government, which makes them a good source for illicit trafficking, as in, for example, the case of drones (Renduchintala et al., 2019).

Data privacy is of utmost importance due to ethical and strategical issues. Like every other crime scene, it is crucial to know whether the system was jeopardized remotely or whether it is malicious by design. There could be involvement from any of the following: the creator, the operator, or the hacker. What if the drone carrying the evidence were given the command to drop it off on the way or to take it to another location (Schneider & Breitinger, 2020)? In such a case, the two challenging tasks would be: (1) to prove that it was intentional and not accidental, and (2) to find the offender (Slak Boštjan, 2016). The crime scene would be bizarre as there is no direct involvement of the perpetrator, so there is no exchange of trace evidence, and one would have to rely upon circumstantial evidence. All the advancement in technologies is as convenient to the hackers as it is to us because, rather than creating new software, they just have to add bugs to the existing software. The time and knowledge required to put a firewall into the existing AI systems are far less than those required for creating a malicious one (Schneider & Breitinger, 2020).

An AI system without a database is as good as an amateur handling the case. The lack of sufficient relevant data available in order to create a good reference database is another setback. Sometimes it takes years to gather and create a particular pattern datum even if all the previous information has been fed correctly.

Charles Kettering once said, "A problem well stated is half solved." Results from AI are entirely dependent on the problems that are well established in the past and require a high volume of data associated with them. It can only outperform humans on the solved problems; what you feed to it is what you get. The unsolved problems with AI might remain unsolved until the human mind intervenes. Even if we have a huge amount of data to feed, the strategy to solve a particular crime won't remain the same as crime evolves, too, with the evolution of technology. So, AI has to be made to learn then unlearn and relearn new aspects, for which, again, a huge amount of data is required. AI in all its forms cannot be replaced with the human mind, but it definitely overcomes its shortcomings of it.

CONCLUSION

To sum up, AI holds its future firmly in forensic investigation. All the techniques have promising results when combined with AI. Once again, AI demands a high volume of data and will always be occupied with a certain level of uncertainty. Until our digital experts figure out a solution to this, AI must be used as an assistant rather than a decision-maker. Undoubtedly, the time it saves by quickly processing the data will always be irreplaceable at any point in time. Once established, it will significantly reduce the number of pending cases due to the lack of timely and adequate processing of evidence worldwide.

Emerging technologies also open the door for its misconduct; therefore, if well programmed, AI could become the critical solution to complex problems.

ACKNOWLEDGMENTS

Sukanya Sachdeva is grateful to the Indian Council of Medical Research (ICMR) for providing the Senior Research Fellowship and would like to acknowledge the Director, ICMR-National Institute of Occupational Health, Ahmedabad for supporting the process. The authors would like to acknowledge Mr. Praveen Mittal CAE Healthcare and their channel partner Hospimedica Group for providing images of the Automated Human Patient Simulator.

REFERENCES

DESPP. (2022). Crime scene reconstruction. Available from: https://portal.ct.gov/DESPP/Division-of-Scientific-Services/_content/Crime-Scene-Reconstruction [last accessed on April 17, 2022].

Dass, G., Pandoh, N., & Choudhary, H. (2020). 3D Crime scene investigation. *International Journal of Research in Engineering, Science and Management, 3*(12), 124–126.

DRDO. (2019). Robotics. Available from: https://www.drdo.gov.in/robotics [last accessed on April 17, 2022].

Everaerts, J. (2008). The use of unmanned aerial vehicles (UAVS) for remote sensing and mapping. *The International Archives of the Photogrammetry, Remote sensing and Spatial Information Services*, 37. www.aerobel.be

Gautam, S., Sharma, N., Sharma, R. K., & Basu, M. (2017). Human Patient Simulator based CBRN casualty management training. *Defence Life Science Journal, 2*(1), 80. doi:10.14429/dlsj.2.11073

Greenwald, S. W., Kulik, A., Beck, S., Newbutt, N., Lee, V., Xia, L., & Maes, P. (2017). *Technology and Applications for Collaborative Learning in Virtual Reality.* CSCL Proceedings. doi:10.22318/CSCL2017.115

Hackney, C., & Clayton, A. I. (2015). Unmanned Aerial Vehicles (UAVs) and their application in geomorphic mapping. *British Society for Geomorphology Geomorphological Techniques, 1*(2).

Houck, M. M., Crispino, F., & McAdam, T. (2018a). CBRN crime scenes. In M. M. Houck, F. Crispino, and T. McAdam, *The Science of Crime Scenes* (pp. 397–408). Elsevier. doi:10.1016/b978-0-12-849878-1.00031-4

Houck, M. M., Crispino, F., & McAdam, T. (2018b). Crime scene reconstruction. In M. M. Houck, F. Crispino, and T. McAdam, *The Science of Crime Scenes* (pp. 341–344). Elsevier. doi:10.1016/b978-0-12-849878-1.00024-7

Interrante, V., Höllerer, T., & Lécuyer, A. (2018). Virtual and Augmented Reality. *IEEE Computer Graphics and Applications, 38*(2), 28–30. IEEE Computer Society. doi:10.1109/MCG.2018.021951630

Koen, W. J., & Goetz, B. (2017). Crime scene reconstruction. In W. J. Coen and C. Michael Bowers (Eds), *Forensic Science Reform: Protecting the Innocent* (pp. 299–329). Elsevier. doi:10.1016/B978-0-12-802719-6.00010-8

Mayne, R., & Green, H. (2020). Virtual reality for teaching and learning in crime scene investigation. *Science and Justice, 60*(5), 466–472. doi:10.1016/j.scijus.2020.07.006

Mendis, N. A. (2017). Use of unmanned aerial vehicles in crime scene investigations— novel concept of crime scene investigations. *Forensic Research & Criminology International Journal, 4*(1). doi:10.15406/frcij.2017.04.00094

NCRB. (2022). NCRB data 2020. Crime in India. Available from: https://ncrb.gov.in/sites/default/files/crime_in_india_table_additional_table_chapter_reports/TABLE%201C.1.pdf [last accessed on April 17, 2022].

Renduchintala, A., Jahan, F., Khanna, R., & Javaid, A. Y. (2019). A comprehensive micro unmanned aerial vehicle (UAV/Drone) forensic framework. *Digital Investigation, 30*, 52–72. doi:10.1016/j.diin.2019.07.002

Rigano, C. (2019). Using artificial intelligence to address criminal justice needs. *NIJ Journal, 280*, https://www.nij.gov/journals/280/Pages/using-artificialintel-ligence-to-address-criminal-justice-needs.aspx

Schneider, J., & Breitinger, F. (2020). *AI Forensics: Did the Artificial Intelligence System Do It? Why?* http://arxiv.org/abs/2005.13635

Shiaeles, S., Chryssanthou, A., & Katos, V. (2013). On-scene triage open source forensic tool chests: Are they effective? *Digital Investigation, 10*(2), 99–115. doi:10.1016/j.diin.2013.04.002

Sieberth, T., Dobay, A., Affolter, R., & Ebert, L. C. (2019). Applying virtual reality in forensics—a virtual scene walkthrough. *Forensic Science, Medicine, and Pathology, 15*(1), 41–47. doi:10.1007/s12024-018-0058-8

Singhal, G., Bansod, B., & Mathew, L. (2018). Unmanned aerial vehicle classification, applications and challenges: A review. *Preprints, 2018*, 2018110601. doi:10.20944/preprints201811.0601.v1

Slak Boštjan. (2016). Drones in criminal investigation. *Kriminalistička teorija I praksa, 3*(2).

Smyth, D. L., Fennell, J., Abinesh, S., Karimi, N. B., Glavin, F. G., Ullah, I., Drury, B., & Madden, M. G. (2018). *A Virtual Environment with Multi-Robot Navigation, Analytics, and Decision Support for Critical Incident Investigation.* http://arxiv.org/abs/1806.04497

Süncksen, M., Teistler, M., Hamester, F., & Ebert, L. C. (2019). Preparing and guiding forensic crime scene inspections in virtual reality. *ACM International Conference Proceeding Series*, 755–758. doi:10.1145/3340764.3344903

UNODC. (2008). Investigation of trafficking in persons. Available from: https://www.unodc.org/documents/human-trafficking/Toolkit-files/08-58296_tool_5-9.pdf [last accessed on April 17, 2022].

Urbanová, P., Jurda, M., Vojtíšek, T., & Krajsa, J. (2017). Using drone-mounted cameras for on-site body documentation: 3D mapping and active survey. *Forensic Science International, 281*, 52–62. doi:10.1016/j.forsciint.2017.10.027

Weiler, N., Kraus, M., Kilian, T., Jentner, W., & Keim, D. A. (2018). *Visual Analytics for Semi-Automatic 4D Crime Scene Reconstruction.* www.victoria-project.eu/.

3

Artificial Intelligence in Fingerprint Identification

Apoorva Singh, Vinay Aseri, Varad Nagar, Sneha Lohar,
Poonam Kumari, Surya Shekhar Daga, Mahipal Singh Sankhla,
Chandra Shekhar Yadav, and Kumud Kant Awasthi

INTRODUCTION

In a lawful climate, criminological science includes utilizing logical ideas to dissect proof at a crime location to reproduce and describe past events. It was intensely impacted by Locard's trade hypothesis, which asserts that a lawbreaker would bring something into the crime location and take something as they fled – the exchange principle – the two items of which might be used as criminological proof. A fingerprint is considered one such item of proof in the field of forensics.

Fingerprints have been reliably used in identification, and criminal identification, applications since the early 19th century. Much research on ridge patterns, finger secretions—and their patterns and marks—was conducted and published by German anthropologist Hermann Welcke, Professor Paul-Jean Coulier, Dr. Henry Faulds, and numerous others. To be useful in criminal investigations, such patterns—Latent Fingerprints (LFPs) as they are termed—must be properly identified, collected, and analyzed. Since under the best of circumstances such processes present

DOI: 10.4324/9781003287810-3

myriad challenges, it's imperative that proper techniques of collection and analysis must be followed and adhered to.

These difficulties can be encountered during fingerprint collection, enhancement and pre-processing, feature extraction, matching, and classification [1]. The optimal answers for some of these issues are still lacking, despite the fact that these issues have been addressed by many scholars utilizing various methodologies to enhance the efficiency of the recognition system as a whole. Artificial neural networks (ANN), support vector machines (SVM), and genetic algorithms (GA) [2] are examples of machine learning approaches that play a significant role in providing unconventional solutions for fingerprint identification challenges. Making a feature vector and tutoring (teaching) the computer how to process it in accordance with predetermined criteria are the objectives of these techniques. This chapter covers the AI-based models used in fingerprint biometrics, latent fingerprint analysis, and various software where artificial intelligence has made it more efficient for forensic scientists to identify fingerprints. Possible future prospects of AI in fingerprint identification and development have also been discussed.

THE ROLE OF AI IN FINGERPRINTING

Many algorithms have been developed, with some of them involving the use of a software procedure that incorporates an artificial neural network. Automatic Fingerprint Verification (AFV) uses a Learning Vector Quantization (LVQ) neural network (NN). This method (shape signatures) uses local (minutiae) and global picture properties. A feature vector that describes the fingerprint is created by digitizing the shape signatures made using the matching minutiae (minute ridge details) as a reference axis. A pair of feature vectors' difference set is used to train an LVQ NN to match fingerprints [3]. Patil and Suralkar [4] and Kashyap and Yadav [16] show how to use a neural network to differentiate fingerprint images into six categories: arch (tented, normal), whorl, and loop (left, right, and twin). The system's classification result has a low rejection ratio and is quite accurate, with an average accuracy of 80.2 percent. It is clear that the given strategy has substantially increased the accuracy of fingerprint image categorization. The suggested method is accurate and effective, according to the simulation findings. Sathiaraj [5] explains how to use an artificial neural network with the backpropagation training network application to determine precise thumb impressions apart from matches to formerly stored photographs. The gadget receives a picture of a person's thumb imprint as input (fingerprint sensor). The fingerprint picture is classified using a neural program as the first stage in the matching procedure. Actually, this categorization procedure is carried out in order to shorten the time it takes to find anything.

The Levenberg-Marquardt backpropagation (LMBP) algorithm is another ANN approach. Because LMBP is the quickest approach for complicated data sets and provides superior performance, it is employed for training purposes. Using the trainlm function, the image being processed is trained to provide a range of outputs, including a performance plot, an input image simulation network, regression results, a histogram graph, and more. Self-organization, fault tolerance, real-time operation, and adaptive learning are only a few of the benefits of adopting neural networks over other approaches. Many applications of neural networks exist, including handwriting and typewriting recognition, fraud detection, criminal punishment, optimization, pattern recognition, and so on. The trainlm function is used to generate distinct result sets for a training network.

The hardware environment includes a 1024-neuron neural network working device known as CM1k Cognimem [6]. The parallel chain of neurons in the neural network must receive the pattern signature in order to function. When this device is used for identifying patterns, the input bus is used. Feature extraction and classification are the two fundamental phases in most classification problems. Many fingerprint classification techniques have been presented in recent decades, integrating various machine learning methodologies [7]. However, information about individual points is frequently taken into account by various algorithms, and it has a tangible effect on the results of the final classification. The failure of categorization is frequently caused by incorrect information on individual points. How can you avoid using solitary points directly while still getting a good categorization result? Deep learning has lately seen a lot of success in various computer vision problems.

Much more complicated characteristics may be achieved using this type of layered structure, which provides a greater capacity for depiction. Restricted Boltzmann machines (RBMs) were used by Hinton [8] to create low-dimensional codes that outperform principal component analysis (PCA). For the purpose of recognizing handwriting, Pascal Vincent et al. [9] developed and used the stacked denoising auto encoders model. The usage of these deep learning methods [10] has expanded to include artificial intelligence [11], natural language processing [12], and visual tasks

[13]. Deep learning methods are currently being applied to address a number of traditional fingerprint recognition challenges, including orientation field estimation and minutiae extraction [14–15].

AI-BASED FINGERPRINT IDENTIFICATION, DEVELOPMENT, AND BIOMETRIC SYSTEMS

In fingerprint identification, minutiae template matching, and the minutiae extraction procedure to get minutiae points, are crucial processes. Various algorithms have been developed, with a few of them using a software method that makes use of an artificial neural network. An AI-based system would provide a better efficiency rate in the identification of fingerprints in different criminal cases, and their details could be saved for a long time. Some of the most advanced biometric system types are currently in use worldwide, and their quality is steadily improving. The world's biggest fingerprint identification automation system uses an AI algorithm for its database. Scientists have been working on many techniques where AI is used for the recognition of LFPs.

Automated Fingerprint Identification System (AFIS)

Recent complications and inaccuracies in fingerprint identification have highlighted the necessity of methodically evaluating the information content of a papillary pattern. In particular, there is an increasing need for an estimation of the statistical uncertainty linked to this kind of information. The methodology employed in this analysis is based on the evaluation of likelihood ratios (LRs). With regard to two mutually incompatible hypotheses, this evaluation tool compares the likelihood of the evidence. Through the calculation of statistical information ratios on a marks database from accepted sources (matching and not matching the unknown mark), it is feasible to estimate the evidential contribution of fingerprint evidence. Only level II features (minutiae) are used in this system. As an equivalent metric between the various arrangements of minutiae, the Artificial Fingerprint Identification System (AFIS) provides an evaluation of any comparison (mark to mark, fingerprint to fingerprint, and mark to fingerprint). The numerator of the LR compares the identical minutiae configuration coming from the same source and treats them within finger variability. Therefore, only comparisons that feature the same minute detail on the mark and print are considered: the LR member's and the configuration of minutiae denominator. Additionally, it demonstrates the misrepresentation rates through cross comparison with a database of prints from various sources independently.

Compared with the evaluation of the LR's denominator (which just requires a significant number of prints from a non-associated population), the estimation of the LR numerator is significantly more difficult in terms of the particular data desired. Therefore, this work only tackles problems relating to the numerator or within finger variability. The aim of this study is to provide explanations of the following issues: (1) What percentage of LRs may be predicted from such a model depends on how the information should be organized, (2) how a database for modelling finger variability should be acquired, (3) whether the visualization technique or the preference of different minutiae arrangements may affect that modelling.

Results indicate that the visualization method applied to the mark has an impact on within-finger variability, according to the numeric evidence. In law enforcement, the fingerprints used are among the most coveted evidence found at crime scene investigations for a number of reasons. Primarily because fingermarks vary so much from person to person, it is possible to identify the individual of these marks even from fragmentary and smeared impressions taken from crime scenes. Second, using chemical and physical detection techniques on pertinent exhibits has improved the quantity and quality of markings found and is beneficial for comparison through their selectivity and sensitivity. Finally, it is relatively easy to classify reference accumulations of prints, which enables the recognition of known offenders who had previously given their fingerprints in the 1970s. Algorithmic research has introduced effective search algorithms to the field, which have been implemented in the majority of countries in the guise of AFIS (Automated Fingerprints, or palm print Identification Systems). With the use of these methods, it is possible to locate a fingertip or palmer region that has been left with a partial print amid thousands of ten-print cards. Based on proximity metrics known as scores, AFIS generates a prioritized list of candidates it deems to be "best matches." The positions and directions of minutiae are usually employed in their computation.

Measuring distances (in a certain way) between minute configurations is the initial step in modelling probability linked to level II features. In order to achieve this, a score will be utilized from AFIS as a stand-in for the comparison of two pattern arrangements. Second, it is important to pay great attention to the fact that there are never two collocations that are an exact match of a given papillary surface in any model for fingerprint feature evaluation. The possibility of an arbitrary association with an independent source and this within-mark distinction are the only factors that may be used to calculate the efficacy of the evidence for an established set of matching level II traits. When using an LR technique, such as that suggested in recent model development [16], this is completely accomplished. The assessment technique under investigation here is applicable in a very specific situation: a mark and a fingerprint are compared, and no discrepancies that would indicate exclusions have been found. The information that has been obtained through comparison of the print and the mark is regarded as valid in this context, and the present approach can be used to assess this concordance. Therefore, it is established how many minutiae there are and how they are arranged topologically. The following ratio of probabilities can be used to express the LR:

$$LR = \frac{P(H, I)}{P(EH, I)}$$

Here, E stands for the observations made between the given print and a mark; H is the notion that the mark and the print were made using the same finger, and as an alternative H means that the mark was created using an unrelated finger from the one that left the print. I is any appropriate background details, such as the gender or race of the mark's donor that could have an impact on the likelihood of the evidence.

In the technique described below, an Automated Fingerprint Identification System is used to access the "evidence." The proximity between two minutiae configurations is measured by the scores the algorithm uses.

The LR therefore becomes:

$$LR = \frac{P(s\ H,\ I)}{P(s\ H,\ I)}$$

Where s is the result of the difference between the print and the mark under consideration. I, H, and H all share the same explanations as above. Be aware that, for the score value acquired, we are evaluating the LR using a ratio of densities. The core of this strategy is the estimation of these two density functions. Initially assuming the set up with a configuration of six minutiae, this chapter will first discuss the density of the numerator and then the denominator. These questions are addressed by this study: (1) How should a database be established for modelling from finger variability? (2) Should different minutiae arrangements be chosen or should the visualization technique have an effect on that modelling? (3) What is the extent that LR can be anticipated from such a model?

AI in Latent Fingerprint Processing

One of the most difficult issues in unique finger impression acknowledgment is contrasting fingermarks with rolled (normal prints of upper digits)/slap (simultaneous plain impressions) fingerprints. Correlation of finger imprints to recommended prints by cutting edge AFIS doesn't normally yield palatable outcomes. This is on the grounds that numerous obscure fingermarks experienced in crime location examinations (1) are incomplete prints with moderately little grating edge region, (2) have unfortunate difference and lucidity with critical mutilation and (3) have huge foundation commotion [17]. Thus, a unique finger impression inspector is regularly expected to physically stamp highlights on a fingermark preceding presenting a question to an AFIS, and to in this way survey the top-K (generally K ¼ 20–50) recoveries to decide whether the obscure fingermark matches against a reference print [18]. When the inquiry submitted to an AFIS has a markup, the probability of observing a match in the reference data set increases, according to the NIST ELFT-EFS 2 assessment [19]. In any event, this presentation benefit depends on the accuracy of the markup provided to the AFIS [20]. When the image alone is a contribution to the AFIS, uncertain markups may cause the matching reference print to rank lower than its rivals among the recovered prints. Moreover, markups for similar fingermarks by various inspectors can essentially fluctuate [21–22].

To defeat the previously mentioned impediments, it very well might be educational to utilize a fingermark distinguishing proof structure where AFIS and unique finger impression analysts work synergistically to further develop the ID precision [17]. Such a system relies on the two conjectures that follow: (1) In order to accurately identify fingermarks of higher quality, manual markup may not be mandatory; if this can be proven, individual finger imprint inspectors will have more time to manually markup tough finger impressions, (2) incorporating the markups made by different inspectors while removing the highlights can help the AFIS functioning. By and large, a gathering of specialists with assorted and corresponding abilities can aggregately take care of a troublesome issue better compared with every individual master (Figure 3.1).

36

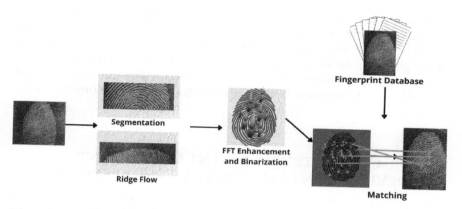

Figure 3.1 Latent fingerprint analysis using an AI-based model.

AI-based Fingerprint Biometrics System

Programmed acknowledgment of people is a vital part of a large number of everyday exchanges in our day-to-day life. Various applications, from cell phone admittance to worldwide boundary-crossing, rely upon the utilization of verification systems to dependably recognize an individual. In general, a person's identity checks are done using identity documents (IDs) and passwords. However, the apparent flaws in these accreditations (what you express and what are your skills) have prompted the use of natural attributes like fingerprints to accurately identify individual people. Biometrics is a method of individualizing people by their physiological or behavioral traits. In terms of loss, theft, fraud, and duplication, biometric identity somewhat compensates for the shortcomings of token- and information-based identification, driven by the security requirements of the electronically connected world.

Iris patterns, retinal scans, voices, fingerprints, and signatures are examples of biometric features. The fingermark impression is one of the most extensively used biometric characteristics because it is individualistic, widely accepted, and inexpensive. Most utilization of AI can be done in biometric systems as they are automated and have large databases which do not require any sort of physical support. AI has been adopted by most companies and organizations all around the world; when specific patterns are disturbed, it stabilizes them and detects dangers, for example when a person's fingerprints don't match those in a database [22]. In the field of forensics, the safeguarding of case files and results of an examination of evidence are a hard a job, so with the use of this system those security protocols can be maintained, limiting the access to important documents as well as their database which can be used in cases to get an idea of the people involved related to the cases. With an everyday increase in the technology's abilities, fingerprint biometrics is also getting more and more advanced, and there is more to be developed in the biometrics with the help of AI.

CONVENTIONAL LATENT FINGERPRINT DEVELOPMENT TECHNIQUE VS THE AI SYSTEM

A latent fingerprint is the most widely available evidence found on the crime scene. Due to this fact, much consideration has been given to advancements in techniques for the development and visualization of these latent fingerprint impressions [23]. Conventionally, the latent fingerprints are developed using various physical and chemical development mediums, and specifically, the physical techniques are applied majorly as they produce good results and negligible tampering to the fingerprint whereas a few chemical techniques are destructive in nature i.e., no method can be used further if the result produced is not significantly efficient for identification in one go.

Once the latent fingerprints are developed, they are subjected to further analysis to identify the individual from the impression. For identification, class and individual characteristics of the fingerprint are traced and recognized. Class characteristics include the pattern types like loops, whorls, arches, composites, and accidental patterns, whereas individual characteristics are the ridge features known as minutiae, which are minute ridge details that have a characteristic formation or shape that makes a fingerprint unique as no two individuals will have the same arrangement of minutiae at the same spots and at the same angle. This is what actually makes fingerprints unique evidence [24]. As far as the AI system is concerned, this method locates and identifies the minutiae digitally using a software tool.

There are various methods being employed in AI systems, like optical scanners, capacitors, or camera-based images. Basically, the ridges are captured either three-dimensionally or two-dimensionally and an image is formed of the ridge pattern in the area that was subjected to the scanner. It identifies and locates the minutiae automatically with the help of software and gives a unique binary code to each fingerprint.

The main differences between the conventional system and the AI system are:

- In the conventional method minutiae are located manually with the help of a magnifying glass, whereas in the AI system the minutiae identification is done using an inbuilt software tool that extracts the ridge characteristics.
- The located minutiae can be stored digitally in unique binary code form in the case of an AI system, whereas this is not possible in conventional methods.
- The conventional method is time consuming and all the minutiae might not necessarily be found, whereas the AI system does this job in seconds.
- Conventionally located minutiae can be very confusing if further analysis is done, and probably, if handed over to a new person, the second time, he/she might have to locate the minutiae again whereas no such issues are encountered in the case of the AI system.
- The chances of error are high in the case of AI systems as software is not always reliable. Manual identification is less prone to errors [25].
- With the aid of an AI, a large number of samples can be analyzed in a remarkably short amount of time, a system that will further aid law enforcement agencies in a speedy investigation [26].
- The application of an AI-based system does not necessarily require an expert in fingerprints, as a person who is adequately trained to use the biometric software would fit the purpose. But an opinion can only be formed with the help of an expert in the field of fingerprints.

CONCLUSION

The use of biometrics or Artificial Intelligence technology is rapidly growing and is being adapted and accepted worldwide for personal identification and verification. It is chosen over traditional methods of verification like passwords, security keys, identification cards, etc. as it provides quick and effective results. The chances of impersonation, forgery, or any kind of digital fraud are very commonly encountered in conventional methods of verification, whereas in the case of AI committing such kinds of fraud becomes extremely difficult as it requires the physical presence of the person. Artificial Intelligence has applications in various sectors like healthcare, manufacturing and production, gaming industries, data mining and knowledge extraction, national security and surveillance, education, and many more. There are a number of technologies that are being combined with AI systems to make things smarter and easier, such as interface technology, molecular biology, nanotechnology, robotics, and communication technology. AI in fingerprint identification plays a major role due to the reality that every person has a distinct fingermark impression and distinguishing ridge patterns that can easily help in the identification of an individual. AFIS is one such tool that basically is a database system that can store multiple fingerprint templates and can compare and verify if the entered data belongs to the same person. AFIS is being used in police organizations and forensic science laboratories for the identification of criminals or the determination of any unknown fingerprint obtained from the scene of the crime. The AI system has various advantages over conventional methods of fingerprint development and identification such as speed, durability, storage, accuracy, acceptability, and universality.

REFERENCES

[1] Maltoni, D., Maio, D., Jain, A. K., & Prabhakar, S. (2009). *Handbook of fingerprint recognition*. Springer Science & Business Media.
[2] Tan, X., & Bhanu, B. (2006). Fingerprint matching by genetic algorithms. *Pattern Recognition, 39*(3): 465–477.
[3] Ceguerra, A., & Koprinska, I. (2002). Automatic fingerprint verification using neural networks. *International Conference on Artificial Neural Networks*. Springer.
[4] Patil Waghjale, S. R., & Suralkar, S. R. (2012). Fingerprint classification using artificial neural network. *Computer Science, 2*(10): 513–517.
[5] Kashyap, K., & Yadav, M. (2013). Fingerprint matching using neural network training. *International Journal of Engineering and Computer Science, 2*(6): 2041–2044.
[6] Sathiaraj, V. (2012). A study on the neural network model for finger print recognition. *International Journal of Computational Engineering Research, 2*(5).
[7] Cognimem, CogniMem_1K (2008). *Neural network chip for high performance pattern recognition, datasheet, Version 1.2.1.* www.recognetics.com.
[8] Galar, M. et al. (2015). A survey of fingerprint classification Part I: Taxonomies on feature extraction methods and learning models. *Knowledge-Based Systems, 81*: 76–97.

[9] Hinton, G. E., & Salakhutdinov, R. R. (2006) Reducing the dimensionality of data with neural networks. *Science, 313*(5786): 504–507.

[10] Vincent, P., Larochelle, H., Bengio, Y., & Manzagol, P.-A. (2008). Extracting and composing robust features with denoising autoencoders. In *Proceedings of the 25th International Conference on Machine Learning*, Helsinki, Finland, June 5–9, 2008. doi:10.1145/1390156.1390294

[11] LeCun, Y., Bengio, Y., & Hinton, G. (2015). Deep learning. *Nature, 521*(7553): 436–444.

[12] Zhang, Z., et al. (2015). Learning deep representation for face alignment with auxiliary attributes. *IEEE Transactions on Pattern Analysis and Machine Intelligence (TPAMI), 38*(5): 918–930.

[13] Yao, K., Zweig, G., Hwang, M.-Y., Shi, Y., & Yu, D. (2013, August). Recurrent neural networks for language understanding. *Interspeech Conference.* doi:10.13140/2.1.2755.3285

[14] Silver, D., et al. (2016). Mastering the game of Go with deep neural networks and tree search. *Nature, 529*(7587): 484–489.

[15] Sankaran, A., Pandey, P., Vatsa, M., & Singh, R. (2014). On latent fingerprint minutiae extraction using stacked denoising sparse AutoEncoders. *2014 IEEE International Joint Conference on Biometrics.* doi:10.1109/BTAS.2014.6996300

[16] Datta, A. K., Lee, H. C., Ramotowski, R., & Gaensslen, R. E. (2001). *Advances in fingerprint technology.* CRC Press.

[17] Paulino, A. A., Feng, J., & Jain, A. K. (2012). Latent fingerprint matching using descriptor-based hough transform. *IEEE Transactions on Information Forensics and Security, 8*(1): 31–45.

[18] Arora, S. S., Cao, K., & Jain, A. K. (2015). Crowd powered latent fingerprint identification: Fusing AFIS with examiner markups. In *2015 International Conference on Biometrics (ICB)*. IEEE.

[19] Indovina, M., Dvornychenko, V., Hicklin, R. A., & Kiebuzinski, G. I. (2012). *ELFT-EFS Evaluation of Latent Fingerprint Technologies: Extended Feature Sets [Evaluation# 2].* 7859: p. 535. NIST. doi:10.6028/NIST.IR.7859

[20] Dror, I. E., Wertheim, K., Fraser-Mackenzie, P., & Walajtys, J. (2012). The impact of human–technology cooperation and distributed cognition in forensic science: Biasing effects of AFIS contextual information on human experts. *Journal of Forensic Sciences, 57*(2): 343–352.

[21] Ulery, B. T., Austin Hicklin, R., Buscaglia, J., & Roberts, M. A. (2012). Repeatability and reproducibility of decisions by latent fingerprint examiners. *PLoS One, 7*(3): e32800.

[22] Kairinos, N. (2019). The integration of biometrics and AI. *Biometric Technology Today, 5*: 8–10.

[23] Wang, M., Li, M., Yu, A., Zhu, Y., Yang, M., & Mao, C. (2017). Fluorescent nanomaterials for the development of latent fingerprints in forensic sciences. *Advanced Functional Materials, 27*(14): 1606243.

[24] Jain, A. K., & Feng, J. (2010). Latent fingerprint matching. *IEEE Transactions on Pattern Analysis and Machine Intelligence, 33*(1): 88–100.

41

[25] Alsaadi, I. M. (2015). Physiological biometric authentication systems, advantages, disadvantages and future development: A review. *International Journal of Scientific & Technology Research*, 4(12): 285–289.

[26] Asha, S., & Chellappan, C. (2012). Biometrics: An overview of the technology, issues and applications. *International Journal of Computer Applications*, 39(10): 35–52.

4

Artificial Intelligence in Multimedia Forensics

Palak Aneja, Parvesh Sharma, Krittika Sood, Kalpesh Solanki,
Sumit Kumar Choudhary, and Surbhi Mathur

INTRODUCTION

Advents and advancements in technology have revolutionized the world, impacting almost everything in all walks of life. Whether we use social media, such as Instagram or Facebook, or emails for formal conversation, artificial intelligence (AI) has a significant role in our day-to-day lives. Digital assistants like Siri, Alexa, Bixbi, and others have become our helping hands. Emails/messages are automatically sorted into primary, social, promotions, spam, or other tags. We rely on these assistants to update news, play music for us, dial calls, or search for any detail from the Internet. We have become dependent on AI for every trivial task of the day.

The term AI was coined back in the mid-1950s by the father of AI, John McCarthy (McCarthy et al., 1955), who defined it as "the science and engineering of making intelligent machines" (McCarthy, 2007). Three terms, AI, machine learning (ML), and deep learning (DL), which we use sometimes as synonyms, are in reality the subfields of AI. AI is a program that can sense, reason, act, and adapt, whereas an algorithm known as

DOI: 10.4324/9781003287810-4

ML improves over time as it gets exposed to more and more data. DL is a multi-layered neural network that learns from a vast amount of data.

The three pillars for the development of AI are:

1. Hardware of computer technology: In the last two decades, the growth in the Central Processing Unit has been remarkable. With these developments in computing technology hardware, computers have become necessary in our everyday lives. It also allows users to train the small DL models using laptops with advanced Graphical Processing Unit.
2. Data: AI is indirectly based on the amount of data used for structuring the model. The Internet revolution has become an added boon for AI. The collection and distribution of data have never been so easy. Developers use the data available on the Internet to enhance their algorithms. For instance, consider how Facebook and Instagram map images to recognize and give an option of tagging without manually labelling a person.
3. Algorithm: Hardware and easy accessibility of data have provided an advantage to developers to develop more accurate algorithms.

These advents and advancements have revolutionized the world, impacting almost everything in all walks of life.

Traditional media has lost ground to online and multimedia material, especially among young people. The Internet, particularly social media, has become a dangerous source of misleading and immoral content. Multimedia manipulation has become a potent tool in the hands of criminals and attackers due to various editing apps, as well as the simplicity of use and retrieval of these tools; phoney news, fake political campaigns, pornographic movies, and other forms of deception are becoming progressively easy to transmit and manufacture with a high level of realism. The ability to distinguish between phoney and real is growing increasingly vital, but it is also becoming increasingly difficult.

Forensic science is no exception. AI has started to impact the very way forensic science is practiced and professed. Forensic science is a comparative science; the questioned samples collected from the crime scene are compared with controlled samples. This includes the examination of audio, videos, images, or CCTV (closed-circuit television) footage. The evidence is sent to the multimedia division of the Forensic Science Laboratory. Multimedia Forensics includes a set of scientific techniques used to examine the multimedia signals; they can be in the form of audio, images, or videos. The multimedia expert aims to identify the source, authenticate the content's integrity, and retrieve information from the signals for examining the content for speaker identification or facial identification from the image or video compared with the control evidence.

Typical editing actions in multimedia evidence include copy/move or splicing/cut-paste, resampling, contrast enhancement and denoising/median filtering.

Copy-move: In the copy-move method, the forger modifies the content by copying it from some part of the media and replacing it at another place of interest. It is frequently done to either hide an object's presence or change the meaning of the media.

Resampling: The mathematical resampling technique is used to create a new version of a media with a different size. It may be downsampling, which is the process of decreasing its size, whereas up-sampling is increasing an image's dimensions. For example, a down-sample in an image removes the information and hence details by computing the image's convolution a low-pass filter (to avoid aliasing) is employed. When up-sampling, however, one convolves the image that has an interpolation kernel, thus the photo-editing software evaluates the original photo's colors and features and creates. Then, new ones are added to the ones that already exist. Resampling can be done using various filters, including nearest neighbourbicubic, windowed sinc, and bilinear functions. Although the presence of resampling proofs throughout an image does not always mean that it has been modified, it does show that it has been processed.

Contrast enhancement: This method is commonly used to change the lighting in a photograph. Contrast enhancement is accomplished by applying a nonlinear, nondecreasing mapping to a signal's values, which means abrupt peaks and gaps introduced into the pixel values of a picture could generate traces. It can be combined with splicing to hide the brightness difference between the image from which the object introduced with the alteration comes and the image from which the object introduced with the manipulation comes, even though it can be used to fix a photo that is too dark or too light.

Denoising/median filtering: This is frequently used to denoise or smooth. It is done using a nonlinear technique that smooths the signal while maintaining the edge content. This strategy causes streaks in the signals by causing a series of observations of nearby signals to all assume the same value.

The use of Al technology improves the possibility of detecting and investigating crime. This enables forensic experts to get to the source of the problem swiftly and effectively. AI assists in solving a crime. AI can discover suspicious and illegal activity by combing through unorganized data collected by investigators. AI offers cognitive-data analytics, allowing users to consume and evaluate data quickly. It may also make it easier for experts to go through felony convictions and find prospective culprits. AI also assists in identifying specific components in pictures and films that are being investigated. Al helps identify similarities in communication, place, and time (Kuwabara & Sagisak, 1995; Chowdhury, 2021).

AUDIO AS EVIDENCE

One of the most crucial types of evidence in multimedia forensics is audio. Audio consists of speech, which is a clue in criminal offences such as ransom calls, threats, kidnapping, hate speech, and others. The science behind the audio examination for speaker recognition is that every individual has unique characteristics in their voice. These characteristics can be used for the identification of that person. Noteworthy qualities of the voice have led to use in biometric systems, voice assistants, voice-controlled services, and speech-based authentication products. Speaker recognition can either be done by speaker identification or speaker verification. Comparing an unknown speaker with a list of known speakers is speaker identification. Verifying a speaker's recognition is a method of speaker verification. Speaker identification can be done by comparing the speaker in two ways.

The first is the open set and closed set examination. In the open set, speaker utterance is compared with multiple speakers; acceptance is only made when an exact match is found. In the case of the closed set, a similarity score is given of the unknown speaker with all of the known speakers. The second is the text-dependent and text-independent way of examination. It is based on the utterance of the content. In text-dependent, the comparison for identification is based on precisely speaking the same utterance, whereas in text-independent the speaker can talk about anything without any constraint.

The replica of speech said by the criminals, and the commission of act crime, are done with the recording system's help. The recording system encodes sound signals and stores them on magnetic tape or optical discs in an analog or digital format. The stored signal can be played again with the help of a playback machine and loudspeaker. The sound wave can be converted into an analog or digital signal and be saved and reproduced accordingly.

Analog recording devices use the diaphragm to study the use of sound waves for measuring changes in atmospheric pressure, and phonographs to record those results. Waves of sound vibrate the microphone diaphragm during magnetic tape recording and are transformed into changing electric current by an electromagnet with changing magnetic field, which creates a plastic tape with a magnetic coating that has magnetized spots to imitate the sound.

Enhancements in technology have also impacted recording devices. Nowadays, smartphones can act as digital recording devices, documenting audio in an effortless process. This has increased audio usage in the court of law as crucial corroboratory evidence. The digital recording devices use pulse code modulation (PCM), with which audio is converted into digital code that a computer can understand. PCM, which involves sampling audio and turning it into a digital code that computers understand, is used to create digital audio thousands of times per second, a computer "listens" to an audio flow at specific times and turns each time sample into a numeric code. Your computer system's conversion speed acts as an indicator of its sample rate. (Jump, 2017). The Nyquist equation states that "a periodic signal must be sampled at more than twice the highest frequency component of the signal." The audio amplitude "describes the resolution of the sound data that is captured and stored in an audio file."

Therefore, the recording process completes in the three steps:

1. With the help of a transducer, sound waves are converted into an electric signal.
2. Storing the signal from the transducer on a recording medium such as magnetic tape, or optical device.
3. The captured signals are made audible using playback machines or loudspeaker systems (Jump, 2017).

Recorded audio is submitted to the forensic science laboratory by the investigating officer to determine the following:

1. Transcription of the questioned audio.
2. How many speakers are present in the questioned audio?
3. Identify the speaker in the questioned audio to known control audio.

Transcription is a systematic representation of the speech in the form of writing or printed document from the audio. Humans can speak 150 words per minute but typically may only type 40 words per minute. Transcription is a crucial part of the investigation. It helps determine the number of speakers, type of conversation, the language of communication, identification of clue words, and most importantly, it becomes easy for the judge to understand the context without listening or playing the audio in the proceedings. Transcription itself is a tedious task and requires the transcriber to be aware of the language of conversation. A person cannot have sound knowledge of all the languages in a particular region. It is a challenge for experts and requires continuous listening and writing while discriminating against different speakers. All these complexities increase the chances of error.

In the 1980s, Dr. Jim Baker and Dr. Janet Baker launched "Dragon Systems," a voice-recognition system based on mathematical models. It used statistics to predict words or phrases, or sentences. In 1990, Dragon dictate was launched, which is general-purpose to speech to text dictation. It required users to pause between words. In 1997 this problem was solved when Dragon Naturally Speaking was launched. At present, there is software that can take write/type at the speed of 160 words per minute with a 99 percent accuracy rate.

Advancements in speech to text have made life so easy now that merely giving instructions to digital devices can prompt them to draft emails and messages; we can even dictate to Microsoft Word and it will type. Speech to text conversion removes language barriers, and automatic subtitles can be added to the live streaming audio/video file.

Transcription of audio is not limited to forensic science scenarios. Medical personnel use it to make records of their surgeries. It is also used for dictation, in courts of law for recording the proceedings, by lawyers to make notes, etc.

After the audio transcription, the next step is the segmentation of the audio and marking the clue words for examination. Segmentation of the audio means creating segments from the heterogenous speaker file into a single-speaker, uniform segment audio file.

Forensic Speaker Identification can be done by three different approaches. The first auditory testing of the audio is its foundation. An analysis of those parameters of speech that are apparent to the human ear is considered appropriate. When approaching the audio for auditory analysis, the parameters to be considered are sound quality, speaking style, background sound, speech disturbances, speech irregularities, pauses, speaking speed, or any other parameter that can be obvious from the speaker-specific. Some studies prove that the listener's method is robust and language-dependent; the speaker should be known; and text-dependent (Kuwabara & Sagisak, 1995; McGehee, 1937; Perrachione et al., 2011). Multiple studies present in the literature prove humans are good speaker recognizers even allowing for degradation of the audio (Doddington, 1985; Lehiste & Meltzer, 1973). Linguistic analyses have been added in the last decade while performing forensic speaker identification. The parameters to be noted, but not limited to, are: accent, dialect, grammar, articulation, geological characteristics, or any specifics are noted and used when comparing audio files.

The second approach of speaker identification is based on studying the acoustic parameters of the audio with the help of a spectrogram. A spectrogram is the detailed view of the audio in a three-dimensional space. The vertical axis of the spectrogram displays frequency, the horizontal axis represents time in seconds, and the dark bands in the spectrogram describe the intensity.

In spectrographic analysis, acoustic parameters such as pitch, formant frequencies of phonemes, energy, and bandwidth are measured on a speech signal spectrogram. The values are compared among control and questioned audio.

The auditory-phonetic-and-acoustic-phonetic technique is used for technical speaker recognition. This technique considers an extensive range of speaker attributes combined with established speaker-distinguishing information. Aural-phonetic processes rely on qualified phoneticians or linguists for evaluating questioned recordings. The similarity of the recordings to the findings in a relevant population is assessed qualitatively or quantitatively (Drygajlo et al., n.d.).

Semi-Automatic Speaker Identification

Semi-automatic identification is an approach that uses both machine and human intervention when performing speaker identification. The parameters for this technique are acquired primarily from linguistic, auditory, acoustic, and phonetic components. Later on the results can be reported by following the "American Board of Recorded Evidence" set guidelines or the established guidelines of the "European Network of Forensic Science Institutes."

Automatic Speaker Identification

Another method of identification is automatic speaker recognition (ASR). This method enables machines to do all the procedures, with no manual interference. The results of this method are in the statement based upon the similarity score or likelihood ratio. For a successful working of an ASR, the following step-by-step processes are used:

1. data collection,
2. signal pre-processing,
3. feature extraction,
4. size reduction,
5. classification model construction,
6. learning models' evaluation.

Forensic speaker recognition (FASR) is another technical examination of audio that uses ASR principles to identify the questioned speaker to the control speaker.

Structure of ASR

ASR is a process of identifying an unknown speaker, with the help of control samples from the suspected speakers and the samples used as population (database) for training the machine.

The database for training the ASR system is critical as low quality will directly impact the performance of the identification system. The databases are available in different languages, but they are not very extensive. The following characteristics indirectly affect the identification system of ASR as population training is crucial for correct identification.

1. Language: Different languages have diverse acoustic properties, affecting the performance of speaker-identification (SI) systems.
2. Demography: Numerous studies have indicated that the SI systems must take into consideration the number of speakers and the demographic information of their representatives, including their age and gender. The number of speakers must be sufficient to improve fidelity of SI systems and requires large-scale datasets featuring higher recognition rates.
3. Lexical variability: The effectiveness of SI systems is based on the quality of the input utterances.
4. Session variability: Session variabilities can be influenced by a variety of factors, including recording time, type of device, channel mismatch, environment, or ambient sound.
5. Recording devices: Due to the various sensors, sensitivities, and recording capacities of different recording devices, each device records voice differently.

Pre-processing of Audio

The primary objective of the pre-processing phase is to get the audio data ready for feature extraction analysis. During speech recording, noise interference often occurs, which degrades the performance. Thus, pre-processing is an essential and necessary step, as poor pre-processing of the recorded speech input results in a drop in classification performance. Numerous noise-reduction algorithms exist, but spectral subtraction and adaptive noise cancellation are the two most commonly employed. Multiple studies emphasize that the kind of feature extraction approach to choose significantly impacts what functionality to apply during the pre-processing step. Pre-emphasis, noise reduction, endpoint recognition, framing, and normalizing are some of the frequently used features (Cutajar et al., 2013; Ibrahim et al., 2017; Jahangir et al., 2021; Suchitha & Bindu, 2015).

Feature Extraction

As Hanifa et al. (2021) state:

> The basic principle of feature extraction is to extract a sequence of features for each short-time frame of the input signal, with the assumption that such a small segment of speech is sufficiently stationary to allow for better modeling. In other words, the process retains useful and relevant information about the speech signal by rejecting redundant and irrelevant information.

The extraction and selection of features results in function matrices that reduce identification errors and identify the most exclusionary traits for speaker identification tasks. Attributes used to identify speakers are classified as (Table 4.1):

1. time domain,
2. frequency domain,
3. prosodic domain characteristics,
4. acoustic characteristics,
5. cepstral domain characteristics.

The primary research and development component in automatic speech recognition is feature extraction. As a result, numerous toolboxes and modules for speech feature extraction have been developed to address various speech-related challenges, such as pre-processing, algorithm competence, etc. (Moffat et al., 2015). Despite significant research in audio processing and feature extraction, little work has been done

Table 4.1   List of features

Feature		Description
Frequency domain feature	Energy (*E*)	The energy of the signal reflects the area under the square magnitude.
	Mean frequency (μF)	Mean frequency measures the mean normalized frequency of the power spectrum of a speech signal.
	Spectral Flux	Spectral Flux differentiates between normalized spectral magnitudes.
	Spectral Roll-Off	Spectral Roll-Off measures the spectral concentration less than threshold.
	Spectral Centroid	Spectral Centroid is the average frequency of speech signal weighted by magnitude.
	Spectral Flatness	Spectral Flatness shows whether the distribution is spiked or smooth.
	Spectral Entropy	Spectral Entropy calculates the regularity of power spectrum of speech signal.
	Spectral Contrast	Spectral Contrast represents the relative distribution of frequency instead of average frequency of speech signal.
Prosodic feature	Fundamental frequency (F0)	F0 is the reciprocal of time interval between two consecutive glottal cycles.
	Pitch	Pitch is a perceptual property of the speech signal with physical characteristics denoted by the F0.
	Intensity	Intensity is the measure of loudness or energy of a signal and is related to amplitude square.

to define and evaluate potential feature extraction toolboxes and their associated applications. Some toolboxes are Markov Model Toolkit (HTK), SIDKIT, openSMILE, Kaldi, Python speech Feature (PSF), jAudio, YAAFE, and LibXtract (see Table 4.2).

Another critical aspect of feature engineering is feature reduction, where inappropriate parameters have been removed to increase the accuracy and reliability of the results. The objective is to reduce the

Table 4.2 Popular feature toolboxes used in Speaker Identification (Jahangir et al., 2021)

	HTK	SIDEKIT	Open SMILE	Kaldi	pyAA	jAudio	YAAFE	Essentia	LibXtract	Librosa
Organization	Cambridge University	LIUM, Universite du Mans	audEERING GmbH	Microsoft Research	Behavioral Signals	QMUL	Telecom ParisTech	Pompeu Fabra University	–	NYU
Platform	Windows LINUX	Windows MacOS LINUX	Windows MacOS LINUX	Windows MacOS LINUX	Windows MacOS LINUX	Windows MacOS LINUX	MacOS LINUX	Windows MacOS LINUX	Cross-Platform	Cross-Platform
Open Source Access	✓ Free[a]	✓ Free[b]	✓ Free[c]	✓ Free[d]	✓ Free[e]	✓ Free[f]	✓ Free[g]	✓ Free[h]	✓ Free[i]	✓ Free[j]
Language Support	Python MATLAB C	Python	C++	C++	Python	Java	Python MATLAB C++	Python C++	C Java	Python
MFCC	✓	✓	✓	✓	✓	✓	✓	✓	✓	✓
LPC	✓	×	✓	×	×	×	✓	✓	✓	✓
LPCC	×	×	×	×	×	×	×	×	×	×
LSF	×	×	×	×	×	×	×	×	×	×
PLP	✓	×	✓	✓	×	×	×	×	×	×
LFCC	×	✓	×	×	×	×	×	×	×	×
ZCR	×	×	✓	×	✓	✓	✓	✓	✓	✓
HNR	×	×	✓	×	×	✓	✓	✓	×	×
RMS	×	×	×	×	×	✓	×	×	×	✓
MoM	×	×	×	×	×	×	×	×	×	×

(Continued)

53

Table 4.2 (Continued)

	HTK	SIDEKIT	Open SMILE	Kaldi	pyAA	jAudio	YAAFE	Essentia	LibXtract	Librosa
Energy	×	×	✓	×	✓	×	✓	✓	×	×
Formant	×	×	✓	×	×	×	×	×	✓	×
Tonal	×	×	✓	×	×	×	×	✓	×	✓
Spectral Flux	×	×	×	×	✓	✓	✓	✓	×	✓
Spectral ROF	×	×	×	×	✓	✓	✓	✓	×	✓
Spectral BW	×	×	×	×	×	×	×	×	×	✓
Mean	×	×	×	×	×	×	×	×	✓	×
Kurtosis	×	×	×	×	×	×	×	×	✓	×
S. Centroid	×	×	×	×	✓	×	×	✓	✓	✓
Spectrogram	×	×	×	×	✓	×	×	×	×	✓
Chroma	×	×	×	×	✓	×	×	×	×	✓
Output	HTK	SPRO4 HTK	Matrix CSV HTK ARFF	Matrix	CSV Matrix	XML ARFF	CSV HDF5	YAML JSON	VAMP XML	CSV TSV

** MFCC = Mel Frequency Cepstral Coefficients, LPC = Linear Predictor Coefficients, LFCC = Linear Frequency Cepstral Coefficients, LPCC = Linear Predictor Cepstral Coefficients, PLP = Perceptual Linear Prediction, MoM = Method of Moments, Spectral ROF = Spectral Rolloff, S. Centr = Spectral Centroid, Spectral BW = Spectral Bandwidth, pyAA = pyAudioAnalysis, QMUL = Queen Mary University of London, NYU = New York University.

Table 4.3 Feature selection methods used in reviewed studies

Methods	Advantages	Disadvantages	References
PCA	Reduces the number of dimensions without losing information	Not scale-invariant	Ali et al. (2018), Indumathi and Chandra (2015)
SFG	Best performs when the optimum feature subset is small	Unable to subtract features that become redundant after adding other features	Sardar and Shirbahadurkar (2018)
SBG	Best performs when the optimum feature subset is big, as it spends most of the time exploring large subsets	Unable to re-evaluate the usefulness of a feature after its removal	Sardar and Shirbahadurkar (2019)
UFSM	Simple to understand, run, and provides a better data understanding	Does not always give optimized feature set	Dhakal et al. (2019)

computational complexity of classification models, source dimensions, and overfitting. The methods for data reduction are shown in Table 4.3.

Classification Model Construction

A classification model is developed using the ML technique based on the training data. The built model is capable of predicting the speaker's unknown utterances. Numerous ML methods have been devised for the purpose of automatically identifying speakers. Gaussian Mixture Model, ML techniques include Support Vector Machine, Naive Bayes, Decision Tree, and artificial neural networks are techniques available which have evidently been used in Speaker Recognition.

Evaluation of Learning Models

DL approaches are characterized as Discriminative or Generative. The bottom-up models for the discriminative DL techniques (convolutional neural networks (CNN), recurrent neural networks (RNN)) have hidden layers connecting input and output layers. These strategies are used in supervised training for problems involving regression and classification. It is used to offer adequate training in the cases of known data, also known as the supervised training method. Restricted Boltzmann Machines (RBMs) and Deep AutoEncoder (DAE) are instances of generative DL methods that use a top-down, counter-flowing data approach, and these models are used for training the unknown data; this kind of training is known as unsupervised training (Lasserre & Bishop, 2007; Shrestha & Mahmood, 2019; Jahangir, et al., 2021).

This completes the structure of the ASR.

Next is speaker identification. The questioned speaker audio and the control speaker audio are used as input files in the ASR and there is a pre-set database present in the software. The database within the system will act as the reference population. After doing the analysis, results will be shown in the one of the following hypothesis statements based on the likelihood value calculated while doing the analysis.

1. Moderately strong evidence against prosecution hypothesis.
2. Moderate evidence against prosecution hypothesis.
3. Limited evidence against prosecution hypothesis.
4. Moderately strong evidence against prosecution hypothesis.
5. Moderately strong evidence to support prosecution hypothesis.

Possible formulation of the defense hypothesis: H_0 = recordings of a Potential Reference Speaker's sources are distinct from those of the in-depth recording.

Possible formulation of the prosecution hypothesis: H_1 = recordings of The Source of the Questioned Recording and the Suspected Reference Speaker is the same.

Challenges and Future Approaches for ASR in Forensic Speaker Identification

The first requirement for the working of the ASR is a database. There is no significant database available with the authorities which can be used as standard. Some databases are available but with a small number of speakers with a single language. Countries with multi-lingual dialects using ASR results needs to be more cautious. There is no standard guideline for the number of speakers, for a particular language, gender, age group etc. to be present in the database. It has given new leads that new research needs to be conducted to create the database. There should be standard protocols for creating and using the database. There is a need for research to be conducted on the multi-lingual system.

Another important challenge for ASR is at the pre-processing step. The background noise, overlapping audio, distortions due to recording device, etc. Signal to noise ratio, loudness in the voice hamper at every step. The similarity or likelihood value can be compromised in such cases. Present ASR systems do not consider the linguistic parameters for feature extraction. The possibility of using these parameters can also be explored in future research.

IMAGE/VIDEO AS EVIDENCE

When an expert examines an image or video, the ultimate goal is to recognize and track altered and created content. There are three approaches to identify modified content:

1. As a classification issue when a picture or video must be determined to be authentic or fraudulent,
2. As a regression issue where you're attempting to find the portion of an image or video that was modified.
3. As an anomaly identification issue, in which a machine is trained on real-world instances to identify these attacks as abnormalities.

When an image/video is put on the Internet, there is a chance it will become viral on social media. The advancement in Deepfakes (modern deep-learning algorithms) creates modification in a manner that new artificial content is created on the basis of content available. Deepfake has also attracted a lot of interest in recent years due to its involvement and engagement algorithm. Autoencoders (AE) and two sophisticated deep-learning methods are adversarial networks that are generative (GANs), architectures that are operated to make very genuine looking forged images and movies. Building trust and making it possible to assess the legitimacy of multimedia information is no longer a choice, but a requirement. Due to growing concern in this field, multimedia forensics brings together principles and methodologies from a variety of fields, including signal processing and computer vision while establishing the veracity and origin of an image or video.

The following are the three most common themes investigated by multimedia forensics:

1. Detection of forgeries entails establishing the validity of a picture or video and establishing no tampering.

2. Source recognition entails reconstructing the history of certain media content, such as the camera type, manufacturer, the particular device that recorded it, and whether it was obtained from a social networking platform.
3. Detection of deepfakes defines a deepfake as any false media used to replace an image or video.

For a long time now, researchers have been researching the topic of forgery detection, because thousands of professionals all over the world utilize fundamental editing products like Photoshop, Lightroom, and Final Cut Pro X, on a daily basis. Researchers have attempted to respond quickly to all of these uses by developing new technologies to detect false content.

Many researchers have recently become interested in the advances of Deepfakes. These artificially generated interventions are creating fresh concerns about fake news manufacturing, and their emergence into the sphere of substantial technological companies has hastened the development of new ways. In today's hyper-connected society, when information is distributed throughout the Internet, this is critical.

In many cases, multimedia content can be used as evidence in court, and it is essential to prove the validity of a picture or video's source and the picture or video itself. Experts can discover dishomogeneities in an image or video and manipulated characteristics that introduce discrepancies from the authentic picture, particularly to those that are not apparent. The content's source credentials can then be utilized to ascertain the camera model or brand used and the device used. This can be achieved by using a camera's operations to convert light entering the camera into a photograph or video. A forensic trail is left on the files that can be used afterward. With the increasing usage of social media and messaging apps, establishing where an image or video originated from has become essential. Using specific editing tools to manipulate an existing image or video can be called forgeries. This could be any standard editing action, such as picture scaling or color activities that include rectification or content editing, including adding a new object to a photograph or altering a movie frame to change its semantic content. Multiple compression and manipulated media (discussed in the introduction) are images and video forgery methods.

To identify between input false and actual photos or video frames, Do et al. (2018) use the feature extractor in the VGGFace (Parkhi et al., 2015).

The architectures in this area are united by the decision to focus on a particular element. However, as forensic tools evolve, deepfake generating methods do as well, making it harder to find these traces. Therefore, we predict the future development of detectors that are more intricate and advanced. Cross-manipulation detectors that can identify any kind of attack are still being developed in terms of forgery detection.

CONCLUSION

In today's scenario almost everything is generated and stored in the form of digital media only. The number of increasing social medias, the use of CCTV footage in almost every city, deepfakes, software that can copy voice and face semantics. All these have not just increased the data on servers and storage but have also given rise to new studies and fields. Multimedia has proven to be a very promising journey and future. If we look at just a decade ago, we can see that there used to be 2 to 3 megapixel smartphone cameras and CCTV but today they almost beat the DSLRs. In this progression of ten years, we can see new domains developing in this field, such as:

CCTV Audit: Due to the limitations of sitting in front of a screen all the time, this field has developed and we now have software that can audit the data of 24 hours in 20 minutes. With the integration of this software with ML and DL, we are already able to track data in footage. With AI we should be able to track anything in footage.

Image processing: Different image formats are available in the field, from generally public available formats to proprietary image formats, which, in effect, change the image compression methods and results with AI, meaning we can study all image processing at once. This will help us with the identification of the origin of any digital image. Also, AI can be utilized to study gate pattern and facial feature identification, which can help us in identifying deepfakes.

Apart from those mentioned above, other approaches could be: batch image processing and identification; data analyzing from the image at the pixel level; the prediction of an object by analyzing and studying its track movements. Due to the necessity to address these issues for forensic purposes as well as the enormous revenue opportunities connected with such applications, the study of multimedia forensic professions will continue to grow and expand. The development of new and more complex generating operations and techniques will make simpler technologies less effective. Multi-stream designs that are more intricate have shown promise in resolving this problem. To make use of all the delicate information available, more complex structures, methods, and data must be integrated to tackle multimedia-forensics problems. AI should be able to adapt to new manipulations without having to totally retrain, which could be challenging due to a lack of training data, or lead to catastrophic forgetting, in order to keep up with the rapid advancements in manipulation technology.

Futuristic Approach of AI

Closed-circuit television (CCTV), which can also be referred to as "the eye of justice," has proved its efficiency and capability of being a reliable tool to ensure the safety and security of the citizens of a country by helping in crime detection and prevention. The applications of CCTV are not limited, and its use is not just confined by law enforcement agencies; the common citizens of a country utilize the same for varied purposes that serve their interests like safeguarding their businesses and monitoring their personal affairs, etc.

According to police personnel, around 80–90 percent of crime is now detected through CCTVs, thus the role of CCTV has been instrumental in paving a way to serve justice at a faster rate. The introduction of CCTV has not only demonstrated the revolution of contemporary policing practices but has also brought massive reform in investigating judicial crimes.

The introduction and adoption of AI mark the beginning of an era of technological advancement that makes machines intelligent enough to achieve results faster with higher accuracy. AI aims to enhance devices by aiding them with the knowledge and skill similar to human intelligence, thereby delivering a performance that can be on par with human aptitude.

Deployment of AI in CCTV cameras can augment the capabilities of CCTV tenfold. Providing CCTV cameras with human intelligence will maximize CCTV's potential in numerous ways that can efficiently increase its utility. The futuristic approach of incorporating AI with CCTV camera systems can help in manufacturing CCTV systems that are smart enough to reduce human labor in achieving several day-to-day tasks, thereby helping in the betterment.

FASTag technology, which incorporates Radio Frequency Identification technology, is now widely used to collect tolls from vehicle owners by the National Highway Authority of India. The FASTag, which is affixed to the front windscreen shield of the vehicle, is scanned by the FASTag scanner, which will automatically deduct the fixed amount of money as a toll from the linked vehicle owner's prepaid account.

CCTV systems can be developed using smart sensors in the future that can scan the FASTag to keep track of and provide details of the vehicle and its owner that have crossed the toll plaza, thereby majorly contributing to prevailing security by monitoring the movement of suspicious vehicles with ease. The CCTV systems can be designed to function with the help of AI tools that aid in alerting the police by scanning the FASTag of the vehicles, predominantly in cases of stolen/blacklisted vehicles.

Existing CCTV systems are not yet operational with technologies to record audio simultaneously while capturing video footage. This is a huge drawback as we can only watch the video without the associated audio. In the future, CCTV systems will be able to be designed with AI technologies that are not only able to record audio but also have algorithms that can, with sound-based trigger mechanisms, notify the police in the case of a car crash/emergency, who can then take the necessary action and assist the person in need.

AI-operated CCTV systems can be deployed in the future to cater to various other purposes that can help common citizens residing in an area to make day-to-day decisions like reservations/booking a hotel based on the crowd, parking, and recommendations to decide the best route to reach a destination based on the traffic conditions, to name a few. AI can thus boost the capacities of the CCTV tool and help in unlocking its vast potential through the use of AI-driven CCTV systems.

AI can also be used to engineer intelligent video tools that can be used in the efficient analyzing and investigation of the contents of a video file, thereby reducing human effort during investigations.

AI tools can be designed to report or flag sexually explicit content/child pornography videos put up by criminals on social media. AI tools can also be designed so that the video files submitted for forensic analysis can automatically apply algorithms that support photogrammetry and gait analysis, which will help in profiling the suspect that will aid in identifying and apprehending the criminal.

REFERENCES

Ali, H., Tran, S. N., Benetos, E., & Garcez, A. S. (2018). Speaker recognition with hybrid features from a deep belief network. *Neural Computing and Applications, 29*, 13–19.

Amerini, I., Uricchio, T., Ballan, L., & Caldelli, R. (2017, July). Localization of JPEG double compression through multi-domain convolutional neural networks. In *2017 IEEE Conference on computer vision and pattern recognition workshops (CVPRW)* (pp. 1865–1871). IEEE.

Bromley, J., Bentz, J. W., Bottou, L., Guyon, I., LeCun, Y., Moore, C., ... & Shah, R. (1993). Signature verification using a "Siamese" time delay neural network. *International Journal of Pattern Recognition and Artificial Intelligence*, 7(4), 669–688.

Chowdhury, M. (2021, August 13). AI in forensic investigation and crime detection. *Analytics Insight*. https://www.analyticsinsight.net/ai-in-forensic-investigation-and-crime-detection/

Cole, S. (2018, January 24). We are truly fucked: Everyone is making AI-generated fake porn now. *Vice*. https://www.vice.com/en/article/bjye8a/reddit-fake-porn-app-daisy-ridley

Cutajar, M., Gatt, E., Grech, I., Casha, O., & Micallef, J. (2013). Comparative study of automatic speech recognition techniques. *IET Signal Processing*, 7(1), 25–46.

Dhakal, P., Damacharla, P., Javaid, A. Y., & Devabhaktuni, V. (2019). A near real-time automatic speaker recognition architecture for voice-based user interface. *Machine Learning and Knowledge Extraction*, 1, 504–520.

Do, N. T., Na, I. S., & Kim, S. H. (2018). Forensics face detection from GANs using convolutional neural network. In *2018 International Symposium on Information Technology Convergence (ISITC 2018)*, South Korea.

Doddington, G. R. (1985). Speaker recognition—Identifying people by their voices. *Proceedings of the IEEE*, 73(11), 1651–1664. doi:10.1109/PROC.1985.13345

Donahue, J., Anne Hendricks, L., Guadarrama, S., Rohrbach, M., Venugopalan, S., Saenko, K., & Darrell, T. (2015). Long-term recurrent convolutional networks for visual recognition and description. In *Proceedings of the IEEE Conference on computer vision and pattern recognition* (pp. 2625–2634).

Drygajlo, A., Jessen, M., Gfroerer, S., Wagner, I., Vermeulen, J., & Niemi, T. (n.d.). *Methodological Guidelines for Best Practice in Forensic Semiautomatic and Automatic Speaker Recognition*. Verlag f. Polizeiwissens.

FakeApp. (2018). https://www.fakeapp.com/.

GitHub. (2018). Deepfakes software for all. Deepfakes Faceswap. https://github.com/deepfakes/faceswap/

Ibrahim, Y. A., Odiketa, J. C., & Ibiyemi, T. S. (2017). Pre-processing technique in automatic speech recognition for human computer interaction: An overview. *Annals. Computer Science Series*, 15(1), 186–191.

Hanifa, R., Isa, K., & Mohamad, S. (2021). A review on speaker recognition: Technology and challenges. *Computers & Electrical Engineering*, 90, 107005.

Indumathi, A., & Chandra, E. (2015). Speaker identification using bagging techniques. In *2015 International Conference on Computers, Communications, and Systems (ICCCS)* (pp. 223–229): IEEE.

Jahangir, R., Teh, Y. W., Nweke, H. F., Mujtaba, G., Al-Garadi, M. A., & Ali, I. (2021). Speaker identification through artificial intelligence techniques: A comprehensive review and research challenges. *Expert Systems with Applications*, 171, 114591. doi:10.1016/j.eswa.2021.114591

Jump, B. (2017, December 30). Audio recording: Definition and process. *Chasing the Chords*. https://brianjump.net/2017/12/29/the-definition-and-history-of-sound-recording/

Karras, T., Aila, T., Laine, S., & Lehtinen, J. (2017). Progressive growing of gans for improved quality, stability, and variation. *arXiv preprint arXiv:1710.10196*.

Kuwabara, H., & Sagisak, Y. (1995). Acoustic characteristics of speaker individuality: Control and conversion. *Speech Communication, 16*(2), 165–173. doi:10.1016/0167-6393(94)00053-D

Lasserre, J., & Bishop, C. M. (2007). Generative or discriminative? Getting the best of both worlds. In Bernardo, J. M., Bayarri, M. J., Berger, J. O., Dawid, A. P., Heckerman, D., Smith, A. F. M., & West, M. (Eds.), *Bayesian statistics* (Vol. 8, pp. 3–24). Oxford University Press.

Lehiste, I., & Meltzer, D. (1973). Vowel and speaker identification in natural and synthetic speech. *Language and Speech, 16*(4), 356–364.

Liu, Z., Luo, P., Wang, X., & Tang, X. (2015). Deep learning face attributes in the wild. In *Proceedings of the IEEE international conference on computer vision* (pp. 3730–3738).

Liy, C. M., & InIctuOculi, L. Y. U. S. (2018). Exposing AI created fake videos by detecting eye blinking. In *2018 IEEE Inter G national Workshop on Information Forensics and Security (WIFS)*. IEEE.

McCarthy, J. (2007). What is artificial intelligence? https://www-formal.stanford.edu/jmc/whatisai.pdf

McCarthy, J., Minksy, M. L., Rochester, N., & Shannon, C. E. (1955/2006). A proposal for the Dartmouth Summer Research Project on artificial intelligence. *AI Magazine, 27*(4): 12.

McGehee, F. (1937). The reliability of the identification of the human voice. *The Journal of General Psychology, 17*(2), 249–271.

Matern, F., Riess, C., & Stamminger, M. (2019, January). Exploiting visual artifacts to expose deepfakes and face manipulations. In *2019 IEEE Winter Applications of Computer Vision Workshops (WACVW)* (pp. 83–92). IEEE.

Moffat, D., Ronan, D., & Reiss, J. D. (2015). An evaluation of audio feature extraction toolboxes. In *18th International Conference on Digital Audio Effects*.

Nguyen, T. T., Nguyen, C. M., Nguyen, D. T., Nguyen, D. T., & Nahavandi, S. (2019). Deep learning for deepfakes creation and detection: A survey. *arXiv preprint arXiv:1909.11573*.

Parkhi, O. M., Vedaldi, A., & Zisserman, A. (2015). Deep face recognition. *Proceedings of the British Machine Vision Conference (BMVC)*. doi:10.5244/c.29.41

Perrachione, T. K., Del Tufo, S. N., & Gabrieli, J. D. E. (2011). Human voice recognition depends on language ability. *Science, 333*(6042), 595. doi:10.1126/science.1207327

Sardar, V. M., & Shirbahadurkar, S. D. (2018). Speaker identification of whispering speech: An investigation on selected timbrel features and KNN distance measures. *International Journal of Speech Technology, 21*(3), 545–553.

Sardar, V. M., & Shirbahadurkar, S. (2019). Timbre features for speaker identification of whispering speech: Selection of optimal audio descriptors. *International Journal of Computers and Applications*, 1–7.

Shrestha, A., & Mahmood, A. (2019). Review of deep learning algorithms and architectures. *IEEE Access, 7*, 53040–53065. doi:10.1109/ACCESS.2019.2912200

Suchitha, T. R., & Bindu, A. T. (2015). Feature extraction using MFCC and classification using GMM. *International Journal for Scientific Research & Development (IJSRD)*, 3(5), 1278–1283.

Thies, J., Zollhofer, M., Stamminger, M., Theobalt, C., & Nießner, M. (2018). Face2Face: Real-time face capture and reenactment of RGB videos. *Communications of the ACM*, 62(1): 96–104. doi:10.1145/3292039

Wang, Q., & Zhang, R. (2016). Double JPEG compression forensics based on a convolutional neural network. *EURASIP Journal on Information Security, 2016*(1), 1–12.

Yang, X., Li, Y., Qi, H., & Lyu, S. (2019a, July). Exposing GAN-synthesized faces using landmark locations. In *Proceedings of the ACM Workshop on Information Hiding and Multimedia Security* (pp. 113–118).

Yang, X., Li, Y., & Lyu, S. (2019b, May). Exposing deep fakes using inconsistent head poses. In *ICASSP 2019 IEEE International Conference on Acoustics, Speech and Signal Processing (ICASSP)* (pp. 8261–8265). IEEE.

5

AI in Post-Mortem Analysis

Mohammed Irfan

INTRODUCTION

Legal medicine is an area that belongs to the legal sciences, however, it is formed of several interdisciplinary lines of knowledge. One of these is artificial intelligence (AI), which, in today's modern era, has helped in paving the way in which the legal process is driven along the right path by complementing the evidentiary means. In this sense, the present chapter makes a complete analysis of the science of AI and post-mortem techniques, relating their importance in expertise, with an emphasis on criminal proceedings and criminal laws [1–4].

The objectives of this chapter are to outline the scope of forensic medicine and AI, seeking to insert them definitively into the curriculum of law/medical/forensic courses and pointing out methods for their improvement in regard to face-to-face scenarios of a crime in the justice system, since any kind of expertise is essential to define a typical fact [1, 5–6]. To do so, I begin with a descriptive research technique, using the method of bibliographic research. This is where the material is analyzed in an exploratory way, i.e., survey the general characteristics of the problem, choose to describe it, and formulate systematic observations through doctrine, legislation, jurisprudence, scientific articles, and electronic website searches.

The chapter provides an epistemological analysis of criminal medicine in connection with AI, with the result that the principle of truth is the true pursuit of this science, as well as being one of the direct guides of the entire criminal and sentence determinant. It is important to note that the interdependence of actions will be in focus, since the analysis of expert activity is a complex system of reactions to a common goal. Finally, it can be concluded that the principle of real truth is formed by a philosophical analysis of the evidential material and that this, in most cases, is collected in the expertise, through medicine and all the sciences it covers, including AI [7–9]. Forensic science is an important endeavor with great significance in society.

Finally, the forensic standard defines the status quo of the rules of the law. Every day, innovations in forensic science make the lives of post-mortem investigators easier. AI has brought endless possibilities which connect forensic science in an interdisciplinary way with other science and technology streams; as a result of such interdisciplinary connections, the innovative technology of forensic post-mortem computed tomography (PMCT) arose, and it is evolving each and every day with new results and probabilities, which are highly accurate [4, 10–13].

PMCT is highly regarded in the field of forensic science. It has proven to be reliable in detecting fractures during post-mortem investigations. In addition, PMCT angiography enhances the images by providing better contrast for soft tissues and organ findings. This feature makes it particularly effective in identifying hemorrhages within the human body. The use of PMCT and post-mortem computed tomography angiography (PMCTA) as triage tools is dependent on the jurisdiction and legal permissions of each country. These techniques can serve as additional investigative methods to complement traditional autopsies [1–4, 10–11, 14–16].

The process of image analysis in PMCT differs greatly from that of regular clinical radiology. In clinical radiology, the focus is typically limited to a specific area of examination to minimize radiation exposure and scanning time for the patient. This targeted approach allows for a more efficient evaluation of a particular region. However, in post-mortem radiology, a distinct methodology is employed. The entire body is captured in high resolution during PMCT scans to ensure comprehensive documentation of all pathologies, anatomical anomalies, and foreign objects. This comprehensive imaging approach aims to capture a thorough representation of the deceased individual's body for the purpose of forensic investigation [3, 6, 10, 14–15, 17–18].

PMCT scans can encompass a substantial number of individual images, sometimes exceeding 10,000. While it is customary for forensic pathologists and professionals to focus solely on relevant findings during their analysis, this can still result in a significant workload. Comparable challenges relating to workload also arise in regular clinical radiology settings, prompting the development of AI and machine learning (ML) approaches as potential solutions [7, 14–15]. Consequently, the automated analysis of PMCT images emerged as a research priority during the inaugural summit on post-mortem radiology and imaging research. This summit was organized by the International Society of Forensic Radiology and Imaging based in the United States of America [2–4, 10–11, 14–16].

The primary factor of utmost importance is the quality of the images, which must meet the necessary standards for identification, visualization, and intricate forensic reconstruction [14–15]. Since there is no need to take radiation doses into account, the scan protocol can be optimized to prioritize higher image quality. This optimization results in more detailed images, consequently generating larger datasets.

Understanding Deep Learning Techniques

Computer science plays a central role in driving today's innovative technologies, and within computer science AI is a specific field that aims to replicate or approximate human intelligence to solve intricate mathematical problems [4, 10]. While many AI techniques rely on algorithms, a subset known as ML takes a more data-driven approach. ML algorithms analyze sample data to adapt their behavior, learning from the data rather than following a predefined procedure [10, 19–21].

Another technique within ML is deep learning (DL), which utilizes artificial neural networks (ANNs) to process and analyze data. ANNs simulate, in a simplified manner, the functioning and communication of nerve cells to comprehend and tackle complex behaviors using elementary building blocks. The fundamental component of an ANN is the artificial neuron [4, 6, 22].

MATERIALS AND METHODS

The software utilized for creating the evaluation interface was Delphi 7®, while the construction of the database involved the MS Access® program, and the database management was handled using the MS SQL Server® program. The information stored in the database adhered to the WHO-CT PG/2003 classification.

From a forensic perspective, the Odonto Forensic Group at Federal University of Pelotas, Brazil initiated their work by assessing and validating images of bovine skulls affected by gunshots. Over time, the forensic ballistic project expanded into a comprehensive research project encompassing multiple documentation and analysis methods, including:

- 3D body surface imaging techniques.
- Multidetector and multislice computed tomography (CT).
- Magnetic resonance imaging (MRI).
- Magnetic resonance spectroscopy (used for determining time of death).
- Development of synthetic body models.

In Figures 5.1, 5.2, and 5.3 you can see the test specimens (bovine mandible) prepared and accordingly numbered to receive the ballistic projectiles of different callibers. As shown in Figure 5.2, these ballistic tests were done under controlled environments maintaining exact firing distances and surrounding protection, as shown in Figure 5.3.

Figure 5.1 Four freshly extracted bovine mandibles were used to test four different ballistic ammunations. (Image taken by author Prof. Dr. Mohammed Irfan at Federal University of Pelotas-Brazil, Department of Forensic Odontology.)

Figure 5.2 Four different ammunitions for the ballistic tests on bovine mandíbula. Equal distance was maintained by using measuring tape from the point of fire to the target mandible distance. (Image taken by author Prof. Dr. Mohammed Irfan at Federal University of Pelotas-Brazil, Department of Forensic Odontology.)

The core emphasis of this project revolves around these five key areas with forensic significance:

1. Reconstruction and explanation for the cause of death based on pathological evidence.
2. Injury reconstruction.

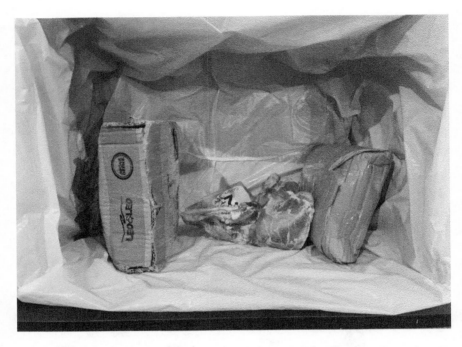

Figure 5.3 Concrete-filled cardboard boxes were maintained to prevent mandible fragment scatter due to ballistic impact. (Image taken by author Prof. Dr. Mohammed Irfan at Federal University of Pelotas-Brazil, Department of Forensic Odontology.)

3. Forensic path-morphologic findings.
4. Reactions (vital).
5. Visualization.

In the above radiological investigation, as shown in Figure 5.4, in contrast to conventional clinical scanning, there are two important points. First there are no respiration artifacts, and second there is no radiation limitation. As a result, the radiological pictures of the examination are not limited or affected by these factors.

The approach outlined above presents numerous significant advantages. First, it allows for observer-independent and objective data archiving, ensuring that the collected information remains unbiased and reliable. Moreover, it is a nondestructive and minimally invasive method, which means that the integrity of the forensic evidence is preserved during the

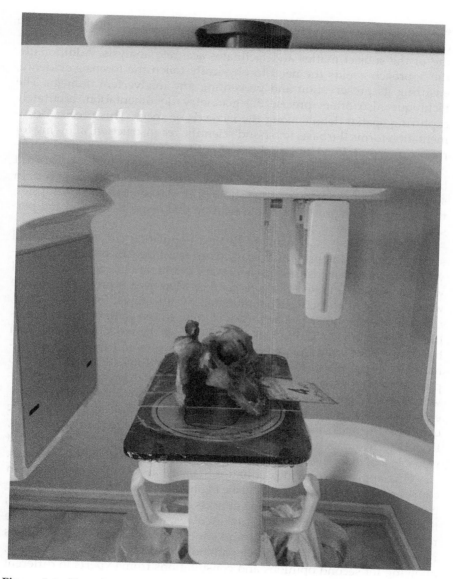

Figure 5.4 Dental tomography of the ballistic wound in the mandible was done and a 3D image was developed for further studies. (Image taken by author Prof. Dr. Mohammed Irfan at Federal University of Pelotas-Brazil, Department of Forensic Odontology.)

examination process. One notable benefit is the provision of actual-size documentation in a 3D format. This enables a comprehensive understanding of the subject matter and facilitates accurate analysis. Additionally, the approach avoids the need to physically touch the forensic evidence, ensuring its preservation and preventing any inadvertent damage. The technique also offers precise 3D geometry documentation, accurately capturing spatial details along the xyz-axis or space. This precise documentation forms the basis for sound scientific reconstruction, allowing for robust interpretations and analyses. Another advantage lies in its application as an alternative or supplementary examination tool for "difficult body area autopsies," such as those involving the face, neck, or pelvis. In situations where religious or psychological reasons preclude autopsies, this approach can provide a viable solution that respects cultural and personal sensitivities.

Furthermore, it is valuable in diverse population cultures and social situations where autopsies may be met with resistance. By offering a noninvasive alternative, it ensures that necessary examinations can be conducted without causing undue distress or conflict. Moreover, it proves invaluable when dealing with bodies contaminated by infections, toxic substances, radionuclides, or other biohazards, including in the context of pandemics like the ongoing Covid-19 crisis. By mitigating the risks associated with handling such hazardous materials, it enables safe and thorough examinations to take place. Finally, the approach facilitates both 2D and 3D post-processing, allowing the findings to be visualized and analyzed by individuals who were not present during the initial examination. This feature enhances collaboration and ensures a broader understanding of the forensic evidence. In conclusion, the above approach offers a range of advantages, from objective data archiving to noninvasive documentation, making it a valuable tool in forensic investigations across various challenging scenarios.

This approach provides enhanced clarity and comprehensibility in court proceedings through scientific explanations, aiding in the effective presentation of evidence. It also supports quality improvement processes through the establishment of digital archives, which can serve as valuable resources for teaching, learning, and education. Additionally, it facilitates remote collaboration through telepathology and teleforensic capabilities, allowing for second opinions and consultations from experts in different locations.

However, it is important to note that the AI approach does come with certain disadvantages that persist to this day. One significant drawback is the substantial initial installation cost, which can be a barrier to implementing this technology widely. Additionally, the tissue resolution of radiology scanners may still be limited, potentially affecting the level of detail that can be obtained during the examination. Another limitation is the inability to visualize organ colors, such as the process of inflammation, which can provide additional information in certain forensic scenarios. Despite these drawbacks, the advancements in this field continue to progress, and ongoing research aims to address these limitations, seeking to improve the cost-effectiveness, resolution, and visualization capabilities of the AI approach in forensic investigations.

CASE STUDY AND APPLICATION

The Application Significance of AI in the Inference of Post-mortem Interval

At present, although there are many post-mortem interval (PMI) inference methods, none of these methods are perfect, and they are highly subjective and influenced by the surrounding environment [6]. There are many disadvantages, such as being large and difficult to quantify, and poor repeatability of some observation objects that use a variety of PMI inference methods artificially and empirically and compare them with each other, which can obtain more accurate time inference results [6, 8–9].

In this process, a large number of observations and inferences can form subjective errors and superimpose and magnify each other, leading to obvious results bias, and, at the same time, the derivation's own relevant knowledge store equipment and work experience will also strongly affect the accuracy of the final inference results [14, 17]. Therefore, attempts to ensure the reliability of single-path derivation results and multi-path the effectiveness of the integration of path results have further improved the accuracy of PMI inference. AI can comprehensively investigate by using multi-dimensional big data, evaluating weights and identifying data changes, establishing an effective "time fingerprint" mathematical model.

Theoretically, through comprehensive face-to-face training, an effective and widely applicable PMI inference model can be established, and actual case data can be inputted into the model for further model training and correction. After the model is stable, PMI inference can be carried out and the case can be resolved. The real PMI obtained after acquisition continues to be fine-tuned. Because of AI work, it is an excellent feature of both "actual combat" and "training," so as the model uses an increase in the number of uses (accumulation of training data sets), with AI-based PMI the validity and universality of inference will continue to improve [1, 3, 14–15, 18].

Research on the Application of AI in the Inference of Post-mortem Interval Time

Due to its rapid development and maturity, AI technology has been applied to much forensic research, including age inference, facial recognition, tracepoints analysis, cause of death analysis, and gene and protein analysis. AI microbial forensics is the basis of corpse-related microbial detection, which is a cross-discipline or interdisciplinary subject that solves forensic problems in association with microbiology [4, 10].

The PMI of a corpse is inferred from the succession of the thriving microorganism diversity after death or during the process of decomposition. A bovine corpus/carcass was placed under soil under laboratory conditions. There are many places (next to the mouth, abdominal skin, and abdominal cavity) that collect microbial samples, and the samples are processed by 16s rRNA and 18s rRNA. Next-generation sequencing (NGS) identification obtained PMI inference with an accuracy of (3.30 ± 2.52) (total observation time 48 days).

The model was found to be most effective in the early stage of decomposition (the first 34 days). It is believed, according to the model, that accurate PMI can be established through AI technology and microbial sequencing, and it is inferred that the model put forward the concept of "microbial clock" for the first time.

Microbial samples were collected from the nasal cavity and external auditory canal of the carcass every 2–3 days, parallel 16s rRNA NGS detection was done, the data run by multiple algorithms ML, with the results showing that a complete data set is most conducive to model training, and the microbial population information of "family" or "genus" is most conducive to the PMI model. Type inference, K-nearest neighbor regression is the optimal algorithm (error ± 2 d).

In another similar experiment, we took pig carcasses as the experimental animal, collected the oral cavity and microbial samples of the skin, and established based on 16s rRNA sequencing data. The model found that the coincidence rate between the predicted PMI and the actual PMI was as high as 94.4 percent. At the same time, some scholars have successfully employed conventional microbial identification methods to analyze the spread and evolution of microbial populations during the decay of corpses using statistical methods. However, when compared with the

74

research method involving AI technology combined with second-generation sequencing, traditional research can only elucidate the general composition mode of microbial populations. As its model framework changes over time, it becomes unable to achieve full quantitative analysis and accurate model prediction.

Multiplanar reconstruction (MPR) serves as a straightforward technique for reconstructing volumetric data. The volume is created by stacking axial slices. Subsequently, specialized reconstruction software cuts slices through the volume in different planes, often orthogonal to the original slices. MPR finds particular utility in the examination of the spine.

When using axial images alone, each slice only displays one vertebral body at a time and fails to reliably reveal compression fractures along the longitudinal axis of the body. By reformulating the volume through MPR, it becomes significantly easier to visualize the structure and determine the position of one vertebral body relative to the others. In addition to MPR, curved-plane reconstruction can be applied to the volume dataset. This technique allows for the "straightening" of bent or curved structures, such as the sacrum, enabling the visualization of the entire length in a single image.

Data Visualization

A DVR Pipeline for Visual Analogue Scales (VASs)
The utilization of volume rendering techniques is gaining popularity within the medical field, and visualization methods have undergone significant advancements. However, there are numerous visually oriented tasks that are unique to Volume Rendered (VA) angiography, and there exists an opportunity to develop specialized methods that cater to these specific requirements. Recent efforts have been made in this direction, and this section has highlighted a selected subset of emerging technologies and rendering techniques that are particularly relevant to VASs [4, 6, 11, 13, 23].

CONCLUSIONS AND THE SCOPE FOR FUTURE RESEARCH

The Forensic Group at the Federal University of Pelotas in Brazil is actively involved in evaluating and validating their AI approach for forensic post-mortem examinations of ballistic wounds in the head and neck area. However, it is important to exercise caution when considering this approach as a standalone procedure in the court system at this stage. While 3D surface scanning has gained acceptance as a method in European courts, further scientific research is needed for the radiological aspect.

DL techniques are being increasingly used to automate the analysis of computerized tomographic (CT) images in various areas of forensic medicine. Studies have demonstrated successful implementation of ML methods for tasks such as classifying CT images to detect fractures, identify ballistic wounds, and detect pathologies like cancer and skin anomalies. Convolutional neural networks (CNNs) are commonly chosen for medical diagnosis, thanks to the availability of frameworks like TensorFlow, Keras, and PyTorch, which facilitate the development of sophisticated CNN systems with minimal programming knowledge. Data collection, preprocessing, and the design of appropriate network architectures are crucial aspects of this work.

While there is ample information on the use of DL techniques in clinical CT image analysis, their application in forensic medicine and post-mortem computed tomography is still relatively limited. Many potential applications in this specific field remain unexplored and warrant further investigation in the future.

REFERENCES

[1] Minsky, M., Papert, S. A., & Bottou, L. (2017). *Perceptrons: An introduction to computational geometry*. Massachusetts: MIT Press.

[2] Lan, Q., Wang, Z., Wen, M., Zhang, C., & Wang, Y. (2017). High-performance implementation of 3D convolutional neural network on a GPU. *Computational Intelligence and Neuroscience*; Article ID 8348671: 1–8.

[3] Kooi, T., Litjens, G., Ginneken, B., Gubern-Mérida, A., Sánchez, C. I., Mann, R., et al. (2017). Large-scale deep learning for computer aided detection of mammographic lesions. *Medical Image Analysis*, 35: 303–312.

[4] Bucci, E. M. (2018). Automatic detection of image manipulations in the biomedical literature. *Cell Death & Disease*, 9(3), article no. 400.

[5] Holzinger, A., Plass, M., Holzinger, K., Crisan, G. C., Pintea, C. M., & Palade, V. (2017). A glass-box interactive machine learning approach for solving NP-hard problems with the human-in-the-loop. *CoRR. arXiv*: 1708.01104.

[6] Atluri, G., Karpatne, A., & Kumar, V. (2018). Spatio-temporal data mining: A survey of problems and methods. *ACM Computing Surveys*, 51(4): 1–83.

[7] Larsson, M., Zhang, Y., & Kahl, F. (2018). Robust abdominal organ segmentation using regional convolutional neural network. *Applied Soft Computing*, 70: 465–471.

[8] Yang, T., You, M., Zhang, H., Zhang, F., Bai, R., Chang, L., Di, S., Guo, Z., Lu, D., Wang, X., Xiang, J., & Xiaofei, E. (2016). Estimation of the postmortem interval by measuring blood oxidation reduction potential values. *Journal of Forensic Science and Medicine*, 2(1): 8–11.

[9] Costa, I., Carvalho, F., Magalhães, T., Guedes de Pinho, P., Silvestre, R., & Dinis-Oliveira, R. J. (2015). Promising blood-derived biomarkers for estimation of the postmortem interval, and standardized nomenclature. *Toxicology Research*, 4: 1443–1452.

[10] Holzinger, A., Malle, B., Kieseberg, P., Roth, P. M., Müller, H., Reihs, R., & Zatloukal, K. (2017). Towards the augmented pathologist: Challenges of explainable-AI in digital pathology. *CoRR. arXiv*: 1712.06657.

[11] Ball, P., & Maxmen, A. (2020). The epic battle against coronavirus misinformation and conspiracy theories. *Nature*, 581(7809), 371–374.

[12] Nelson, G. S. (2019). Bias in artificial intelligence. *North Carolina Medical Journal*, 80(4): 220–222.

[13] Padilha, R. et al. (2021). Unraveling the Notre Dame cathedral fire in space and time: An x-coherence approach. In Padilha, R., Andaló, F. A., Pereira, L. A. M., & Anderson, R. (Eds), *Crime science and digital forensics: A holistic view*. CRC Press.

[14] Becker, A. S., Marcon, M., Ghafoor, S., Warning, M. C., Frauenfelder, T., & Boss, A. (2017). Deep learning in mammography: Diagnostic accuracy of a multipurpose image analysis software in the detection of breast cancer. *Investigative Radiology*, 52: 434–440.

[15] Wang, X., Li, R., Zhou, Y., & Kambhamettu, C. (2017). A study of convolutional sparse feature learning for human age estimate. *12th IEEE International Conference on Automatic Face & Gesture Recognition (FG 2017)*, Washington, DC, pp. 566–572, doi:10.1109/FG.2017.141.

[16] Chilamkurthy, S., Ghosh, R., Tanamala, S., Biviji, M., Campeau, N. G., Venugopal, V. K., et al. 2018). Deep learning algorithms for detection of critical findings in head CT scans a retrospective study. *Lancet*, 392: 2388–2396.

[17] Arbabshirani, M. R., Fornwalt, B. K., Mongelluzzo, G. J., Suever, J. D., Geise, B. D., Patel, A. A., et al. (2018). Advanced machine learning in action: Identification of intracranial hemorrhage on computed tomography scans of the head with clinical workflow integration. *NPJ Digital Medicine*, 1: 9.

[18] Gilpin, L. H. et al. (2018). Explaining explanations: An overview of interpretability of machine learning. In: *IEEE International Conference On Data Science And Advanced AnalyticS (DSAA)*, 2018, pp. 80–89.

[19] Theoflas, P., Ehrenberg, A. J., Dunlop, S., Alho, A. T. D. L., Nguy, A., Leite, R. E. P., Rodriguez, R. D., Mejia, M. B., Suemoto, C. K., Ferretti-Rebustini, R. E. D. L., et al. (2017). Locus coeruleus volume and cell population changes during Alzheimer's disease progression: A stereological study in human postmortem brains with potential implication for early-stage biomarker discovery. *Alzheimer's & Dementia*, 13(3): 236–246.

[20] Rutty, G. N., Morgan, B., Robinson, C., Raj, V., Pakkal, M., Amoroso, J., Visser, T., Saunders, S., Biggs, M., Hollingbury, F., et al. (2017). Diagnostic accuracy of post-mortem CT with targeted coronary angiography versus autopsy for coroner-requested post-mortem investigations: A prospective, masked, comparison study. *The Lancet* 390(10090): 145–154.

[21] Theóphilo, A., Pereira, L. A., & Rocha, A. (2019). A needle in a haystack? Harnessing onomatopoeia and user-specific stylometrics for authorship attribution of micro-messages. In: *IEEE International Conference on Acoustics, Speech and Signal Processing (ICASSP)*, 2019, pp. 2692–2696.

[22] Kilimann, I., Hausner, L., Fellgiebel, A., Filippi, M., Würdemann, T. J., Heinsen, H., & Teipel, S. J. (2017). Parallel atrophy of cortex and basal forebrain cholinergic system in mild cognitive impairment. *Cerebral Cortex*, 27(3): 1841–1848.

[23] Song, L. et al. (2020). Unsupervised domain adaptive re-identification: Theory and practice. *Pattern Recognition*, 102, 107–173.

6

Artificial Intelligence in Forensic Linguistics

Vernika Mehta, Palak Aneja, Krittika Sood,
Surbhi Mathur, and Sumit Kumar Choudhary

INTRODUCTION

John McCarthy was the first to use the term "artificial intelligence" at the Dartmouth Conference in 1956. It is, according to him, "The study of the science and engineering of creating intelligent machines" (McCarthy et al., 1955; McCarthy, 2007).

Artificial intelligence (AI) is increasingly becoming used in various fields, including linguistics. This use of AI has created an important way to investigate the connection between society and language. The current methods for studying language are dependent on sociolinguistic human subjects, so they can be time consuming and expensive. This is where AI comes in.

AI involves creating computer programs that mimic the thought processes and behaviors of humans. A number of applications of artificial intelligence are already being used in today's world, such as Internet shopping, weather forecasting, image processing, logistics, search engine optimization (SEO), robotics, and medicine. The addition of games, speech recognition, natural language understanding, expert

DOI: 10.4324/9781003287810-6

systems, and heuristic classification to the list of AI applications is the cherry on top.

The Internet's infrastructure and computers are useful in linguistics, as they permit far greater access and manipulation of data than could otherwise be achieved, as well as collaborating with more people across greater distances. Because computational methods enable us to take a broader view of data and manage the complexity that results, we can ask questions that would otherwise seem completely impossible. The truth is that this is true in all subfields of linguistics, although the current state of the existing infrastructure (and, accordingly, existing practice) may vary from one to another (Bender & Langendoen, 2010).

Prior to examining the details of AI in linguistics, we must understand the techniques by which AI has been adapted for the purpose of linguistics. Following are some processes/techniques that can be employed to apply AI to solving real-world problems.

AI attempts to emulate human intelligence using a computer. Human intelligence can be expressed primarily through language. The acquisition of language is regarded as one of the greatest achievements of human intellect. Among the major fields of AI, natural language processing (NLP) overlaps heavily with computational linguistics, one of the most important fields of the study of language (Hein, n.d.). NLP will be thoroughly covered in the sections that follow. In order to understand the use of AI in linguistics, we first need to understand key concepts in linguistics.

The role of AI in forensic linguistics is to help with the translation and interpretation process. This can be done through machine learning (ML), deep neural networks, or NLP. AI has been used for many purposes including—but not limited to—Automated Translation (e.g., Google Translate) or Text Mining & Sentiment Analysis (e.g., sentiment analysis on Twitter).

LINGUISTICS

Linguistics is the name given to the scientific study of language. Language is studied in linguistics in society, including its structure and use. It deals with:

1. Knowing what we know about human languages in general.
2. Documenting the structure of particular languages.
3. Examining how languages work in individual cases.
4. Exploring how knowledge of one language can illuminate the understanding of other languages. (Merriam-Webster, n.d.)

Having a better knowledge of the linguistics and forensic linguistics fields enables the researchers to better understand recent advancements in *forensic stylistics* for authorship identification. The scientific examination of particular stylistic cues present in a particular author's idiolect is known as linguistic stylistics, and some stylistic indicators that can be detected among populations that speak the same language or dialect. Linguistic stylistics in forensics refers to the science of applying stylistics to forensic purposes and contexts (McMenamin, 2002).

Major branches of linguistics include *psycholinguistics*, which is the study of the relationship between psychological processes and linguistic behavior, and *sociolinguistics*, which examines the interaction of languages among people with different cultures and historical backgrounds. The application of linguistics to solving real-world problems is known as *applied linguistics*. A relatively new field of linguistics, *computational linguistics*, deals with how computers use language to communicate. Computer science plays a key role in linguistics, analyzing, modeling, and producing speech. *Comparative linguistics* explores the similarities and differences among languages that were derived from the same source. *Historical linguistics* studies the development of languages over time and analyzes the changes that have occurred in them, and the study of a language's style and rhetoric is known as *stylistics*, as applied by different authors (Careers 360, 2021).

There is the need to understand some more related study areas for linguistics. The study of speech sounds and their physical properties is *phonetics*. *Phonology* studies the rules of how sounds are produced and used in different languages. The study of word structure is known as *morphology* and it deals with the different ways that words are formed from smaller units such as prefixes and suffixes. *Syntax* deals with the rules of how sentences are formed and used in a language. Linguists can work in various areas of academia, such as academia and business, law, and medicine. A study of *semantics* includes the study of semiotics, formal logic, programming languages, and language meaning within a linguistic and philosophical perspective.

While other disciplines are also connected, here there is an instant connection between linguistics and programming languages. As part of semantics, words, phrases, signs, and symbols are studied in relation to their denotations i.e., what they represent in reality. In this interpretation, semantics is concerned with essential meanings. *Pragmatics*, meanwhile, is concerned with the context in which words are used (Moltzau, 2020). Let us analyze linguistic AI possibilities to better grasp how we use linguistic

AI. To do so, we must return to the fundamental building blocks of dealing with language:

1. *Language understanding* is the process of utilizing a variety of deep learning (DL) algorithms to understand the meaning behind the noise. Using language understanding, humans and machines can interact in a meaningful way so we can understand the vast amounts of content we deal with every day.
2. *Language transformation* is the part that involves a machine-first approach in order to enable another machine or human to produce a new, altered output.
3. *Language creation* occurs both at the end of the process and at the beginning. It is necessary to have content in order for linguistic AI to understand and transform, and the technology can be used to create new content as well. Linguistic AI can provide a jump start for writers because it is already proven and has been tested well. Linguistic AI can help the writer get an edge by leveraging what has been done successfully across a variety of domains (Hendricks, 2019).

The term language is often used to refer simultaneously to a particular set of human languages. A computational linguistics studies how people understand, translate, and create language and the language faculty, a component of which is language creation. Linguists study and analyze many different things. For instance, they can study the origins of words, and even the variations on certain words in different languages across the globe. They can also examine the history of languages and how they are constructed.

In the field of linguistics, the goal of a linguist is to comprehend language units, their potential rule-governed combinations, usage contexts, and standards of appropriate language for a given speech group. Similarly, a court-appointed linguistic expert has a similar objective in that they examine and describe during a case, educating everyone in the courtroom with a fundamental foundation of language usage and what language users know and do (McMenamin, 2002).

Computational Linguistics

Computers are used in the discipline of computational linguistics to create language models. Subtle patterns in the structure of languages can be explained by using these models. Taking advantage of these models allows computers to read what we type and respond to it. They can also hear and respond to what we say. Computational linguistics is essential for voice recognition, text-to-speech, and AI in search engines (McShane & Nirenburg, 2021). In the past, computational linguistics was closely related to linguistics, but today it is more closely related to computer science (engineering), particularly ML.

Computing linguistics aims to develop information regarding the syntactic and semantic structure of language that enables the computational analysis of that structure; identifying the distributional and structural properties of language to infer strategies for language processing and learning; and creating cognitive and neuroscientific computational models that explain how language is possessed and learned (Schubert, 2020). In addition, machine translation (MT), that is done instantly, uses computational linguistics, speech recognition (SR), speech synthesizers (TTS), and interactive voice response (IVR) systems, links to text editors, search engines, and educational resources. Computational linguistics is a discipline that includes modeling natural language as well as studying computational approaches to linguistic problems (Yasar et al., 2023).

Computational linguistics aims to accomplish the following practical applications: finding text efficiently on a preferred topic; answering questions, good MT; varying from straightforward open-ended inquiries to those requiring inference and discursive or descriptive responses (perhaps with explanations); the development of computer systems that possess human-like capabilities in dialogue, in learning languages, etc.

The field of applied computational linguistics like *sentiment analysis* has become very popular thanks to its potential applications in ranking and product marketing, social network analysis, political analysis, an analysis of writing samples to determine personality types and disorders, and many other fields. These techniques are typically built around sentiment lexicons that categorize vocabulary items according to their affective polarity, and application of supervised ML methods to texts employing word and phrasal data that have been manually labeled as representing favorable or unfavorable sentiments toward a particular theme (Schubert, 2020). A key term in computational linguistics circles has been called ML, which is more accurately known as statistical pattern recognition (SPR), although historically it has referred to a variety of learning and reasoning techniques, many of which are not statistical, and drawn from psychology, cognitive science, probability, and information theory.

In addition to speech recognition systems, instant MTs, IVRs, text editors, text-to-speech synthesizers, search engines, and materials for language instruction, computational linguistics also finds application in text editors, search engines, and language learning resources. ML, DL, AI, cognitive computing, and neuroscience knowledge are necessary to prepare for the interdisciplinary field of research (Yasar et al., 2023).

History of AI in Linguistics and Forensic Linguistics

The first time that AI was used in linguistics was in 1957, when MT programs were created. Later, in 1962, MT programs were created to translate Russian into English. These programs made it possible for the first time for people who did not speak Russian to read it. In 1965, researchers at California Institute of Technology announced that they had created a program that could converse with a person about their thoughts and feelings. Linguistics is a broad field that includes both formal and informal aspects of language structure, from phonetics to morphology to syntax. By the middle of the 1960s, researchers had begun developing systems for full language comprehension and dialogue, inspired by the vision of AI on a par with that of humans and made possible by the growing strength and accessibility of general purpose computers (Schubert, 2020). AI writing assistants are becoming increasingly popular in the workplace. When a company needs to develop content for a specific topic or niche, they use them. They're used by digital agencies to create a variety of content for their clients.

Jan Svartvik, a linguist, coined the phrase "forensic linguistics" in his 1968 book, *The Evans Statements: A Case for Forensic Linguistics*, which describes the study of language and speech in a judicial setting. It wasn't until 1980 that linguists in Australia began to consider how it might be used in legal contexts. They learned that expressions like "the same language" are ambiguous. In 1988, the BKA of the German Federal Criminal Police organized a two-day seminar on forensic phonetics (Ariani et al., 2014). Forensic linguists have been in existence since the late 1800s, but they weren't formally recognized as a profession until 1984. The history begins with a man named William Chester Minor, who is considered to be the father or forensic linguistics. FL is relatively young when considered in the context of "the significance of language to both life in general and law specifically" (Derin et al., 2019).

The 1980s saw the beginning of AI in forensic linguistics, with efforts including some early works on authorship attribution by Schumann et al. (1987), and the use of NLP techniques in forensic authorship attribution. Several authors have since used ML methods for forensic authorship attribution. They have applied supervised learning methods like support vector machines (SVMs) and Bayesian networks, semi-supervised learning methods like hidden semi-markov models (HSMM), or unsupervised approaches like infinite mixture models (IMM) (e.g., Smith, Durham, & Richards, 2013).

Technology is rapidly developing and becoming more involved in the lives of people, so real-time intelligence will soon be supported by forensic linguistics in cyberspace. As of now, it is legal to take a sample of a suspect's audio recording, but if they refuse to give it to law enforcement, forensic linguistics may be able to obtain voice records from social networks. This will allow law enforcement to maximize their efficiency. In the future, social media will help solve crimes and corruption. Deception and fraud will be predicted and avoided before they even occur (Derin et al., 2019).

HUMAN SPEECH PRODUCTION

Speech Production

A human's ability to articulate sounds or words is referred to as speech production. The auditory system, perception, and nervous system, as well as the brain, are involved in this complex feedback process (Docio-Fernandez & García Mateo, 2015). The process of producing human-sounding speech from text is known as synthetic speech production. This process has been around since the 1950s, but it was not until recently that it became a real possibility.

The human speech production system is the process by which spoken language is generated. It consists of three stages:

1. Planning: The process of selecting and organizing thoughts before they are spoken, such as deciding what to say and in what order.
2. Articulation: The production of the sounds that form words and sentences, such as the movement of air from lungs through the larynx to produce voice.
3. Reception: The process by which listeners understand what someone else has said, such as interpreting a speaker's tone or facial expressions.

A speech signal is produced during the process of speech generation, which assembles the sounds of language. Air from the lungs is forced into the larynx to create the sound of human speech. This vibration causes sound waves to be formed in the vocal tract. A linear system with sound pressure as the output and air pressure as the input can be used to represent the vocal tract.

The larynx is located at the top of the trachea or windpipe and sits just below where it enters the neck. It houses a set of vocal folds which are composed of two membranes that vibrate with each other to produce a sound waveform. These membranes are called vocal cords or vocal bands and are made up of muscle tissue that can be contracted or relaxed to control their tension and hence their width.

The human speech production system is a complex and intricate system, which starts with an idea in the brain and ends with the speech sounds emerging from the mouth. The study of this system is called phonetics. Phonetics is concerned with how we produce speech sounds when we speak. It is also concerned with how we perceive the speech sounds that other people produce. Phonetics includes:

- The physical properties of speech sounds (e.g., their loudness, pitch, duration).
- The way in which these properties are modified by our vocal tract (e.g., by changing our tongue position or jaw position).
- The way in which these properties are modified by our hearing and knowledge of language.

Speech Analysis

Voice analysis is the process of studying a voice signal in an attempt to extract pertinent information in a more condensed form than the original speech signal. Voice analysis seeks to extract any or all of the parameters listed below (and potentially more) from a speech recording.

The strength or volume of the sound: The amount of air released by the lungs and the amount of muscle tension in the articulators that produce sound are what largely define the volume or power of a speaking sound. One prosodic metric that relates to emotion is loudness or intensity.

Phoneme duration: Durations of phonemes are determined by a coordinated behavior of the speech production system across time. This is a prosodic characteristic that provides useful information for identifying phonemes and speakers.

Voicing: In voices sound, the vocal cords vibrate at fundamental frequency F0. The fundamental frequency, one of the most crucial prosodic factors, is established by the pressure placed on the vocal cords and the lungs' airflow. One of the most crucial prosodic factors, it can be modified to give a sentence a particular tone.

Spectral envelope: For tonal languages like Chinese, this is done with the use of voicing and fundamental frequency, the spectral envelope alone is capable of differentiating between various phonemes of a language as well as between different speakers (Docio-Fernandez & García Mateo, 2015).

SYNTHETIC SPEECH PRODUCTION

According to a study published in the journal *Nature* on April 24, 2019, the novel system being developed by Edward Chang's lab, MD, demonstrates the creation of a synthesized voice that can be controlled by the human language center (Anumanchipalli et al., 2019). Scientists at the University of California, San Francisco, have created and advanced a brain-computer interface that uses brain activity to control virtual vocal tracts—a computer simulation of lip movements, jaw movements, tongue movements, and throat movements that produces natural-sounding synthetic speech, voice, or other sounds. This can be accomplished by using either software or hardware products called *speech computers* or *speech synthesizers* (ScienceDirect, n.d.).

In the second part of the eighteenth century, the first attempts to produce human voice by machine were undertaken. Some comparable devices were built in the nineteenth century, but there were no truly revolutionary advances in the field of voice synthesis. The gadget built by Joseph Faber in 1835, on the other hand, can be considered a step forward in that it comprised a model of the tongue and a pharyngeal chamber whose form could be regulated (*History of Speech Synthesis, 1770–1970*, n.d.).

The ability to create synthetic speech production is an important part of AI. It is a form of NLP that will be used to generate speech for chatbots, voice assistants, and other automated systems. The three main types of artificial speech production are concatenative synthesis, parametric synthesis, and unit selection. The first two methods use recordings of human voices to create the desired sound. Unit selection uses a set number of words or syllables to produce the desired words. The more advanced form of synthesis is statistical synthesis, which uses a database of sounds to generate words in a sentence. This method can produce more realistic sounding voices because it can use all the phonemes in a language, not just the ones from one voice actor's recording.

Speech Synthesis

Sound can be synthesized by decoders using structured input. With the text-to-speech (TTS) coder, text is converted into speech, and some more general sounds, like music, can be synthesized with extremely low bit rates. It is possible to synthesize or generate speech using the speech production model. Allophones play an essential role in ensuring the sound of synthetic speech. Even though different allophones sound the same, if the wrong allophone is selected, the synthesized speech will sound unnatural. There are usually rules to guide the translation from phonemes to allophones. Timing is also crucial in determining whether a word sounds right. However, these rules are not controlled by digital signal processing (ScienceDirect, n.d.).

Using speech synthesis, we can artificially produce human speech. Speech computing systems are typically implemented in the form of hardware or software products, which are called speech computers or speech synthesizers. Concatenating recorded speech pieces from a database can be used to create synthesized speech. A number of technologies have been developed to produce synthetic speech. The most popular one is concatenative synthesis, which breaks down words into small segments and then recombines them to create a voice that sounds natural. The most common use for synthetic speech production is in movies and video games where the creators want the computer to speak like a person.

FORENSIC LINGUISTICS

Forensic linguistics is the practice of using language expertise and techniques in criminal investigations and court cases. Forensic Linguistics (also called FoLi) aims to use linguistics to demonstrate truth and deliver justice. It is true that language can hide and reveal information. A language may hold evidence of a truth. Language can therefore be used for criminal investigation, justice, and rule of law.

Forensic linguists can be involved in many different types of legal cases, such as murder, kidnapping, extortion, or fraud. A linguistic expert is capable of analyzing a perpetrator's oral and written language to infer the perpetrator's age, gender, income, ethnicity, socio-economic background, even faith and spiritual beliefs. Linguistic experts meticulously go over forensic documents, including death row statements, ransom demands, suicide notes, and emergency calls, in their capacity as forensic investigators. Forensic linguists study language and how that can be used to investigate past events. For example, a forensic linguist might be able to identify an accent from a different region, what someone is talking about in a given sentence, and whether they're being truthful.

Forensic linguistics is often used in courtrooms to examine whether or not statements made by witnesses or defendants are true. For example, if one person says that they were at home the entire day while another claims that they saw this person shopping earlier in the day, forensic linguists may be called upon to examine the language usage of both individuals and determine which story seems more plausible based on their findings. It's also common for forensic linguists to work alongside investigators to investigate written documents for clues about their origin or authenticity. Focusing on legal issues while acquiring abilities, credentials, and knowledge from other related fields would help linguists in forensic linguistics succeed and better prepare them for working in and with courts (Ariani et al., 2014).

Role of AI in Forensic Linguistics

In the discipline of forensic linguistics, AI is used to analyze language and text using computer programs. The goal of forensic linguists is to extract information from documents, such as the author's identity or the time period in which the documents were written, by examining linguistic patterns found within them. Since it has been in use for a while, this technology has lately been more generally accessible as a result of developments in ML algorithms and NLP techniques. AI in forensic linguistics is the use of AI algorithms to process linguistic data. Its goal is to provide a tool that can be used by forensic linguists and other researchers, as well as law enforcement agencies, for analyzing text evidence such as crime scene or victim statements. The algorithm uses ML techniques on large amounts of textual information that has been manually annotated with comments like "he said," "she said," etc., so it can learn how language works from its own training corpus without any human intervention.

AI is a tool that can be used to help with the identification and analysis of linguistic evidence. It has been applied by linguists for decades, but it was not until recently that AI became more widely available as an option for forensic linguists. The use of AI tools allows us to explore datasets previously difficult or impossible to analyze manually (Ariani et al., 2014).

Natural Language Processing (NLP)

In the same way that ML and DL are subsets of AI, so is NLP. Computational linguistics and computer science are used in the AI discipline known as NLP to convert human speech into computer language. Computers and human language are interconnected through NLP. In more detail, NLP refers to the understanding, analysis, manipulation, and/or generation of natural language by computers. A branch of AI, NLP allows humans to talk to machines: by detecting, interpreting, and manipulating human language, computers can understand, interpret, and act upon it.

NLP is the study of deriving knowledge from human language to enhance business operations. It is used in techniques like AI and ML. The NLP algorithm is used in Twitter's tweets to filter out terrorist language. In Amazon customer reviews, the NLP algorithm is applied to improve the user experience (Lateef, 2023).

Statistical semantics, probabilistic grammar modeling and parsing, discourse modeling, plan recognition, and knowledge extraction from text are just a few of the computing problems that have been tackled using a wide range of statistical models and methods. We need to understand the modeling techniques and algorithms that have dominated statistical NLP in the past few years, wherein the traditional view of computational linguistics is challenged (Schubert, 2020).

Historically, statistical NLP's primary focus was on assigning sequences, labels, syntax trees, and the translation of linguistic inputs using statistical language models that have been trained on vast datasets of observed language use. A more detailed view of the tasks addressed can be given as follows (where the appended keywords refer to typical applications).

> *Text and document classification*: Large publications can be categorized using the normalized frequency rates of specific words (or word classes) and punctuation. A wide range of traditional pattern recognition algorithms may be used regarding the difficulty of learning to assign brand new documents (as vectors) to the appropriate class (e.g., Sebestyen et al., 1962; Duda & Hart, 1973; Schubert, 2020).
>
> *Classification of particular words or phrases in more general or sentential settings*: This includes any term or word used in the context of the work that has to be categorized. As a result, traits are chosen to reflect the qualities of the target word or phrase as well as how it interacts with its surroundings. These traits include nearby words

or word categories, (possibly) local syntactic dependency links, and traits with a wider scope, like word frequencies or document class (Schubert, 2020).

Sequence labeling: A common NLP problem is sequence labeling, which gives a class or label to each character in a given input sequence. A single word will be referred to as a "token" in this context. These tags or labels can be employed in additional downstream models as token features or to improve search quality by designating token spans.

SIGNIFICANCE OF AI IN LINGUISTICS

The significance of AI in linguistics can be seen through various examples. One is the development of language acquisition models, which has been a major focus for many researchers and developers since the 1950s when Chomsky published his seminal work on generative grammar. Another example is how ML algorithms are used to automatically generate sentences from texts that have already been translated into other languages. On top of these linguistic developments, there's also an increasing use of AI-based text analysis tools such as sentiment analysis or NLP systems like IBM Watson and Google Translate. AI has a significant impact on the field of linguistics. It is used to improve language translation, speech synthesis, and text-to-speech technology. Additionally, it can be applied to NLP. This includes some tasks such as machine comprehension and understanding meaning from written or spoken texts with intentionality, which humans are capable of doing naturally.

- Language scientists are discovering that AI is one of the most powerful new tools at their disposal. Corpus linguists rely on AI to collect and refine data. Psycholinguists make use of neural networks to build realistic brain models.
- AI offers researchers a fast and scalable alternative to study linguistic patterns at scale, so that they can reach conclusions faster than ever before.
- The use of AI by linguists includes tracking the movements of our eyes during reading, measuring the tone of our voice, and measuring the movement of our faces when talking.
- AI is being used to do linguistic analyses including translation and speech recognition with far better accuracy than humans can achieve with these tasks alone, which gives it a variety of

applications across many industries such as law enforcement, healthcare, and disaster relief.

SIGNIFICANCE OF AI IN FORENSIC LINGUISTICS

AI is a branch of computer science and engineering that involves the creation of intelligent machines. It is not just a new concept that we have only begun to explore in recent years; it has been in existence for decades and has changed the world we live in in many significant and drastic ways. One such field of research where AI has taken a front seat is forensic linguistics.

In forensic linguistics, AI has been used to develop artificial neural networks for language analysis. Artificial neural networks are mathematical models which can be applied to various areas including NLP, voice recognition, and MT from one human language into another. The goal is not only linguistic accuracy but also rapid response speed. AI has been used to aid forensic linguists. This is because the ML techniques that are central to AI offer a way for computer programs, which use algorithms and datasets, to be applied with more accuracy than traditional human-based analysis methods. These tools have also helped law enforcement agencies detect patterns in speech or text that might otherwise go unnoticed by humans.

AI offers an opportunity to create new tools, algorithms, and techniques to improve the process of forensic linguistics. The significance of this technology is huge as it can help solve crimes which might otherwise go unsolved due to lack of evidence or because there was no one available who could do linguistic analysis before.

AI can help to identify dialects as well as detect emotions such as sarcasm or aggression in order to better identify what someone is trying to say. AI also has applications for detecting false statements.

ADVANTAGES OF AI IN FORENSIC LINGUISTICS

In 1968, linguistics professor Jan Svartvik recorded his first analysis of the "statement of Timothy John Evans" given at Notting Hill police station to police officers in 1953. He did a methodical examination of Evans' statement and observed that it contained two different styles. This led to questions on the *Judges' Rules*, which state that the suspect/witness must narrate the incident to a police officer, who is not allowed to interrupt the suspect, and who is not to ask anything of the suspect at the statement stage except for minor clarifications. But, in reality, this never happened. Instead, police officers used to ask questions and, based on the answers, make their own responses.

Forensic linguistics began to establish itself as one of the investigative sciences, questioning witness and defendant statements; linguistics professionals were called upon as experts in cases related to the interpretation of meaning in legal and other documents, the analysis of text messages and emails, and this practice continues to grow (Olsson & Luchjenbroers, 2013).

As discussed in the introduction, Forensic Linguistics is the branch of applied linguistics that examines language evidence in a criminal or civil matter. Forensic linguists use their knowledge to answer questions during the investigation, trial, or appeal stages (Olsson & Luchjenbroers, 2013). The observation skills in identifying the author, understanding the stylistics of spoken words and written content, discourse analysis, studying dialects, and transcription of the speech are some of the significant applications of Forensic Linguistics (Ariani et al., 2014). The language in question constitutes a language in the crime, such as threats, bribery, hate speech, or clarifying the context in the interpretation of the message, the manner in which the spoken or written words are delivered (Bruinsma & Weisburd, 2014). According to linguist Malcolm Coulthard, a person's writing style "will manifest itself in distinctive and cumulatively unique rule-governed choices for encoding meaning linguistically in written and spoken communications they produce" (2013, p. 446). Various studies conducted in the late 1990s suggested that detecting the authorship average word length would be helpful (Coulthard, 2004; Mosteller & Wallace, 1964/2007; Mendenhall, 1887). The use of "stop words" or "function words" has proved accurate in authorship detection (Stamatatos, 2009; Tweedie et al., 1996).

Detection of authorship is a very time-consuming chore. Multiple studies have been done to detect authorship with the help of AI, deep neural networks, and ML (Kurtukova et al., 2020). Techniques used could be "Feed-forward neural network," "Radial basis function network," or "Support Vector Machines" (Nirkhi & Dharaskar, 2013). In one of the studies conducted in 2007, the author was detected in a Portuguese written document using Support Vector Machine, and the study achieved a recognition rate of 78 percent (Oliveira et al., 2007).

Every year, PAN conducts scientific events and shares tasks on digital text forensics and stylometry. At these scientific events, multiple participants develop algorithms; the performance of these algorithms assesses results accuracy. Numerous experiments have been conducted for Authorship Identification on this platform worldwide over the last decade. During the last five years, these events have also included studies on Author Profiling, Multi-Author analysis, and Author Verification (PAN Data, n.d.).

Another vital aspect is emotion recognition from language. Forensically this is used in cases of hate speech analysis. In multiple types of research, it has been found that emotions are moderated by speech, voice tone, sentence collection, breathing, etc. (Abdullah et al., 2021; Dou et al., 2020; Fortuna & Nunes, 2019; Ibrahim et al., 2019).

CONS OF USING AI IN LINGUISTICS

Technology has made our life easier today; we humans live, thrive, and depend on technology. With the rapid advancement in technology, we humans have evolved to introduce and achieve new know-hows in the field of science today. The introduction of AI was one such invention that paved the way for other fascinating creations like Alexa, Siri, Automated Maps, Google Maps, etc. AI-based machines have become so efficient in mimicking human activities and augmenting the efficiency of delivering tasks that our lives now seem impossible without their presence, and with the way our life is intertwined with the same, it is sometimes worrying to ponder what effect does it have on us, that it makes us so dependent?

According to some people, the development of numerous programs of the sorts we are currently writing, and the creation of vast knowledge bases of facts in the languages that are currently utilized to represent information, are necessary to achieve human-level intelligence. Most AI researchers think that novel approaches are required to achieve human-level intelligence. Therefore, human-level intelligence cannot be predicted (McCarthy, 2007).

According to a 2018 research survey conducted by PwC Consumer Intelligent Series Voice Assistants, the introduction of smart voice assistants like Siri and Alexa, which use components of AI linguistics such as Natural Processing language and ML, has made users between the ages of 25 and 49 heavily dependent on them (PwC, 2018). This is problematic as it can have a significant effect on the creativity of a person, creating dependencies and encouraging laziness.

Automated tools using AI linguistic tools are now used so extensively everywhere, as many organizations and companies want efficient AI tools and algorithms in place of humans, that many fear it will cause mass unemployment. By 2030, 30 percent of the world's existing work force might be replaced by robots and intelligent agents, according to a McKinsey Global Institute report. The study states: "by 2030, automation will displace between 400 and 800 million jobs, requiring as many as 375 million people to switch job categories entirely." As a result of the observations, it is certain that AIs will result in less human involvement, potentially causing major disruption in employment standards (Proschool, 2019).

Technology is designed to make our lives more convenient. However, the existing powerful AI tools, like intelligent conversation bots—voice assistants that are manufactured and programmed to deliver and achieve outstanding results by understanding the language spoken by humans—fail to attain their maximum efficiency and are prone to many errors. The technology lacks the needed intellect and creativity of humans with which it can function. Humans possess a high emotional quotient and intellect which the AI tools clearly lack, thus their capabilities are confined to the ability of the programmers who design them.

AI tools have made machines highly skilled; however, they remain unmatchable to human minds and fail to be 100 percent efficient in performing in the same way. Also, the production and set up of AI tools are very expensive. Huge costs are incurred during the research and development, engineering etc. of AI tools. The amount of money spent to acquire and set up the virtual assistant Siri by Apple was around a whopping $200 million, whereas, Alexa was acquired by Amazon for $26 million in 2013. The huge sum spent was due to the high costs of AI implementation. A large sum of money is also required for its maintenance and repair.

Another major concern following the implementation and adoption of AI linguistics tools available today is the alarming issue of privacy. The popular IoT (Internet of Things) devices available on the market today are equipped with powerful AI linguistic tools; these tools are used in a wide range of devices like smartphones, smart lightbulbs, security cameras etc. and have become an integral part of our day-to-day lives. However, the convenience of adopting them comes at a cost in terms of privacy: IoT devices, due to their lack of security features, can pose serious security risks. They enable a hacker to potentially invade the user's privacy in a variety of ways, from smart TV spying to hijacking smart speakers. IoT devices are connected to the user's home through WiFi connection, giving the hacker the opportunity to hack smart devices or routers to give a cybercriminal control of the user's smart home, which can be a major threat concerning the privacy of the user (Avast Academy, n.d.).

FUTURISTIC APPROACHES OF AI IN LINGUISTICS

The advancement of technology has made machines faster and smarter with time. Currently, machines can be trained and used to logically interact and, with experience, perform human-like tasks. This has led to a revolution in the way we interact and use technology. One of the most significant advancements is a component of AI, natural language processing (NLP), which can be described as the machine's ability to understand and perceive language as it is spoken by humans. With the introduction of NLP we now have smart assistants like Siri and Alexa that efficiently understand what we speak and present us with the answers or results we seek.

Conversational bots, virtual traveling booking agents, etc. are all advancements of AI in linguistics. The sole aim of the AI linguistics tool is to comprehend the language spoken by the user and assist the user. In future, with the development of more AI linguistic tools, we can achieve the manufacturing of more intelligent machines that can improve the quality of our lives and make our life easier than ever before. Much research is currently ongoing to make the benefits of AI accessible to everybody and to introduce the use of AI in linguistics in new domains with the help of IoT devices etc.

The world is battling loneliness. Although we all seem to be connected to each other just a click or text away, loneliness persists and is a major cause of depression. Loneliness can be termed as an unpleasant emotional state that is born out of isolation. In a world where we could go to great lengths to introduce new technologies to connect people, we remain oblivious to eradicating the unwanted feeling of being lonely. Technology could be used to solve this problem. In future, intelligent bots could be developed that can be used specifically for social interactions. They could be designed to act like humans, to offer comfort to the user so that they don't feel lonely. Intelligent bots could also be designed and used in healing/rehabilitation centers as trainers to humans seeking rehabilitation and help.

AI linguistic tools can also be developed to respond to emergencies and can be used as smart security tools. The IoT devices/AI tools can alert law enforcement agencies whenever trigger words like HELP, SAVE ME etc., are uttered by the user. This development could be very helpful in preventing or detecting crime.

AI tools can also be designed in such a way that they can be used as smart translators globally. Even though there are AI tools like Google Translate available online, for such a purpose, they are inefficient and fail to achieve the required task. The need for human translators could be replaced with the use of smart AI tool devices capable of interpreting all languages spoken globally and of translating the language of the user into the language requested. This would dispel the need to rely on another person.

FUTURISTIC APPROACHES OF AI IN FORENSIC LINGUISTICS

Future forensic linguists will be more successful if they concentrate on legal concerns and get training, expertise, and knowledge in other legal fields to better prepare them for employment in and with the legal system (Ariani et al., 2014).

"Language itself can prove to be very strong Forensic evidence" (Tuck, n.d.); the same was demonstrated by Jan Svartvik in 1968, after the thorough analysis and scrutiny of the four statements made by Timothy Evans, who lied about confessing to the 1949 murders of his wife and little daughter. The study that he published after examining the Evans statements paved the way in providing compelling observations depicting the importance of forensic linguistics.

An area of applied linguistics known as forensic linguistics is concerned with the analysis of language, as language can be deemed an important piece of evidence in the forensic context and the investigation of criminal or civil cases. The use of forensic linguistics in assisting the law is now done extensively around the world. However, this is a tedious task that requires immense skill and expertise. With the advent of technology and the powerful evolution of mankind with science, anything and everything is surmountable. The problems of the fast-paced world are now easily conceivable, as machines are given the ultimate power of "Human Intelligence." Humans are the most intelligent beings that are endowed with consciousness, cognitive abilities, understanding, and intellect to perform tasks. Machines, on the contrary, lack consciousness and perform different functions, as they are manufactured to do so. Machines were invented by man to assist us to perform complex tasks at a faster rate. Today, machines are manufactured with the aim of making them smarter to enable them to carry out tasks that require the need of human intelligence.

AI, which is frequently described as the simulation of intelligence in machines, personifies the concept in which machines are trained to learn and mimic humans with experience to deliver commendable results to human-like tasks (Great Learning Team, n.d.). AI can be used in forensic linguistics to detect potential crimes. The future holds limitless possibilities in this context in which to investigate language as evidence with the help of AI.

The Internet and social media have fascinated humans around the world. At this point in time there are approximately 3.5 billion people online, using the Internet, with Facebook, the extremely popular social networking site, having 2.4 billion subscribers. More than 1 billion people are using YouTube and WhatsApp, the two further admired social media. The world population is 7.7 billion people, which means that social media accounts for one-third of the global population and more than two-thirds of Internet users.

Social media has had a significant impact on the globe. The speedy and extensive adoption of the tools available on the Internet has transformed how we connect with people, perceive and access news, and also react to current socioeconomic situations and political changes (Ritchie et al., 2023). The Internet is both a safe and a dangerous space to be in. According to the American Community Survey (ACS), around 95 percent of children aged 3 to 18 in the United States had access to the Internet at home in 2019 (NCES, n.d.). Children using the Internet are vulnerable and easily lured by fraudsters and are subjected to cyberbullying amongst the other crimes that frequently occur through the Internet.

Cyberbullying has plagued the users of the world. Even though there is no age group that is specifically targeted by the bullies on the Internet, the teens are often the ones who are frequently subjected to online bullying. As a result, they are susceptible to social anxiety and mental health problems, which can even lead to suicidal tendencies, and therefore need assistance. Cyberbullying is a grave problem and currently there is no foolproof system or method designed to curb it or identify the culprits who engage and are responsible for it.

With the use of AI-developed algorithms by social media platforms, in the near future this problem could get a permanent fix, or at least the much-needed attention that it requires. Even though there are some NLP tools available that are used by some social media sites, these tools are not efficient and do not solve the existing problem. AI-developed tools can be used to analyze and investigate the chats/comments/posts posted online to alert and notify if there is any cyberbullying/harassment done online with the help of the language used by users to communicate with each other. This could help solve some of the underlying problems that cyberbullying victims face online.

The implementation of AI in forensic linguistics can also be useful in analyzing fraud/scam emails that are sent online by potential fraudsters who send malicious emails to people for various malicious intentions. There are many cases in which fraudsters have stolen money/crucial data by convincing users to believe the email/message is genuine. A tool with the employ of AI can help clients mark their emails/messages as threats so as to avoid potential scams.

AI tools can also be used to identify propagandists and rebels who instigate violence through their posts/comments in the name of freedom of expression.

A game known as the "Blue Whale Game," also known as the "Suicide Game," was developed and available on the Internet. The game was abetting the players to attempt suicide (NCES, n.d.). It was believed that it was disseminated among hidden groups on social media networks, according to numerous Internet reports. The developers would identify depressed players/victims and invite them to join the game by convincing them that it would be fun. The challenge is based on an anonymous "group administrator," sometimes known as "the curator," assigning 50 tasks to selected "players" during a 50-day period that must be performed, documented, and posted. Players of the challenge are blackmailed and cyber harassed into completing the "game" once they begin. No player could stop playing the game as the player would be harassed online. Due to this dangerous game, many children and teens have ended their lives. AI-developed tools can be used to investigate the linguistics used in the legal terms and conditions/the adware/chatbot etc. of the apps available online so that these dangerous apps/games can come to notice.

REFERENCES

Abdullah, S. M. S. A., Ameen, S. Y. A., Sadeeq, M. A., & Zeebaree, S. (2021). Multimodal emotion recognition using deep learning. *Journal of Applied Science and Technology Trends*, 2(2): 52–58.

Anumanchipalli, J. C., Chartier, J., & Chang, E. F. (2019). Speech synthesis from neural decoding of spoken sentences. *Nature*, 568: 493–498 doi:10.1038/s41586-019-1119-1

Ariani, M. G., Sajedi, F., & Sajedi, M. (2014). Forensic linguistics: A brief overview of the key elements. *Procedia—Social and Behavioral Sciences*, 158: 222–225. doi:10.1016/j.sbspro.2014.12.078

Avast Academy. (n.d.). Is Alexa always listening? How to protect your privacy (n.d.). *Avast Academy*. Retrieved January 8, 2022, from https://www.avast.com/c-amazon-alexa-listening#gref

Bender, E. M., & Langendoen, D. T. (2010). Computational linguistics in support of linguistic theory. *Linguistic Issues in Language Technology*, 3.

Bruinsma, G., & Weisburd, D. (Eds.). (2014). *Encyclopedia of criminology and criminal justice*. Springer New York. doi:10.1007/978-1-4614-5690-2

Careers 360 (2021). Branches of linguistics—meaning, scope, types, FAQs. Retrieved January 9, 2022, from https://www.careers360.com/articles/branches-of-inguistics-counar

Coulthard, M. (2013). On admissible linguistic evidence. *Journal of Law and Policy*, 21(2): 441–466. Retrieved December 14, 2023, from https://brooklynworks.brooklaw.edu/jlp/vol21/iss2/8

Coulthard, M. (2004). Author identification, idiolect, and linguistic uniqueness. *Applied Linguistics*, 25(4): 431–447. doi:10.1093/applin/25.4.431

Derin, T., Evizareza, Deliani, S., & Hamuddin, B. (2019, February). Exploring the past, present, and future of forensic linguistics study: A brief overview. In: *The First Conference of Indonesian Community for Forensic Linguistics (KLFI-1) At: Trenz Hotel Panamz, Pekanbaru, Riau.*

Docio-Fernandez, L., & García Mateo, C. (2015). Speech production. In S. Z. Li & A. K. Jain (Eds.), *Encyclopedia of biometrics* (pp. 1493–1498). Springer US. doi:10.1007/978-1-4899-7488-4_199

Dou, S., Feng, Z., Yang, X., & Tian, J. (2020). Real-time multimodal emotion recognition system based on elderly accompanying robot. *Journal of Physics: Conference Series*, 1453, 012093. doi:10.1088/1742-6596/1453/1/012093

Duda, R. O., & Hart, P. E. (1973). *Pattern classification and scene analysis* (Vol. 3, pp. 731–739). Wiley.

Fortuna, P., & Nunes, S. (2019). A survey on automatic detection of hate speech in text. *ACM Computing Surveys*, 51(4): 1–30. doi:10.1145/3232676

Great Learning Team. (n.d.). What is Artificial Intelligence? How does AI work, applications and future? (n.d.). *Great Learning*. Retrieved January 6, 2022, from https://www.mygreatlearning.com/blog/what-is-artificial-intelligence/

Hein, A. S. (2010). Achievements of AI in linguistics. Retrieved January 6, 2022, from https://ep.liu.se/ecp/048/003/ecp1048003.pdf

Hendricks, J. (2019, May 21). What linguistic AI has learned. *RWS Blog*. Retrieved January 10, 2022, from https://www.rws.com/blog/what-linguistic-AI-has-learned/

History of speech synthesis, 1770–1970. (n.d.). Retrieved January 11, 2022, from https://www2.ling.su.se/staff/hartmut/kemplne.htm

Ibrahim, R., Zeebaree, S., & Jacksi, K. (2019). Survey on semantic similarity based on document clustering. *Advances in Science, Technology and Engineering Systems Journal*, 4: 115–122. doi:10.25046/aj040515

Kurtukova, A., Romanov, A., & Shelupanov, A. (2020). Source code authorship identification using deep neural networks. *Symmetry*, 12(12): 2044. doi:10.3390/sym12122044

Lateef, Z. (2023). Types of Artificial Intelligence you should know, *Edureka*. Retrieved December 13, 2023, from https://www.edureka.co/blog/types-of-artificial-intelligence/

McCarthy, J. (2007). What is artificial intelligence? Retrieved December 14, 2023, from https://www-formal.stanford.edu/jmc/whatisai.pdf

McCarthy, J., Minksy, M. L., Rochester, N., & Shannon, C. E. (1955/2006). A proposal for the Dartmouth Summer Research Project on artificial intelligence. *AI Magazine*, 27(4): 12.

McMenamin, G. R. (2002). *Forensic linguistics: Advances in forensic stylistics*. CRC Press.

McShane, M., & Nirenburg, S. (2021). *Linguistics for the age of AI*. MIT Press.

Mendenhall, T. C. (1887). The characteristic curves of composition. *Science*, 9(214): 237–249.

Merriam-Webster. (n.d.). "Linguistics" definition and meaning. Retrieved January 6, 2022, from https://www.merriam-webster.com/dictionary/linguistics

Moltzau, A. (2020). Artificial intelligence and linguistics. *Medium*, 17 July. Retrieved January 8, 2022, from https://medium.datadriveninvestor.com/artificial-intelligence-and-linguistics-dc9eeee775dd

Mosteller, F., & Wallace, D. L. (1964/2007). *Inference and disputed authorship: The Federalist Papers*. CSLI Publications. Retrieved January 6, 2022, from https://web.stanford.edu/group/cslipublications/cslipublications/site/1575865521.shtml

NCES (n.d.). Fast facts: Access to the internet. (n.d.). *National Center for Education Statistics*. Retrieved January 6, 2022, from https://nces.ed.gov/fastfacts/display.asp?id=46

Nirkhi, S., & Dharaskar, R. V. (2013). Comparative study of authorship identification techniques for cyber forensics analysis. *International Journal of Advanced Computer Science and Applications*, 4(5). doi:10.14569/IJACSA.2013.040505

Oliveira, L. S., Pavelec, D., & Justino, E. (2007). Author identification using stylometric features. *Inteligencia Artificial: Revista Iberoamericana de Inteligencia Artificial*, 11(36): 59–65. doi:10.4114/ia.v11i36.892

Olsson, J., & Luchjenbroers, J. (2013). *Forensic linguistics*. A&C Black.

PAN Data. (n.d.). Retrieved January 7, 2022, from https://pan.webis.de/data.html

Proschool (2019, November). Is AI coming to take our jobs? Top 5 disadvantages of AI today. *Proschool*. Retrieved January 8, 2022, from https://www.proschoolonline.com/blog/what-are-the-disadvantages-of-ai

PwC. (2018). The impact of voice assistants on consumer behavior. *PwC*. Retrieved January 8, 2022, from https://www.pwc.com/us/en/services/consulting/library/consumer-intelligence-series/voice-assistants.html

Ritchie, H., Mathieu, E., Roser, M., & Ortiz-Ospina, E. (2023). Internet. *Our World in Data*. Retrieved December 14, 2023, from https://ourworldindata.org/internet

Schubert, L. (2020). Computational linguistics. In E. N. Zalta (Ed.), *The Stanford encyclopedia of philosophy* (Spring 2020 edn), https://plato.stanford.edu/archives/spr2020/entries/computational-linguistics/

Schumann, J. H. (1987). The expression of temporality in basilang speech. *Studies in Second Language Acquisition*, 9(1), 21–41.

ScienceDirect (n.d.). Synthetic speech. Retrieved January 11, 2022, from https://www.sciencedirect.com/topics/computer-science/synthetic-speech

Sebestyen, G. S., Van Meter, D., & Air Force Cambridge Research Labs Hanscom AFB MA. (1962). *Investigation of automation of speech processing for voice communication*. PN Publishers.

Smith, J., Durham, M., & Richards, H. (2013). The social and linguistic in the acquisition of sociolinguistic norms: Caregivers, children, and variation. *Linguistics*, 51(2), 285–324.

Stamatatos, E. (2009). A survey of modern authorship attribution methods. *Journal of the American Society for Information Science and Technology*, 60(3): 538–556. doi:10.1002/asi.21001

Svartvik, J. (1968). *The Evans statements: A case for forensic linguistics*. University of Göteborg.

Tuck, B. M. (n.d.). Preserving facts, form, and function when a deaf witness with minimal language skills testifies in court. *University of Pennsylvania Law Review*, 158: 52.

Tweedie, F. J., Singh, S., & Holmes, D. I. (1996). Neural network applications in stylometry: The Federalist Papers. *Computers and the Humanities*, 30(1): 1–10. doi:10.1007/BF00054024

Yasar, K., Gillis, A. S., & Bernstein, C. (2023, June). What is computational linguistics (CL)? *TechTarget*. Retrieved December 13, 2023, from https://www.techtarget.com/searchenterpriseai/definition/computational-linguistics-CL

7

Artificial Intelligence in Forensic Biology

Neha Gupta, Kunwar Veer Vikram Srivastav, Sneha
Lohar, Vaibhav Sharma, and Rajesh Kumar

INTRODUCTION

As the field of forensic science continues to advance, it offers the opportunity to process complex evidence with unprecedented precision, sensitivity, and efficiency. Traditional forensic identification methods heavily rely on the manual extraction of information by forensic experts, who provide insights based on their knowledge and personal experience. However, this approach can be both time-consuming and subject to various influences that are difficult to overcome. In the era of vast amounts of data, the rapid development of Artificial Intelligence (AI) introduces new possibilities in the field of forensic biology. AI techniques have been applied to various aspects such as estimating post-mortem interval, DNA analysis, facial recognition for age and gender identification, cause of death determination, injury analysis, and identification of individuals. These advancements demonstrate the potential and benefits of utilizing AI in forensic science, injecting new energy into the field. However, they also come with challenges that need to be addressed. The integration of AI in forensic science holds great promise for improving efficiency and objectivity in analyzing

DOI: 10.4324/9781003287810-7

evidence. It has the potential to streamline processes, enhance accuracy, and provide valuable insights. Nonetheless, careful consideration and further research are required to ensure the ethical and reliable use of AI in forensic investigations (Fang et al., 2020).

The term "artificial intelligence" (AI) was coined by John McCarthy, widely recognized as the father of AI, during the Dartmouth Conference in 1956. It marked the beginning of a field within computer science dedicated to solving highly complex problems that cannot be easily tackled through direct calculations or traditional mathematical methods. AI aims to enable computers to approach problems in a manner like human thinking, taking on a "human-like" approach to finding innovative solutions (Cho et al., 2016; Dale, Popescu, & Karp, 2010; McCarthy et al., 2006).

To grasp the concept of artificial intelligence, it is important to understand a few key aspects. First, AI refers to the capability of machines to exhibit their own form of intelligence. This intelligence allows machines to process information, make decisions, and perform tasks without explicit human input. Machine learning is a subset of AI that relies on algorithms to analyze datasets and predict outcomes. By learning from the data, machines can autonomously resolve issues and improve their performance over time.

Neural networks are algorithms designed to simulate the functioning of the human brain. They consist of artificial neurons that compute signals, enabling the network to process and analyze complex information. Neural networks are a crucial component of AI, as they contribute to creating systems that can emulate human-like intelligence and behavior.

Deep learning, on the other hand, is a specific branch of machine learning that employs deep neural networks with multiple layers of computation. This approach allows for the automatic identification of patterns in input data, enhancing feature detection and enabling more sophisticated analysis. Deep learning techniques have proven effective in various domains, including image recognition, natural language processing, and data analysis.

In summary, artificial intelligence encompasses a broad range of techniques and methodologies aimed at solving complex problems by imitating human-like intelligence. Machine learning, neural networks, and deep learning are integral components of AI, each serving a specific purpose in enhancing computational capabilities and enabling machines to perform tasks that were once exclusive to humans. The field of AI continues to advance rapidly, with ongoing research and development driving innovation and expanding its potential applications in various domains (Akst, 2019).

Artificial intelligence technologies, specifically neural networks, offer significant opportunities for their application in expert tasks, such as pattern recognition of symbols, sounds, images, and other complex problems. These technologies utilize heuristic analysis to process vast amounts of information. Artificial neural networks (ANNs) serve as a model for data processing, designed to emulate the functioning of the human brain. Their capacity to learn from newly acquired information reduces the potential for errors in forensic examinations, enhancing the accuracy and reliability of the results (Taylor & Powers, 2016; Polyakov et al., 2019).

Forensic investigations are conducted by the experts to serve justice to involved parties. A variety of evidence is found from different locations of a crime scene, amongst which the most commonly found is blood. Forensic Biology involves the utilization of biological science principles and methodologies within a legal framework. Forensic biologists examine cellular and tissue samples, along with physiological fluids, that are pertinent to legal investigations. This multidisciplinary field encompasses specialized areas such as DNA analysis, forensic anthropology, forensic pathology, forensic entomology, forensic odontology, forensic botany, forensic serology, and forensic microbiology. The integration of artificial intelligence technologies into forensic practices is gaining momentum and offers extensive potential for their application. In this chapter, we will discuss the possible application of artificial intelligence covering each area of forensic biology.

ARTIFICIAL INTELLIGENCE IN FORENSIC DNA ANALYSIS

After the generation of the Short Tandem Repeat (STR) profiles by using Polymerase Chain Reaction i.e. PCR, an analyst needs to decide whether the data generated in the form of profiles correctly shows the components of DNA extract, or if it is just the mishaps in the process which may affect the result. Looking for and understanding an electropherogram (EPG) may take significant time and can cause differences of opinion. In some instances, stutter can be caused which means an error in the DNA replication process of the PCR, that results in the generation of copies of different numbers of repeats than intended. Also, sometimes it may cause pull-ups, which means that commercial kits having the different fluorophores that emit certain wavelengths get mixed in the process.

As Taylor & Powers (2016) state, the analyst must:

recognise and remove artefacts such as pull-up that have not automatically been identified by an expert system. For stutters (they) ... require removal in reference samples as it is only the alleles that are of interest for most applications. For evidence samples the removal of stutter peaks will depend on the downstream system being used to interpret the profile.

If the system incorporates stutter peaks in its modeling, such as a continuous system, the analyst would want them to remain in the EPG. Otherwise, they must be eliminated, and expert systems can automate this removal by identifying most stutter peaks. The integration of ANNs into expert EPG reading systems shows significant promise. The structured nature of the data, characterized by clear features and patterns, makes it well suited for processing through ANNs. Implementing ANNs could eliminate the need for multiple manual removals by analysts and potentially save significant reading time. The ultimate goal would be to train an ANN to a level where no human intervention is required at all, an attainable objective considering the diverse achievements demonstrated by ANNs in various fields (Taylor & Powers, 2016).

ARTIFICIAL INTELLIGENCE IN FORENSIC ODONTOLOGY

Forensic odontology is an emerging field that has made remarkable advancements in the identification of individuals involved in crimes such as child abuse, sexual assault, mass disasters, and other legal matters. Its practitioners hold a strong sense of moral responsibility to deliver justice to victims and their families, particularly in cases where dental remains are the only available evidence. Through their expertise in dental analysis and identification techniques, forensic odontologists play a crucial role in providing closure and resolving complex legal issues. Their dedication to upholding justice is evident in their unwavering commitment to using dental evidence to bring perpetrators to account and ensure the rights of victims are protected. Age and gender determination from teeth using third molar development (De Tobel et al., 2017) and mandibular morphometric parameters (Niño-Sandoval et al., 2017) respectively, with the help of artificial intelligence based on artificial neural networks, has been extensively used in the field of forensic science for a long time. In the field of forensic odontology, automated methods have emerged as a promising approach. These methods involve utilizing software to perform several key tasks: first, identifying the region of interest within the image(s); second, assessing the level of development observed in that region; and, finally, correlating this information with the age of the individual based on a reference population. By leveraging AI, these automated systems can assist in making more accurate decisions in cases where traditional forensic odontologists may face challenges. AI acts as a guiding tool, aiding in the analysis and interpretation of dental evidence, ultimately improving the accuracy and efficiency of age estimation processes in forensic investigations.

ARTIFICIAL INTELLIGENCE IN FORENSIC ENTOMOLOGY

Forensic entomology focuses on the utilization of insects (and other arthropods) in legal affairs. The most frequent applications are in the estimation of post-mortem interval (time that has passed since death) as well as other aspects related to the facts of the place and circumstances of death. To serve this purpose, the first and foremost requirement is the proper identification of those forensically relevant insects. For the acquisition of developmental data and insect succession patterns in an investigation, accurate determination of insect species is necessary; failure to do so can lead to an incorrect estimation of the post-mortem interval (PMI). Succession studies play a crucial role in providing valuable insights into the insect species present in specific geographic areas and during particular seasons. This information becomes particularly useful in estimating the timing and location of specific cases. By studying the succession patterns of insects and their interactions with decomposition processes, forensic entomologists can make informed assessments about the season and region in which a particular incident has occurred. This knowledge enhances the ability to reconstruct crime scenes and contributes to the overall understanding of forensic investigations (Wang et al., 2021). Traditional identification of insects is accomplished by the analysis of their morphological features such as texture, color, and shape but this process takes considerable time and is also complicated for experts. Hence it becomes mandatory to develop a tool that assists the entomologist in identifying the insect based on computational techniques (Luquin et al., 2017). In the present scenario, the use of artificial neural network algorithms emerged as new field of study focussing on image recognition and feature extraction and has proved to be a boon to overcoming the shortcomings of traditional identification methods.

ARTIFICIAL INTELLIGENCE IN FORENSIC MEDICINE AND FORENSIC PATHOLOGY

Forensic medicine serves as a crucial link between the medical field and the justice system, specifically within the context of criminal law. This interdisciplinary field can be broadly categorized into two main streams: clinical forensic medicine and forensic pathology.

Clinical forensic medicine encompasses the evaluation and examination of living individuals who are engaged in legal matters, with a specific focus on the scientific investigation for the administration of justice. It involves various tasks such as assessing and documenting injuries, collecting evidence, conducting sexual assault examinations, and offering expert medical opinions in legal proceedings. By ensuring the rights of victims, providing necessary medical care, and aiding in the investigation and prosecution of crimes, clinical forensic medicine plays a crucial role in the legal system. The primary responsibility of clinical forensic scientists is to conduct examinations on both victims and suspects involved in criminal assault cases, including rape, child abuse, and domestic violence. Their expertise lies in the scientific investigation of living individuals to gather evidence and contribute to the pursuit of justice. By examining the victims and suspects, clinical forensic scientists play a critical role in gathering important information that can support legal proceedings and assist in the resolution of these cases (Pollak & Saukko, 2013; Sharma et al., 2005).

Forensic pathology plays a critical role in determining the cause and manner of death in cases of suspicious or unexplained deaths, such as homicides. Forensic pathologists employ both anatomical and clinical pathology techniques to investigate these cases. However, the integration of AI in forensic pathology encounters two primary challenges. First, it is essential to establish a clear understanding of evidence, differentiating between scientific evidence and legal evidence in both upstream and downstream processes. Second, the challenge lies in individualization or identification. In the field of forensic medicine, the application of statistical knowledge based on homogeneous groups to specific cases becomes more complex. It requires ensuring the validity of algorithms without biases and individualizing legal reasoning and sentences (DiMaio & Molina, 2021).

AI can serve as a supportive tool to enhance the decision-making capabilities of forensic pathologists. It acts as a confidence booster, providing valuable insights and assisting in the structuring of research for the advancement of scientific knowledge in forensic medicine. However, it is important to note that the current use of AI in decision support for forensic medicine is still in its early stages of development. Continued research and refinement are necessary to ensure its effectiveness and reliability in this field (Lefèvre, 2021).

ARTIFICIAL INTELLIGENCE IN FORENSIC MICROBIOLOGY

Micro-organisms emerged approximately 3.5 billion years ago, making them among the earliest life forms on Earth. They can be broadly classified into two types based on their morphology (Nannipieri et al., 2003).

The first type consists of non-cellular organisms, such as viruses. The second type comprises cellular organisms, which can be further divided into two categories: prokaryotes and eukaryotes. Prokaryotes include groups like Achaea and Eubacteria. These micro-organisms lack a well-defined nucleus and other membrane-bound organelles. They are characterized by their simplicity and are found in various environments, ranging from extreme habitats to the human body.

On the other hand, eukaryotes encompass micro-organisms such as fungi and unicellular algae. These organisms possess a distinct nucleus and other membrane-bound organelles within their cells. Eukaryotes exhibit a greater complexity compared with prokaryotes and have a wide range of ecological roles, including symbiosis, decomposition, and photosynthesis. Understanding the diversity and characteristics of micro-organisms is essential in fields such as microbiology, ecology, and health sciences. These tiny organisms play critical roles in various ecological processes, nutrient cycling, and the maintenance of global ecosystems. Additionally, their study helps in addressing infectious diseases, developing biotechnological applications, and exploring the origins and evolution of life on Earth (Maiden et al., 1998; Nowrousian, 2010; Weinbauer, 2004; Yeom & Javidi, 2006).

Prediction of Human Micro-biome By Environmental and Host Phenotypes

With the development of next-generation sequencing and high-throughput of microbial sequencing, a new area of forensic microbiology has been generated. The main job of the forensic microbiologist is to link microbial populations to phenotypes and ecological environments (Atlas, 1998). A micro-biome is the community of micro-organisms. Due to the uniqueness of an individual's micro-biome, we can easily predict the presence of particular micro-organisms with next-generation sequencing. We can correlate between victim, crime scene, and suspect.

CONCLUSION

This involves considering relevant social and cultural differences among the coder's perspective and that of the target population, as well as the coder's latent and inherent biases. Such an outcome will liberate AI's capacity to improve lives everywhere and help us achieve the United Nations' sustainable development goals. AI improves the judgment power of a court of law. Reports of forensic biology and DNA are permissible in a court of justice due to the major role of AI.

REFERENCES

Akst, J. (2019). A primer: artificial intelligence versus neural networks. *Inspiring Innovation: The Scientist Exploring Life, 65802.*

Atlas, R. M. (1998). *Microbial ecology: fundamentals and applications.* Pearson Education India.

Cho, S., Seo, H. J., Lee, J., Yu, H. J., & Lee, S. D. (2016). Kinship testing based on SNPs using microarray system. *Transfusion Medicine and Hemotherapy, 43*(6): 429–432.

Dale, J. M., Popescu, L., & Karp, P. D. (2010). Machine learning methods for metabolic pathway prediction. *BMC Bioinformatics, 11*(1): 1–14.

De Tobel, J., Radesh, P., Vandermeulen, D., & Thevissen, P. W. (2017). An automated technique to stage lower third molar development on panoramic radiographs for age estimation: a pilot study. *The Journal of Forensic Odonto-Stomatology, 35*(2): 42.

DiMaio, V. J. M., & Molina, D. K. (2021). *DiMaio's forensic pathology.* CRC press.

Fang, Y. T., Lan, Q., Xie, T., Liu, Y. F., Mei, S. Y., & Zhu, B. F. (2020). New opportunities and challenges for forensic medicine in the era of artificial intelligence technology. *Fa Yi Xue Za Zhi, 36*(1): 77–85.

Lefèvre, T. (2021). Artificial intelligence in forensic medicine. In *Artificial Intelligence in Medicine* (pp. 1–9). Springer.

Luquin, M. F. H., Santacruz, E. V., Morales, R. A. L., Vázquez, C. N., & Zúñiga, M. G. (2017). Development of intelligent tools for recognizing cockroaches in the forensic entomology context. *2017 Intelligent Systems Conference (IntelliSys)*, 1117–1121.

Maiden, M. C. J., Bygraves, J. A., Feil, E., Morelli, G., Russell, J. E., Urwin, R., Zhang, Q., Zhou, J., Zurth, K., & Caugant, D. A. (1998). Multilocus sequence typing: A portable approach to the identification of clones within populations of pathogenic microorganisms. *Proceedings of the National Academy of Sciences*, 95(6): 3140–3145.

McCarthy, J., Minksy, M. L., Rochester, N., & Shannon, C. E. (1955/2006). A proposal for the Dartmouth Summer Research Project on artificial intelligence. *AI Magazine*, 27(4): 12.

Nannipieri, P., Ascher, J., Ceccherini, M., Landi, L., Pietramellara, G., & Renella, G. (2003). Microbial diversity and soil functions. *European Journal of Soil Science*, 54(4): 655–670.

Niño-Sandoval, T. C., Pérez, S. V. G., González, F. A., Jaque, R. A., & Infante-Contreras, C. (2017). Use of automated learning techniques for predicting mandibular morphology in skeletal class I, II and III. *Forensic Science International*, 281: 187–e1.

Nowrousian, M. (2010). Next-generation sequencing techniques for eukaryotic microorganisms: Sequencing-based solutions to biological problems. *Eukaryotic Cell*, 9(9): 1300–1310.

Pollak, S., & Saukko, P. (2013). Clinical forensic medicine—overview. In S. Pollak & P. Saukko, *Encyclopedia of forensic sciences* (pp. 83–88; 2nd ed.). Elsevier. doi:10.1016/B978-0-12-382165-2.00166-5

Polyakov, V. V, Bespechniy, O. V, & Neymark, M. A. (2019). Artificial intelligence as an object of forensic study: Perspectives from a border region. *The Role of Transnational Corporations in the Globalization of the Economy. Advances in Social Science, Education and Humanities Research*, 364: 637–640.

Sharma, B. R., Harish, D., & Chavali, K. H. (2005). Teaching, training and practice of forensic medicine in India—an overview. *Journal of Indian Academy of Forensic Medicine*, 27(4): 247–251.

Taylor, D., & Powers, D. (2016). Teaching artificial intelligence to read electropherograms. *Forensic Science International: Genetics*, 25: 10–18.

Wang, Y., Wang, Y., Wang, M., Xu, W., Zhang, Y., & Wang, J. (2021). Forensic entomology in China and its challenges. *Insects*, 12(3): 230.

Weinbauer, M. G. (2004). Ecology of prokaryotic viruses. *FEMS Microbiology Reviews*, 28(2): 127–181.

Yeom, S., & Javidi, B. (2006). Automatic identification of biological microorganisms using three-dimensional complex morphology. *Journal of Biomedical Optics*, 11(2): 24017.

8

Artificial Intelligence in Wildlife Forensics

Gaurav Kumar Singh, Shubham Saini, Muskan,
Ankita, Navjot Kaur, and Saurabh Shukla

WILDLIFE FORENSICS

Wildlife forensics is a field of criminal examination. It typically utilizes logical strategies to examine, distinguish, and compare evidence collected from crime locations to associate this evidential data with a suspect and a victim. Wildlife forensics likewise is considered to be the application of forensic science to the preservation and assurance of wild animals. The illegal killing of non-domesticated animals that are threatened by hunting, also called poaching, is quite possibly the most serious crime examined by wildlife forensics researchers. Other crimes regarding wildlife include the trading of rare animals and items produced using these secured animals. Wildlife crime is a billion-dollar industry that traverses nations and continents [1].

Wildlife forensics science is science applied to legitimate inquiries including wildlife crimes. Forensic science contributes to settling wildlife crime through investigative activities. Such activities incorporate deciding the reason for wildlife death, recognizing suspects, and tracking down missing wildlife and profiling wildlife. Wildlife forensics tries to interface

DOI: 10.4324/9781003287810-8

the crime location, the suspect, and the victim. It does this in a manner that is permissible in court [2]. More explicitly, forensic science in these sorts of examinations can be utilized to follow and recognize criminals by the utilization of evidentiary investigation, whether it be DNA, trace evidence like hair or feathers, creature tracks, characterization of animal items or imported, exported, or exchanged products, or the simple recognition of what establishes unquestionable, definitive proof. Time after time these things are ignored or overlooked or are inappropriately evaluated [3].

Most frequently, mitochondrial DNA (passed from mother to posterity) is utilized, as it gives the best molecular markers. After sequencing, individual profiling is done wherein microsatellite markers are utilized to develop the person's (victim's and additional culprit's) profile. This profile is incredibly valuable, as it can recognize not only an animal but additionally its biological family members. On the other hand, human DNA profiling and ballistics are generally used to recognize the culprit [4]. These strategies are likewise supported by microscopic devices including the investigation of fingerprints, soil, and hair.

WILDLIFE CRIMES

Wildlife crime takes numerous structures from managing with live examples, discordant hunting, brutality to creatures, environment annihilation, poaching of animals for meat and prizes; the variety of illegal activities that entail hunting animals to use their parts in medicines, their horns and tusks for ornaments and decorations, etc., is endless [5].

There are basically two main problems that are focused on in crimes related to wildlife, and these connect with expressing the different types of regulation. The first is the ability to identify a certain animal type, and the second is the ability to ascertain if the natural material can be definitively linked to a particular member of that species [6, 7].

Wildlife crime might be viewed as functioning on a modest level (for instance, resource trafficking and isolated incidents of cruelty), meso-level (particularly domestic trading in native susceptible species and coordinated illicit pursuits), and on a large scale (import and export of vulnerable species for international trade) [7]. It is hard to learn what specifically drives wildlife exchange, but it is thought that various factors, such as style, peculiarity of different breeds, trends in elective treatments, and both medication and criminal activity, have an impact. Style can have a significant effect and is a profound factor. Endangered animals, in particular,

Table 8.1 Showing different parts of animals, birds, and plants for identification using different methods

Serial No.	Wildlife	Parts	Method
1.	Animal	Paw prints	Image processing and measurements of paw print
		Skin pattern	Image processing
		Horns	Measurements
		Face	Feature extraction and image processing
2.	Birds	Feathers	Image processing
		Sound	Sound recording and analysis
		Claw	Image processing and measurements
3.	Plants	Flowers	Image processing
		Petals	Count of petals and image processing
		Leaves	Pattern analysis
		Stem	Structural analysis
		Fruits	Shape, size, and color analysis

are more expensive, making them more desirable to consumers because the advantages outweigh the risks and penalties they face [3].

Government authorities and international organizations worldwide may make efforts to protect an endangered species. Poaching and the destruction of the ecosystem for a species could be prohibited by laws. Individuals and organizations who violate these regulations risk receiving hefty fines. Due to these activities, numerous varieties of plants and animals have recuperated from their endangered status [8, 9]. Meanwhile the trade bans increase the risk of black marketing prices for endangered species [10, 11].

ARTIFICIAL INTELLIGENCE IN ANIMAL IDENTIFICATION

Populations of wild animals decline very rapidly [12, 13]. This loss is not only due to genetic changes but also to the diversity and ecology of animals. According to the IUCN Red List, there are more than 100,000 threatened species of animals on which we lack data [14]. Valuable data about animals are mostly obtained manually by field observation and patrolling.

These methods are very time consuming and expensive [15]. The results are also very biased because of different challenges in data collection [16–17]. The presence of humans in the wild also causes risks to human lives and animal lives and their habitats [18–19]. There have been incidents of conservationists who have tried to capture data from the air in aircraft who have crashed and consequently died in such incidents [20]. The data collected by humans have a number of limitations in that someone cannot count a large group of animals at the same time and only a few areas can be covered by themselves [21–22]. These impact greatly on the observations of animal ecology, their habitat, and their rapid decline in numbers [23–24]. Similarly, because of inaccurate and false data, some conservation efforts are ineffective [25]. To conserve primates and other endangered species of animals, the major problem is data collection and its cost [26]. In the same manner, to protect other endangered animals from poaching requires very rigorous monitoring of animals. Governments have invested a lot to protect animals from poaching by using manpower but they are still not able to control illegal poaching [27].

To overcome these problems, recent advancements in technology like camera sensors and artificial intelligence have emerged as very valuable tools. They have increased the data collection capacity and reduced the cost of data collection, opening new roads for wildlife conservation [28]. Many areas that were not accessible to humans can now be studied using remote sensing techniques [29], and very large amounts of data can be collected without any intrusion into animal habitats using camera traps [30], public cameras [31], and voice identification systems [32]. New types of small animal tags which track animals [33–34], and detector systems which can detect their movements and sounds, help in tracking and monitoring animals to a very high accuracy [35].

The use of artificial intelligence helps to identify animals in different ways, like using pugmarks for individual animal identification [36] and by using their skin pattern to identify species of animals [37]. Researchers have also identified different birds species from their sounds using artificial intelligence [38].

Animal Identification from Pugmarks

To curb wildlife crime, the use of pugmarks for animal identification is very helpful as every animal has its individual pugmarks, like fingerprints in humans. Scientists have identified individual tigers using their pugmarks [39]. The conventional method for the identification of pugmarks is using manual measurements to identify them. With the development of machine learning and image processing techniques, it is now possible to identify pugmarks automatically using a variety of tools. It has an advantage over conventional manual methods as it reduces the time and increases the accuracy of the identification [40]. The new research in wildlife conservation is that in which a footprint identification technique (FIT) based on machine learning can identify pugmarks of different animals at individual and species levels [41]. The FIT can identify individual cheetah from their pugmarks [42]; it can also identify rhinoceros species [43]. There are different studies in which scientists have used machine learning and artificial intelligence algorithms to identify different animals such as tigers [39], pumas [44], and Amur tigers using their pugmark images.

Animal Identification from Images

The advancement in sensor technology and in cameras has generated a number of useful applications which can identify species of animals from their images [45]. The advancement in computer science has triggered the creation of software, based on deep CNNs (convolutional neural networks) and machine learning, which can be installed on multiple devices like drone cameras, camera traps, acoustic sensors, and animal tags and collars [33–34]. The camera traps and drone cameras can count the number of individual animals from still images and videos using artificial intelligence models [46]; this helps to monitor and track animals in the wild and protect them from possible threats.

The different studies present different CNN architecture models, which can, for example, identify individual tigers from the stripe patterns of their skin [37] and species of animals from their skin pattern and size [47]. Artificial intelligence models can identify different animals from millions of image datasets in a very short time, which can be impossible to do manually [48]. Primates are also identifying automatically from their facial images [49]. This new advancement in technology is helping scientists and governments to protect wild animals from poaching and illegal hunting [50] and preserving the wildlife diversity.

Bird Identification

Birds are the most important part of our biodiversity; with the increase in human urbanization and climate change, the numbers of endangered species of birds are increasing. To study the ecology of birds, a number of different artificial intelligence-based systems have been developed [51]. Acoustic systems have been made which record the sounds of different birds and then identify them automatically based on their sound [38]. This system can differentiate between the sounds of different birds and amphibians [52]. The advancement in computer science technology has made different programs which can identify different species and subspecies of birds from their images also [53]. This advancement helps ecologists to study the population and habitat of birds, and wildlife conservationists to protect them from illegal trade and hunting.

IDENTIFICATION OF PLANTS USING ARTIFICIAL INTELLIGENCE

Biodiversity is becoming affected day by day and declining all over the world [54]. There are different species which are on the verge of extinction and many species have already become extinct, which is a result directly or indirectly of human activity [55]. While seeing different damage to the biodiversity, it can be said that there is a need for identification and conservation [56].

Generally, botanists use a manual approach for the identification of plant species. In this technique there is a manual identification of characteristics known as identification keys. These identification keys have questions to answer e.g., shape, color, existence of hair or thorns, number of petals on a flower etc., which are to be answered to narrow down the suspected species. The person who identifies the species of plants or animals is known as a taxonomist, and even the taxonomists find it difficult to identify the species manually. There is a shortage of qualified taxonomists, which has led to this predicament [57]. The general public's lack of understanding of taxonomy has been referred to as a taxonomic crisis [58].

The methods which are based on image processing are reliable for the identification of species [59]. Different developments have been made in this particular field by using image processing and pattern recognition systems. Using artificial intelligence models, it has become much easier to identify the species using image processing because anyone can click a picture of any plant while roaming around by using a phone's camera and can identify the plant from pattern recognition techniques. This image

117

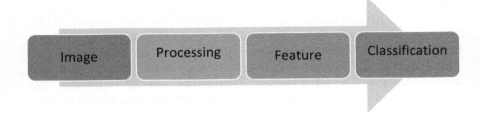

Figure 8.1   Process depicting species identification using AI.

processing and pattern recognition carries four simple steps, as shown in Figure 8.1.

- *Image acquisition*: This step includes the picture of the plant as whole, or its organs, after which the evaluation is to be done.
- *Processing*: Image processing is done to enhance the image data to suppress the undesired distortions. It requires an image as an input. It then processes the image and generates the better quality image as output for further processing. This step includes different operations like image enhancement, image denoising, and segmentation of image. This procedure is done until the picture quality is acceptable [60–61].
- *Feature extraction*: Extraction of features refers to measurements of segmented and meaningful parts of the image. The characterization of image feature is done by extracting the properties of the plant, or parts of the plant, from the plant image.
- *Classification*: All the retrieved features are summed up into a feature vector for classification, after which the feature vector is classified.

Plant Parts Used for the Identification Process

Plant traits must be linked to a common or scientific plant name in order to identify a species of plant. Different parts of plant can be used for identification such as the whole plant, flowers, stem, fruits, and its leaves from their shape, size, color, position, and texture [62].

- *Leaf*: In most plants, a leaf is basically a green, flat structure attached to the stem, which is an organ performing photosynthesis and transpiration. This part of the plant is one of those parts

118

that collectively constitute the plant's foliage [63–64]. A plant can be identified using different leaf parts like the blade, petiole, apex, or base [65–72]; it can also be identified using the margins of the leaf [73–77].

- *Flower:* The flower is usually the most beautiful part of the plant, having various colors, shapes, and sizes. The identification of a plant using flowers can be done using the whole flower [78–92] or by using parts of the flower [82]. Even the shape of blooming flower petals [76] and labellum region [78] have been used for identification. Some features, such as color, texture, petal shape, and petal arrangement, can also be significant in identification processes [93–94].

ARTIFICIAL INTELLIGENCE TOOLS TO COUNTER WILDLIFE CRIME

The illegal trade of wildlife is now ranked the fourth largest illegal trade around the world, worth around 15 billion pounds annually [95]. It has massively decreased some animal populations and has brought others to the verge of extinction [96]. AI has developed as an important tool in wildlife conservation. Just like other artificial intelligence-powered programs such as Google's predictions, Gmail's spam filter, and Apple's Siri, AI is now being used in wildlife conservation and protection and helps in completing tasks automatically which normally need to be done manually [97].

The different AI tools are listed below:

- ChimpFace: An artificial intelligence-powered software which can detect Chimpanzees from the images that are posted online for the illegal trading of endangered primates [98].
- PAWS (Protection Assistance for Wildlife Securities): An artificial intelligence-enabled program which uses previous data to identify the most likely places where poaching can happen in a wildlife area and suggest best patrolling routes to wildlife rangers to protect against threats to animals [99].
- CAPTURE (Comprehensive Anti-Poaching Tool with Temporal and Observation Uncertainty Reasoning): An artificial intelligence-based algorithm which collects real poaching data and predicts poaching activities [100].

Table 8.2   Different AI tools and their working

S. No.	Tool	Work
1.	ChimpFace	This software detects primates from images posted online for the selling of chimpanzees.
2.	PAWS (Protection Assistance for Wildlife Securities)	This software suggests patrolling routes to rangers for the detection of poaching activities.
3.	CAPTURE (Comprehensive Anti-Poaching Tool with Temporal and observation Uncertainty Reasoning)	This software helps to prognosticate poaching activities and detect them.
4.	RFCx (Rainforest Connection)	This software detects illegal activity sounds and alerts the authorities.
5.	Wildbook	This software identifies individual animals from images.
6.	Microsoft AI for Earth MegaDetector	This software detects any type of activity in the protected area.

- RFCx (Rainforest Connection): A mobile application based on artificial intelligence which can detect the poacher's vehicle sounds, chainsaw sounds, and gunshot sounds. It sends a mobile alert, thus protecting against the illegal hunting and felling of trees in a protected area [101].
- Wildbook: A machine learning database management system which collects images of different animals from many sources, such as tourist-posted images of animals, images clicked by scientists, field assistants, camera traps, and drones. It then identifies an animal's species, age, sex, and location from them and suggests a possible management system to protect those animals [102].
- Microsoft AI for Earth MegaDetector: An artificial intelligence-based program developed by Microsoft to protect animals in the wild. It is a detection model that can detect animals, humans, and vehicles, and is now implemented in over 30 organizations' wildlife monitoring systems to detect possible threats on wild animals [103].

There many other software programs based on machine learning and artificial intelligence which are currently used by different organizations and scientific groups to study animal ecology and animal habitats [104]. AI-enabled camera traps and drone cameras are also used to monitor and study different animals and protect them from extinction [105].

CONCLUSION

AI performs important functions in the identification and conservation of wildlife. It reduces the time of identifying any species as it detects automatically by specific features, whereas identifying any species manually takes up a lot of time and effort of taxonomists. Also, there is a limited number of skilled taxonomists available who are not able to identify species because of work overload. In this era, when everyone has a smartphone and uses it regularly, it becomes much easier to identify anything just by clicking a picture through one's phone camera. There are many smartphone applications and websites available that can help the identification process, which reduces time and effort as well. Different tools are also available that have been made using artificial intelligence, like ChimpFace, PAWS, CAPTURE, and RFCx, which have the capacity to identify specific species by different parts of the body. Parts of plants and animals have a different morphology and are specific to the species e.g., the petals of a rose and a lotus are different in color, shape, and size, therefore they are specific to their species. Plants can be identified from all their parts like the flower, stem, petals, and leaves, and different softwares use different parts or the whole plant picture to identify with accuracy. Also, different body parts of animals and birds can be used in the identification process, like the skin patterns, horns, paws of animals, and the feathers, claws, and sounds of birds. To conclude, it is safe to say that the use of artificial intelligence in identification and conservation is an extremely accurate, and much easier, method which can create evolution in the field.

REFERENCES

1. Cook, D., Roberts, M., & Lowther, J. (2002) *The International Wildlife Trade and Organised Crime: A review of the evidence and the role of the UK.* Godalming: WWF-UK.
2. Li, Y.M., Gao, Z., Li, X., Wang, S. (2000) Illegal wildlife trade in the Himalayan region of China. *Biodiversity Conservation*, 9(7): 901–918.

3. Christy, B. (2010) Wildlife Smuggling: Why Does Wildlife Crime Reporting Suck? *The Huffington Post*. Available at http://www.huffingtonpost.com/2010/01/04/wildlifesmuggling-why-do_n_410269.html.
4. Yadav, S., & Dixit, A. K. (2016) Forensic approaches in the solution of wildlife crime. *International Journal of Multidisciplinary Research and Development*, 3: 89–93.
5. Sellar, J. M. (2009) Illegal trade and the Convention on International Trade in Endangered Species of Wild Fauna and Flora (CITES). In A. Linacre (Ed.), *Forensic science in wildlife investigations*. CRC Press, London and Boca Raton, 11–18.
6. World Wildlife Fund (2010) Tiger Overview. Available at http://www.world wildlife.org/species/finder/tigers/index.html.
7. IUCN Red List Quadrennial Report 2017–2020. Available at https://nc.iucnredlist.org/redlist/resources/files/1630480997-IUCN_RED_LIST_QUADRENNIAL_REPORT_2017-2020.pdf
8. Zimmerman, M. E. (2003) The black market for wildlife; Combating transnational organized crime in the illegal wildlife trade. *Vanderbilt Journal of Transnational Law*, 36: 1657–1690.
9. White, R. (2005) Environmental crime in global context; Exploring the theoretical and empirical complexities. *Current Issues in Criminal Justice*, 16(3): 271–285.
10. Comstock, K. E., Ostrander, E. A., & Wasser, S. K. (2003) Amplifying nuclear and mitochondrial DNA from African elephant ivory: A tool for monitoring the ivory trade. *Conservation Biology*, 17(6): 1840–1843.
11. Cowdrey, D. (2002) *Switching channels; Wildlife trade routes into Europe and the UK*. A WWF/TRAFFIC report. Godalming: WWF-UK.
12. BBC News (2010) Emperor Exmoor deer kill brings call for protection. October 27. Available at http://www.bbc.co.uk/news/uk-england-devon-11633614 (accessed October 29, 2010).
13. Ceballos, G., Ehrlich, P. R., & Raven, P. H. (2020) Vertebrates on the brink as indicators of biological annihilation and the sixth mass extinction. *Proceedings of the National Academy of Science*, 117(24): 13596–13602.
14. The IUCN Red List Committee (2017) The IUCN Red List of Threatened Species—Strategic Plan 2017–2020. Technical report, IUCN.
15. Witmer, G. W. (2005) Wildlife population monitoring: Some practical considerations. *Wildlife Research*, 32(3): 259–263.
16. McEvoy, J. F., Hall, G. P., & McDonald, P. G. (2016) Evaluation of unmanned aerial vehicle shape, flight path and camera type for waterfowl surveys: Disturbance effects and species recognition. *PeerJ*, 4: e1831.
17. Burghardt, G. M., Bartmess-LeVasseur, J. N., Browning, S. A., Morrison, K. E., Stec, C. L., Zachau, C. E., & Freeberg, T. M. (2012) Perspectives—minimizing observer bias in behavioral studies: A review and recommendations. *Ethology*, 118(6): 511–517.
18. Giese, M. (1996) Effects of human activity on adelie penguin Pygoscelis adeliae breeding success. *Biological Conservation*, 75(2): 157–164. doi:10.1016/0006-3207(95)00060-7.

19. Köndgen, S., Kühl, H., Paul, K., N'Goran, P. K. et al. (2008) Pandemic human viruses cause decline of endangered great apes. *Current Biology*, 18(4): 260–264. doi:10.1016/j.cub.2008.01.012.
20. Weissensteiner, M. H., Poelstra, J. W., & Wolf, J. B. W. (2015) Low budget ready-to-fly unmanned aerial vehicles: An effective tool for evaluating the nesting status of canopy-breeding bird species. *Journal of Avian Biology*, 46(4): 425–430. doi:10.1111/jav.00619.
21. Sasse, D. B. (2003) Job-related mortality of wildlife workers in the United States, 1937–2000. *Wildlife Society Bulletin*, pp. 1015–1020.
22. Kays, R., Crofoot, M. C., Jetz, W. & Wikelski, M. (2015) Terrestrial animal tracking as an eye on life and planet. *Science*, 348(6240).
23. Altmann, J. (1974) Observational study of behavior: Sampling methods. *Behaviour*, 49(3/4): 227–266.
24. Hodgson, J. C., Mott, R., Baylis, S. M. et al. (2018) Drones count wildlife more accurately and precisely than humans. *Methods in Ecology and Evolution*, 9(5): 1160–1167.
25. Betke, M., Hirsh, D. E., Makris, N. C. et al. (2008) Thermal imaging reveals significantly smaller Brazilian free-tailed bat colonies than previously estimated. *Journal of Mammalogy*, 89(1): 18–24.
26. Rollinson, C. R., O Finley, A., Ross Alexander, M. et al. (2021) Working across space and time: Nonstationarity in ecological research and application. *Frontiers in Ecology and the Environment*, 19(1): 66–72.
27. Junker, J., Petrovan, S. O., Arroyo-Rodríguez, V. et al. (2020) A severe lack of evidence limits effective conservation of the world's primates. *BioScience*, 70(9): 794–803.
28. O'Donoghue, P., & Rutz, C. (2016) Real-time anti-poaching tags could help prevent imminent species extinctions. *Journal of Applied Ecology*, 53(1): 5–10.
29. Lahoz-Monfort, J. J., & Magrath, M. J. L. (2021) A comprehensive overview of technologies for species and habitat monitoring and conservation. *BioScience*, 71(10): 1038–1062. doi:10.1093/biosci/biab073.
30. Gottschalk, T. K., Huettmann, F., & Ehlers, M. (2005) Thirty years of analysing and modelling avian habitat relationships using satellite imagery data: A review. *International Journal of Remote Sensing*, 26(12): 2631–2656.
31. Steenweg, R., Hebblewhite, M., Kays, R. et al. (2017) Scaling-up camera traps: Monitoring the planet's biodiversity with networks of remote sensors. *Frontiers in Ecology and the Environment*, 15(1): 26–34.
32. Hausmann, A., Toivonen, T., Slotow, R. et al. (2018) Social media data can be used to understand tourists' preferences for nature-based experiences in protected areas. *Conservation Letters*, 11(1): e12343.
33. Sayuri Moreira Sugai, L., Sanna Freire Silva, T., Wagner Ribeiro Jr, J., & Llusia, D. (2018) Terrestrial passive acoustic monitoring: Review and perspectives. *BioScience*, 69(1): 15–25.
34. Wikelski, M., Kays, R. W., Kasdin, N. J., Thorup, K., Smith, J. A., & Swenson, G. W. (2007) Going wild: What a global small-animal tracking system could do for experimental biologists. *Journal of Experimental Biology*, 210(2): 181–186.

35. Belyaev, M. Y., Volkov, O. N., Solomina, O. N., et al. (2020) Development of technology for monitoring animal migration on Earth using scientific equipment on the ISS RS. In: 2020 27th Saint Petersburg International Conference on Integrated Navigation Systems (ICINS), pp. 1–7. IEEE.
36. Harel, R., Carter Loftus, J., & Crofoot, M.C. (2021) Locomotor compromises maintain group cohesion in baboon troops on the move. *Proceedings of the Royal Society B*, 288(1955): 20210839.
37. Sharma, S., Jhala, Y., & Sawarkar, V. B. (2005) Identification of individual tigers (*Panthera tigris*) from their pugmarks. *Journal of Zoology*, 267(1): 9–18. doi:10.1017/s0952836905007119.
38. Shi, C., Liu, D., Cui, Y., Xie, J., Roberts, N. J., & Jiang, G. (2020) Amur tiger stripes: Individual identification based on deep Convolutional Neural Network. *Integrative Zoology*, 15(6): 461–470. doi:10.1111/1749-4877.12453.
39. Lopes, M. T., Gioppo, L. L., Higushi, T. T., Kaestner, C. A. A., Silla Jr., C. N., & Koerich, A. L. (2011) Automatic bird species identification for large number of species. IEEE International Symposium on Multimedia, Dana Point, CA, USA, December 5–7. doi:10.1109/ism.2011.27.
40. Raj, A., Choudhary, P., & Suman, P. (2015) Identification of tigers through their pugmark using pattern recognition. *Open International Journal of Technology Innovation Research*, 15: 1–8.
41. Singh, R., Qureshi, Q., Sankar, K., Krausman, P. R., Joshi, B. D., & Goyal, S. P. (2014) Distinguishing sex of free-ranging tigers using pugmark measurements, *Italian Journal of Zoology*, 81(2): 304–309. doi:10.1080/11250003.2014.910276.
42. Jewell, Z. C., Alibhai, S. K., & Law, P. R. (2001) Censusing and monitoring black rhino (*Diceros bicornis*) using an objective spoor (footprint) identification technique. *Journal of Zoology*, 254(1): 1–16.
43. Jewell, Z. C., Alibhai, S. K., Weise, F., Munro, S., Van Vuuren, M., & Van Vuuren, R. (2016) Spotting cheetahs: Identifying individuals by their footprints. *Journal of Visualized Experiments (JoVE)*, 111: 54034.
44. Jewell, Z. C., Alibhai, S., Law, P. R., Uiseb, K., & Lee, S. (2020) Monitoring rhinoceroses in Namibia's private custodianship properties. *PeerJ*, 8: e9670.
45. Alibhai, S., Jewell, Z., & Evans, J. (2017) The challenge of monitoring elusive large carnivores: An accurate and cost-effective tool to identify and sex pumas (*Puma concolor*) from footprints. *PloS One*, 12(3): e0172065.
46. Wäldchen, J., & Mäder, P. (2018) Machine learning for image based species identification. *Methods in Ecology and Evolution*, 9(11): 2216–2225. doi:10.1111/2041-210X.13075.
47. Gonzalez, L. F., Montes, G. A., Puig, E., Johnson, S., Mengersen, K., & Gaston, K. J. (2016) Unmanned aerial vehicles (UAVs) and artificial intelligence revolutionizing wildlife monitoring and conservation. *Sensors*, 16(1): 97.
48. Chen, G., Han, T. X., He, Z., Kays, R., & Forrester, T. (2014, October) Deep convolutional neural network based species recognition for wild animal monitoring. In: *2014 IEEE International Conference on Image Processing (ICIP)* (pp. 858–862). IEEE.

49. Gomez Villa, A., Salazar, A., & Vargas, F. (2017) Towards automatic wild animal monitoring: Identification of animal species in camera-trap images using very deep convolutional neural networks, *Ecological Informatics*, 41: 24–32. doi:10.1016/j.ecoinf.2017.07.004.

50. Deb, D., Wiper, S., Gong, S., Shi, Y., Tymoszek, C., Fletcher, A., & Jain, A. K. (2018, October) Face recognition: Primates in the wild. In: *2018 IEEE 9th International Conference on Biometrics Theory, Applications and Systems (BTAS)* (pp. 1–10).

51. Norouzzadeh, M. S., Nguyen, A., Kosmala, M. et al. (2018) Automatically identifying, counting, and describing wild animals in camera-trap images with deep learning, *Proceedings of the National Academy of Science USA*, 115(25): E5716–E5725. doi:10.1073/pnas.1719367115.

52. Neal, L., Briggs, F., Raich, R., & Fern, X. Z. (2011, May) Time-frequency segmentation of bird song in noisy acoustic environments. In 2011 IEEE International Conference on Acoustics, Speech and Signal Processing (ICASSP) (pp. 2012–2015).

53. Acevedo, M. A., & Villanueva-Rivera, L. J. (2006) From the field: Using automated digital recording systems as effective tools for the monitoring of birds and amphibians. *Wildlife Society Bulletin*, 34(1): 211–214. doi:10.2193/0091-7648(2006)34[211:UADRSA]2.0.CO;2.

54. Jang, W., & Lee, E. C. (2021) Multi-class parrot image classification including subspecies with similar appearance. *Biology*, 10(11): 1140.

55. Pimm, S. L., Jenkins, C. N., Abell, R. et al. (2014) The biodiversity of species and their rates of extinction, distribution, and protection. *Science*, 344(6187). doi:10.1126/science.1246752.

56. Murphy, G. E., & Romanuk, T. N. (2014) A meta-analysis of declines in local species richness from human disturbances. *Ecology and Evolution*, 4(1): 91–103. doi:10.1002/ece3.909.

57. Joly, A., Müller, H., Goëau, H. et al. (2014) LifeCLEF: Multimedia life species identification. In: International Workshop on Environmental Multimedia Retrieval, Glasgow.

58. Gaston, K. J., & O'Neill, M. A. (2004) Automated species identification: Why not? *Philosophical Transactions of the Royal Society of London, Series B Biological Sciences*, 359(1444): 655–667. doi:10.1098/rstb.2003.1442.

59. Dayrat, B. (2005) Towards integrative taxonomy. *Biological Journal of the Linnean Society*, 85(3): 407–415. doi:10.1111/j.1095-8312.2005.00503.

60. Wäldchen, J., Thuille, A., Seeland, M. et al. (2016) Flora Incognita— Halbautomatische Bestimmung der Pflanzenarten Thüringens mit dem Smartphone. *Landschaftspflege und Naturschutz in Thüringen*, 53(3): 121–125.

61. Gonzalez, R. C., & Woods, R. E. (2007) *Digital image processing*, 3rd edn. Pearson Prentice-Hall, New Jersey.

62. Santana, F. S., Costa, A. H. R., Truzzi, F. S., et al. (2014) A reference process for automating bee species identification based on wing images and digital image processing. *Ecological Informatics*, 24: 248–260. doi:10.1016/j.ecoinf.2013.12.001.

63. Prasad, S., Kudiri, K. M., & Tripathi, R. C. (2011) Relative subimage based features for leaf recognition using support vector machine. In: *Proceedings of the 2011 international conference on communication, computing and security, ACM, New York, NY, USA* (ICCCS 2011), pp. 343–346. doi:10.1145/1947940.1948012.

64. Ellis, B., Daly, D. C., Hickey, L. J., Johnson, K. R., Mitchell, J. D., Wilf, P., & Wing, S. L. (2009) *Manual of leaf architecture*. Cornell University Press, Ithaca.

65. Rudall, P. J. (2007) *Anatomy of flowering plants: an introduction to structure and development*. Cambridge University Press, Cambridge.

66. Cerutti, G., Tougne, L., Mille, J., Vacavant, A., & Coquin, D. (2013) A model-based approach for compound leaves understanding and identification. In: *2013 20th IEEE international conference on image processing (ICIP)*, pp. 1471–1475. doi:10.1109/ICIP.2013.6738302.

67. Liu, H., Coquin, D., Valet, L., & Cerutti, G. (2014) Leaf species classification based on a botanical shape sub-classifier strategy. In: 2014 22nd International conference on pattern recognition (ICPR), pp. 1496–1501. doi:10.1109/ICPR.2014.266.

68. Mzoughi, O., Yahiaoui, I., & Boujemaa, N. (2012) Petiole shape detection for advanced leaf identification. In: 2012 19th IEEE international conference on image processing (ICIP), pp. 1033–1036. doi:10.1109/ICIP.2012.6467039.

69. Mzoughi, O., Yahiaoui, I., Boujemaa, N., & Zagrouba, E. (2013) Advanced tree species identification using multiple leaf parts image queries. In: *2013 20th IEEE international conference on image processing (ICIP)*, pp. 3967–3971. doi:10.1109/ICIP.2013.6738817.

70. Mzoughi, O., Yahiaoui, I., Boujemaa, N., & Zagrouba, E. (2016) Semantic-based automatic structuring of leaf images for advanced plant species identification. *Multimedia Tools and Applications*, 75(3): 1615–1646. doi:10.1007/s11042-015-2603-8.

71. Rejeb Sfar, A., Boujemaa, N., & Geman, D. (2013) Identification of plants from multiple images and botanical idkeys. In: *Proceedings of the 3rd ACM conference on international conference on multimedia retrieval, ACM, New York, NY, USA* (ICMR 2013), pp. 191–198. doi:10.1145/2461466.2461499.

72. Rejeb Sfar, A., Boujemaa, N., & Geman, D. (2015) Confidence sets for fine-grained categorization and plant species identification. *International Journal of Computer Vision*, 111(3): 255–275. doi:10.1007/s11263-014-0743-3.

73. Zhao, C., Chan, S. S., Cham, W. K., & Chu, L. (2015) Plant identification using leaf shapes? A pattern counting approach. *Pattern Recogn*, 48(10): 3203–3215. doi:10.1016/j.patcog.2015.04.004.

74. Cerutti, G., Tougne, L., Coquin, D., Vacavant, A. et al. (2013) Curvature-scale-based contour understanding for leaf margin shape recognition and species identification. In: *Proceedings of the international conference on computer vision theory and applications*, vol 1, pp. 277–284.

75. Cerutti, G., Tougne, L., Coquin, D., Vacavant, A. (2014) Leaf margins as sequences: A structural approach to leaf identification. *Pattern Recognition Letters*, 49: 177–184. doi:10.1016/j.patrec.2014.07.016.

76. Cope, J., & Remagnino, P. (2012) Classifying plant leaves from their margins using dynamic time warping. In: Blanc-Talon, J., Philips, W., Popescu, D., Scheunders, P., & Zemc, K.P. (Eds), *Advanced concepts for intelligent vision systems, lecture notes in computer science, vol 7517.* Springer, Berlin pp. 258–267. doi:10.1007/978-3-642-33140-4_23.

77. Jin, T., Hou, X., Li, P., & Zhou, F. (2015) A novel method of automatic plant species identification using sparse representation of leaf tooth features. *PLoS ONE,* 10(10): e0139482. doi:10.1371/journal.pone.0139482.

78. Mouine, S., Yahiaoui, I., & Verroust-Blondet, A. (2013) Plant species recognition using spatial correlation between the leaf margin and the leaf salient points. In: *2013 20th IEEE international conference on image processing (ICIP),* pp. 1466–1470. doi:10.1109/ICIP.2013.6738301.

79. Apriyanti, D., Arymurthy, A., & Handoko, L. (2013) Identification of orchid species using content-based flower image retrieval. In: *2013 International conference on computer, control, informatics and its applications (IC3INA),* pp. 53–57. doi:10.1109/IC3INA.2013.6819148.

80. Cho, S. Y. (2012) Content-based structural recognition for flower image classification. In: *2012 7th IEEE conference on industrial electronics and applications (ICIEA),* pp. 541–546. doi:10.1109/ICIEA.2012.6360787.

81. Cho, S. Y., & Lim, P. T. (2006) A novel virus infection clustering for flower images identification. In: *18th International conference on pattern recognition, 2006 (ICPR 2006),* vol. 2, pp. 1038–1041. doi:10.1109/ICPR.2006.144.

82. Hong, S. W., & Choi, L. (2012) Automatic recognition of flowers through color and edge based contour detection. In: *2012 3rd International conference on image processing theory, tools and applications (IPTA),* pp. 141–146. doi:10.1109/IPTA.2012.6469535.

83. Hsu, T. H., Lee, C. H., & Chen, L. H. (2011) An interactive flower image recognition system. *Multimedia Tools Application,* 53(1): 53–73. doi:10.1007/s11042-010-0490-6.

84. Huang, R. G., Jin, S. H., Kim, J. H., & Hong, K. S. (2009) Flower image recognition using difference image entropy. In: *Proceedings of the 7th international conference on advances in mobile computing and multimedia (MoMM '09).* ACM, New York, pp. 618–621. doi:10.1145/1821748.1821868.

85. Nilsback, M. E., & Zisserman, A. (2006) A visual vocabulary for flower classification. In: *2006 IEEE computer society conference on computer vision and pattern recognition,* vol. 2, pp. 1447–1454. doi:10.1109/CVPR.2006.42.

86. Nilsback, M. E., & Zisserman, A. (2008) Automated flower classification over a large number of classes. In: *2008 Sixth Indian Conference on Computer Vision, Graphics & Image Processing.* IEEE, pp. 722–729. doi:10.1109/ICVGIP.2008.47.

87. Phyu, K. H., Kutics, A., & Nakagawa, A. (2012) Self-adaptive feature extraction scheme for mobile image retrieval of flowers. In: *2012 Eighth international conference on signal image technology and internet based systems (SITIS),* pp. 366–373. doi:10.1109/SITIS.2012.60.

88. Qi, W., Liu, X., & Zhao, J. (2012) Flower classification based on local and spatial visual cues. In: *2012 IEEE international conference on computer science and automation engineering (CSAE)*, vol. 3, pp. 670–674. doi:10.1109/CSAE.2012.6273040.

89. Tan, W. N., Tan, Y. F., Koo, A. C., & Lim, Y. P. (2012) Petals' shape descriptor for blooming flowers recognition. In: *Proceedings of SPIE—International Society for Optics and Photonics*, 8334. doi:10.1117/12.966367.

90. Tan, W. N., Sem, R., & Tan, Y. F. (2014) Blooming flower recognition by using eigenvalues of shape features. In: *Sixth international conference on digital image processing, International Society for Optics and Photonics*, pp. 91591R–91591R. doi:10.1117/12.2064504.

91. Zawbaa, H. M., Abbass, M., Basha, S. H., Hazman, M., & Hassenian, A. E. (2014) An automatic flower classification approach using machine learning algorithms. In: *2014 International conference on advances in computing, communications and informatics (ICACCI)*, IEEE, pp. 895–901. doi:10.1109/ICACCI.2014.6968612.

92. Wyler, L. S., & Sheikh, P. A. (2008, August) *International illegal trade in wildlife: Threats and US policy*. Library of Congress Washington, DC, Congressional Research Service.

93. Hughes, A. C. (2021). Wildlife trade. *Current Biology*, 31(19): R1218–R1224.

94. Wearn, O. R., Freeman, R., & Jacoby, D. M. (2019) Responsible AI for conservation. *Nature Machine Intelligence*, 1(2): 72–73.

95. Sandwell, R. C., & Burghardt, T. (2013) Chimpanzee face detection: An automated system for images captured from natural environments. In: *9th international conference on behaviour, physiology and genetics of wildlife. Leibnitz Institute for Zoo and Wildlife Research*.

96. Ford, B., Kar, D., Delle Fave, F. M., Yang, R., & Tambe, M. (2014, May) PAWS: Adaptive game-theoretic patrolling for wildlife protection. In: *Proceedings of the 2014 international conference on Autonomous agents and multi-agent systems* (pp. 1641–1642).

97. Nguyen, T. H., Sinha, A., Gholami, S. et al. (2016) CAPTURE: A new predictive anti-poaching tool for wildlife protection. In: *AAMAS 2016—Proceedings of the 2016 international conference on autonomous agents and multiagent systems* (pp. 767–775). International Foundation for Autonomous Agents and Multiagent Systems (IFAAMAS). http://dl.acm.org/citation.cfm?id=2937037

98. Sathya Sri, R., & Vithya, G. (2019) Securing ecosystem by RFCX Cloud API. *International Journal of Engineering Research & Technology (IJERT)*, 7(11). doi:10.17577/IJERTCONV7IS11051.

99. Berger-Wolf, T. Y., Rubenstein, D. I., Stewart, C. V. et al. (2017) Wildbook: Crowdsourcing, computer vision, and data science for conservation. arXiv preprint arXiv:1710.08880.

100. Beery, S., Morris, D., & Yang, S. (2019) Efficient pipeline for camera trap image review. arXiv preprint arXiv:1907.06772.

101. Falzon, G., Lawson, C., Cheung, K. W., et al. (2020) ClassifyMe: A field-scouting software for the identification of wildlife in camera trap images. *Animals*, 10(1): 58.

102. Tuia, D., Kellenberger, B., Beery, S. et al. (2021) Seeing biodiversity: Perspectives in machine learning for wildlife conservation. arXiv preprint arXiv:2110.12951.

103. Norouzzadeh, M. S., Nguyen, A., Kosmala, M., Swanson, A., Palmer, M. S., Packer, C., et al. (2018). Automatically identifying, counting, and describing wild animals in camera-trap images with deep learning. *Proceedings of the National Academy of Sciences of the United States of America*, 115(25): E5716–25.

104. Tuia, D., Kellenberger, B., Beery, S., Costelloe, B. R., Zuffi, S., Risse, B., et al. (2022). Seeing biodiversity: Perspectives in machine learning for wildlife conservation. *Nature Communications*, 13(1): 792.

105. Green, S. E., Rees, J. P., Stephens, P. A., Hill, R. A., & Giordano, A. J. (2020). Innovations in camera trapping technology and approaches: The integration of citizen science and Artificial Intelligence. *Animals*, 10(1): Article 132. doi:10.3390/ani10010132

9

Artificial Intelligence in Forensic Psychology

Badal Mavry, Vinay Aseri, Varad Nagar, Abhishek R. Rai,
Divyansh Jain, Anuj Sharma, Dipak Kumar Mahida,
Mahipal Singh Sankhla, and Kapil Parihar

INTRODUCTION

The three pillars of criminal justice success are effective criminal investigations, accurate forensic examinations, and an impartial court system. But even solving a murder case, tracking down sexual abusers, or digging for proof of document fraud necessitates tenacious police work. Examining a single fingerprint may need a considerable quantity of suspected fingerprint data, which is a difficult and time-consuming operation when done manually and, as a result, the employment of digital instruments and AI is becoming increasingly necessary in order to reduce labor load and complete time-consuming processes quickly [1, 2]. Computer science, engineering, criminology, and psychology—every field uses artificial intelligence (AI) [3, 4]. In this chapter, we'll talk about how AI is used in forensic psychology, in addition to every other subject. There is a significant link between human psychological functioning and AI, which is rapidly developing. In psychology, intelligence is described as a person's capacity to use their knowledge to affect their

DOI: 10.4324/9781003287810-9

surroundings [5, 6]. A defendant may be submitted to a forensic psychiatric evaluation to see if he or she has a serious mental illness, significant cognitive impairment, or intellectual disability. Some offenders overstate or deliberate mental illnesses or fail cognitive tests in order to avoid a traditional punishment [7]. Now, in various cases, there are numerous issues that make it difficult for a forensic psychologist to comprehend the mentality of a criminal. In order to address these issues, we can say that AI can assist because machines work on calculations and sensors, and when someone pretends to be someone else [8], AI sensors can calculate the mental process of that person and provide an accurate result [1]. In this chapter, you'll learn how the criminal justice system has evolved, as well as how modern systems may assist in delivering justice and obtaining reliable test findings. This chapter will introduce you to the benefits of AI and how we can apply it to the field of forensic psychology, which is in high demand these days because people are controlled by their brains, and in order to understand how the brain works, we must be able to detect its messages, in which AI can assist with high accuracy (Figure 9.1).

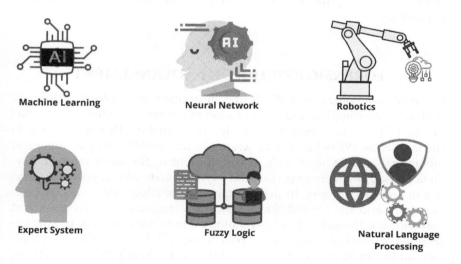

Machine Learning   **Neural Network**   **Robotics**

Expert System   **Fuzzy Logic**   **Natural Language Processing**

Figure 9.1   Different aspects of artificial intelligence (AI).

CURRENT TRENDS IN ARTIFICIAL INTELLIGENCE

The goal of AI is to create intelligent computers which can observe and adapt to new conditions without being programmed. As per the AI experts, these machines' cognitive decision-making and automation capabilities might be comparable to human intelligence [1, 9]. For the past 20 years, AI has been a rapidly re-emerging subject of computer science [10, 11]. Traditionally, AI has only been used in the context of the digital world. However, outside of the digital world, we are seeing an increasing trend for AI applications. In the real world, for example, AI systems have grown increasingly ubiquitous, particularly as industry and services move toward increased automation of labor. Medical diagnostics, robotics, and financial applications are among the most extensively utilized applications [11].

Currently, AI is becoming a part of the forensic field in various divisions. However, it is at a developing stage in the area of forensic psychology. This is because so many aspects of forensic psychology can be done with the help of AI, but there are further requirements that need to be fulfilled for the future era so that AI can perform every therapy and session easily and quickly. There are several advances in the field of AI as far as current trends in AI are concerned. AI can perform the majority of tasks in practically every discipline, and it also comprehends and learns from human psychology.

FORENSIC PSYCHOLOGY ADVANCEMENT

Forensic psychology is a discipline of applied psychology concerned with the investigation and presentation of gathered evidence in a court of law [12]. It has a lengthy and illustrious history that dates back to the late 1800s. Wilhelm Wundt, who built the world's first psychological laboratory in Leipzig in 1879, was a student of the early forensic psychologists. They were experimental psychologists who tried, with varying degrees of success, to bring applied psychology into the courts in Germany and the United States [13]. Individual mental processes and behavior are the subjects of psychology. There are a variety of specializations or areas of study within psychology [5]. Take cognitive psychology, for example, which investigates how the brain thinks and functions. Learning, memory, perception, language, and reasoning are all included in this category [14–17]. There's also developmental psychology, which evaluates how a person adapts and evolves as they progress through distinct developmental stages, as well as what is suitable to think about a human depending on development [15, 18–20]. A psychiatrist conducts clinical and diagnostic interviews and analyzes available data to prepare a forensic psychiatric report. This report includes recommendations that assist the court in determining the appropriate course of action for the defendant, such as imprisonment, psychiatric treatment, or community services. In some cases, a referral for a comprehensive psychiatric examination may be necessary to further assess mental symptoms, cognitive functioning, and the potential for future criminal behavior. The purpose of these evaluations is to provide a thorough understanding of the individual's mental state and aid in making informed decisions within the legal system. The forensic psychiatric report contains the psychological evaluation's conclusion. These days, this process is being changed from manual to machine-based, in which AI will measure various types of biological and physical activity of a person and, on the basis of the calculations, will give its results. These processes have been used for a long time, but manually, which consumes time and sometimes affects the results (Figure 9.2).

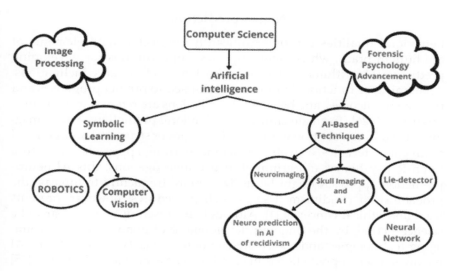

Figure 9.2   Connections and parts of AI and forensic psychology.

AI-BASED TECHNIQUES IN FORENSIC PSYCHOLOGY

Some of the AI-based tests that are used in the field of forensic psychology are listed below.

Neuroimaging

The increasing presence of AI technologies has generated interest in combining brain imaging with AI for improved risk assessment and prediction of future violent behavior [21]. In recent years, advancements in non-invasive neuroimaging technologies have produced large amounts of data, and the application of machine learning statistical techniques has become crucial for effectively analyzing complex brain datasets [22, 23]. One such approach is multi-voxel pattern analysis (MVPA), which employs machine learning methods to examine neuroimaging data [24]. Unlike traditional univariate approaches that focus on analyzing one location at a time, MVPA allows for the identification of temporal and spatial patterns in the data, enabling more precise differentiation between cognitive tasks or subject groups by integrating information from multiple voxels within a region [8, 25].

Neuro-prediction

Behavioral qualities can be significantly connected with elements of the human brain, which opens up new opportunities for developing predictive algorithms that can forecast an individual's inclinations. Anatomical or functional brain traits are used to predict prognoses and treatment outcomes, and behavioral predictions are referred to as "neuro-prediction" [26]. To create clinical or behavioral predictions, neuroimaging is used in conjunction with AI technologies or structural or functional brain characteristics, as well as machine learning approaches. In future forensic psychiatry and criminal justice investigations, this AI neuro-prediction approach might be utilized more frequently to forecast the probability of recidivism. Use of such procedures, however, presents legal and ethical concerns [1]. Although at present it may appear to be science fiction, by the ongoing development of non-invasive neuroimaging technologies and the rising computer capacity of algorithms, AI recidivism neuro-prediction is likely to become available in the future [25] (Figure 9.3).

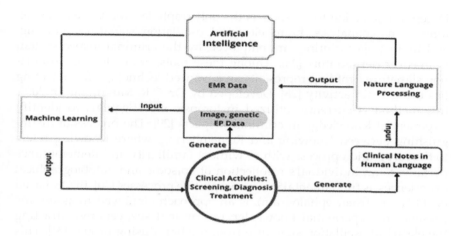

Figure 9.3 Working of the neuro-prediction model.

Lie-detectors

Stress and lying (in the context of bluffing) can be linked using Artificial Neural Networks (ANNs). Thus, ANNs can detect lying, as well as high-stress scenarios, utilizing a range of physiological parameters [27]. When a person tells a falsehood, the system uses machine learning and AI to analyze minute variations in muscular activity. Changes in face muscles and eyebrows are among the motions. Stickers printed on soft surfaces with electrodes that monitor nerves and muscles are used to track the facial muscles. These stickers were placed on the cheek muscles around the lips and the muscles above the brows for the study. The volunteers were then requested to sit in pairs, wear headphones, and face each other before hearing the words "line" or "tree" uttered into their ears. The participants were then asked to tell the truth or lie about what they heard via the headphones.

Brain Electrical Oscillation Signature Profiling (BEOS)

Lies are the most fundamental type of deceit, and they are all around us. Deception may take many forms, from children's harmless falsehoods to community-wide dread. The moral, scientific, clinical, and legal consequences of lie detection are all significant. Human dishonesty may be detected using a variety of approaches in the field of forensic psychology.

Deception detection tools, such as the polygraph, layered voice analyzer, forensic narcoanalysis, brain electrical oscillation signature profiling, and brain fingerprinting, are employed by the criminal justice system to uncover perpetrators [28]. Among these tools, brain electrical oscillation signature profiling represents an advanced technology for detecting lies using brain activity [28]. Developed by Dr. C.R. Mukundan in 2003, this method is currently utilized in forensic investigations to identify Experiential Knowledge in criminal suspects [29]. The process of distinguishing between Knowing and Remembering, where Knowing refers to the recognition process with or without familiarity and Remembrance pertains to an individual's recollection of episodic and autobiographical experiences, is fundamental in neurocognitive processes [30]. BEOS, based on EEG (electroencephalogram), is an approach employed to assess the presence of experiential knowledge in criminal suspects by extracting the electrical oscillation signature from the brain using probes [31]. This method involves the use of a 32-channel electrode head helmet, applying a head cap on the scalp, injecting conducting gel into the electrode discs, and monitoring the subject using webcams [28].

Minnesota Multiphasic Personality Inventory-2 (MMPI-2)

The MMPI-2 (Minnesota Multiphasic Personality Inventory-2) is widely recognized as the primary assessment tool for examining psychopathology and emotional functioning [32–34]. Given its extensive usage among psychologists and mental health professionals involved in forensic assessments, its prominence in forensic cases such as personal injury, competence to stand trial, and child custody is not surprising [35–38]. With 567 true/false items, the MMPI-2 evaluates reaction style, emotional/behavioral functioning, and psychopathology through various scales including validity, clinical, content, additional, component, and research scales [39]. Recent research indicates that forensic psychologists consider the MMPI-2 to meet the admissibility criteria, satisfying both the Frye test (general acceptability) and the Daubert standard (peer-reviewed) [40, 41].

Layered Voice Analysis (LVA)

It is widely accepted that human verbal communication possesses traits that may be used to transmit indexical knowledge about a speaker in addition to the literal translation, or context, of what's being said, and this intertextual information can be immensely valuable in forensic work [42]. In other terms, indexical data includes not just the meaning of the speech but also all features of the speech signal. The speaker's name, age, even if they're drunk or not, and the language and dialect they speak are all provided [43, 44]. Human emotion (including stress) is also highly essential, as it represents another area in which relevant actions may be observed [45]. Many of the impacts of stress, including lying, have been demonstrated. While it is recognized that deception does not just result in verbal distress (due to sociopathic situations, tension concealed by certain pharmaceutical drugs, and so on), it is still considered the foundation for deception in the vast majority of cases, and LVA is utilized to identify such actions [46–52]. Nemesysco manufactures the layered voice analysis instrument (Natania, Israel). LVA's responsiveness to a wide variety of cognitive and emotional states, according to Nemesysco, is based on methodologies that are distinct from those used by prior voice stress analyzers including the Mental Stress Analyzer, the Computerized Voice Stress Analyser, and other commercial precursors [42].

TECHNOLOGICAL LIMITATIONS AND FAILURES IN PREDICTIVE ANALYSIS

Despite the advantages previously highlighted about the future potential employment of AI neuroprotection approaches, there are numerous restrictions to consider; in fact, research into prediction models and their effective implementation remains a difficult undertaking [53]. In the field of machine learning psychiatry, investigations integrating machine learning algorithms with brain-imaging single topic prediction of brain diseases strive to identify individuals with diverse conditions [54]. Surprisingly, these investigations indicated various degrees of accuracy [25], raising concerns about the methodology [55]. Best practices in predictive modeling are required. One issue of neuroprotection systems is that, despite their ability to handle complicated data like neuroimaging scans, they require best practices to maintain sufficient statistical power to evaluate them [56].

There are a few issues that need to be addressed here. For starters, using neuroprotection approaches necessitated extrapolating the group-level to individual predictions [57]. Another issue is validating the findings in a fresh group that is unrelated to the dataset used to train an algorithm. The capacity to generalize is used to assess the validity of estimation techniques; for most machine learning, one typical approach is to assess the generalization performance using a method known as "cross-validation," in which the information is separated into different phases, a training phase and a test phase [58], and portions of the information are iteratively utilized to train and assess the model's predicted performance. Cross-validation with tiny samples, for example, might result in extremely variable and exaggerated estimations of prediction accuracy [56, 59]. Large volumes of data are required to train machine learning algorithms; utilizing a small sample size may result in overfitting, in which the system fits precisely to the particular dataset used to train it but poorly to new and unknown data [56]. There is still no consensus on the appropriate dataset size, however running prediction studies with samples of no fewer than several hundred observations is recommended [55]. Obtaining a large number of samples, on the other hand, is typically difficult and expensive, particularly when neuroimaging data is involved [53].

REFERENCES

1. Jadhav, E.B., M.S. Sankhla, and R. Kumar, Artificial Intelligence: Advancing automation in forensic science & criminal investigation. *Journal of Seybold Report*, 2020. 15(8): pp. 2064–2075.
2. Baraniuk, C., The new weapon in the fight against crime. BBC Online, March, 2019.
3. Jeong, D., Artificial intelligence security threat, crime, and forensics: Taxonomy and open issues. *IEEE Access*, 2020. 8: pp. 184560–184574.
4. LeCun, Y., Y. Bengio, and G. Hinton, Deep learning. *Nature*, 2015. 521(7553): pp. 436–444.
5. Crowder, J.A. and S. Friess, Artificial psychology: The psychology of AI. *People*, 2012. 2(3): pp. 4–5.
6. Coward, W.M. and P.R. Sackett, Linearity of ability-performance relationships: A reconfirmation. *Journal of Applied Psychology*, 1990. 75(3): p. 297.
7. Gudmundsson, S., E.L. Mortensen, and D. Sestoft, The use of psychological assessment and validity tests in forensic psychiatric examinations. *Journal of Forensic Psychology Research and Practice*, 2021. 21(2): pp. 118–130.
8. Haynes, J.-D. and G. Rees, Decoding mental states from brain activity in humans. *Nature Reviews Neuroscience*, 2006. 7(7): pp. 523–534.
9. Kok, J.N., et al., Artificial intelligence: Definition, trends, techniques, and cases. *Artificial Intelligence*, 2009. 1: pp. 270–299.
10. Kurzweil, R., *The singularity is near: When humans transcend biology*. 2005: Penguin.
11. Broadhurst, R., et al., *Artificial intelligence and crime*. Available at SSRN, 2019, doi:10.2139/ssrn.3407779.
12. Gudjonsson, G.H. and L.R. Haward, *Forensic psychology: A guide to practice*. 2016: Routledge.

13. Gudjonsson, G.H., Psychology brings justice: The science of forensic psychology. *Criminal Behaviour and Mental Health*, 2003. 13(3): pp. 159–167.
14. Carbone, J.N. and J.A. Crowder, The great migration: Information content to knowledge using cognition based frameworks, in J.N. Carbone, *Biomedical engineering: Health care systems, technology and techniques*. 2011, Springer. pp. 17–46.
15. Crowder, J.A. and N. Shelli Friess, The artificial prefrontal cortex: Artificial consciousness. In *Proceedings on the International Conference on Artificial Intelligence (ICAI)*. 2011.
16. Davis, M. and P.J. Whalen, The amygdala: Vigilance and emotion. *Molecular Psychiatry*, 2001. 6(1): pp. 13–34.
17. Eichenbaum, H., *The cognitive neuroscience of memory: An introduction*. 2011, Oxford University Press.
18. LeDoux, J., *The emotional brain [Le cerveau des émotions: Les mystérieux fondements de notre vie émotionnelle]*. 1996, Simon & Schuster, New York.
19. LeDoux, J.E., Emotion circuits in the brain. *Annual Review of Neuroscience*, 2000. 23(1): pp. 155–184.
20. LeDoux, J., *Synaptic self: How our brains become who we are*. 2002: Viking, New York.
21. Berk, R., et al., Fairness in criminal justice risk assessments: The state of the art. *Sociological Methods & Research*, 2021. 50(1): pp. 3–44.
22. Lemm, S., et al., Introduction to machine learning for brain imaging. *Neuroimage*, 2011. 56(2): pp. 387–399.
23. Abraham, A., et al., Machine learning for neuroimaging with scikit-learn. *Frontiers in Neuroinformatics*, 2014. 8: p. 14.
24. Ombao, H., et al., *Handbook of neuroimaging data analysis*. 2016: Chapman and Hall/CRC Press.
25. Tortora, L., et al., Neuroprediction and ai in forensic psychiatry and criminal justice: A neurolaw perspective. *Frontiers in Psychology*, 2020. 11: p. 220.
26. Morse, S. Neuroprediction: New technology, old problems. *Bioethica Forum*, 2015. 8: p. 128.
27. Srivastava, N., Lie detection system using artificial neural network. *Journal of Global Research in Computer Science*, 2014. 5(8): pp. 9–13.
28. Savithri, K.K. and P. Kacker, When brain tells the deception: A literature review on brain electrical oscillation signature profiling. *Mind & Society*, 2021. 10(1/2): pp. 27–30.
29. Puranik, D., et al. Brain signature profiling in India: Its status as an aid in investigation and as corroborative evidence: As seen from judgments. In *Proceedings of XX All India Forensic Science Conference*. 2009.
30. Mukundan, C., *Brain electrical oscillations signature profiling for crime investigation*. Selective & Scientific Books, New Delhi, 2008: pp. 123–146.
31. Mukundan, C. *Brain electrical oscillation signature profiling for forensic applications*. In *International Conference of Association of Forensic Sciences*. 2005.
32. Greene, R.L., *The MMPI-2: An interpretive manual*. 2000: Allyn & Bacon.

33. Watkins, C.E., et al., Contemporary practice of psychological assessment by clinical psychologists. *Professional Psychology: Research and Practice*, 1995. 26(1): p. 54.

34. Lubin, B., et al., Psychological test usage patterns in five professional settings. *American Psychologist*, 1985. 40(7): p. 857.

35. Otto, R.K., Use of the MMPI-2 in forensic settings. *Journal of Forensic Psychology Practice*, 2002. 2(3): pp. 71–91.

36. Boccaccini, M.T. and S.L. Brodsky, Diagnostic test usage by forensic psychologists in emotional injury cases. *Professional Psychology: Research and Practice*, 1999. 30(3): p. 253.

37. Borum, R. and T. Grisso, Psychological test use in criminal forensic evaluations. *Professional Psychology: Research and Practice*, 1995. 26(5): p. 465.

38. Bow, J.N. and F.A. Quinnell, Psychologists' current practices and procedures in child custody evaluations: Five years after American Psychological Association guidelines. *Professional Psychology: Research and Practice*, 2001. 32(3): p. 261.

39. Bow, J.N., J.R. Flens, and J.W. Gould, MMPI-2 and MCMI-III in forensic evaluations: A survey of psychologists. *Journal of Forensic Psychology Practice*, 2010. 10(1): pp. 37–52.

40. Bow, J.N., et al., An analysis of administration, scoring, and interpretation of the MMPI-2 and MCMI-II/III in child custody evaluations. *Journal of Child Custody*, 2006. 2(4): pp. 1–22.

41. Lally, S.J., What tests are acceptable for use in forensic evaluations? A survey of experts. *Professional Psychology: Research and Practice*, 2003. 34(5): p. 491.

42. Harnsberger, J.D., et al., Stress and deception in speech: Evaluating layered voice analysis. *Journal of Forensic Sciences*, 2009. 54(3): pp. 642–650.

43. Chen, Y., Cepstral domain talker stress compensation for robust speech recognition. *IEEE Transactions on Acoustics, Speech, and Signal Processing*, 1988. 36(4): pp. 433–439.

44. Cummings, K.E. and M.A. Clements. Analysis of glottal waveforms across stress styles. In *International Conference on Acoustics, Speech, and Signal Processing*. 1990. IEEE.

45. Cummings, K.E. and M.A. Clements, Analysis of the glottal excitation of emotionally styled and stressed speech. *The Journal of the Acoustical Society of America*, 1995. 98(1): pp. 88–98.

46. Frick, R.W., The prosodic expression of anger: Differentiating threat and frustration. *Aggressive Behavior*, 1986. 12(2): pp. 121–128.

47. Hicks, J. and H. Hollien. The reflection of stress in voice-1: Understanding the basic correlates. In *Proceedings of the Carnahan Conference on Crime Countermeasures*. 1981.

48. Hollien, H., Vocal indicators of psychological stress. *Forensic Psychology and Psychiatry*, 1980. 347(1): pp. 47–71.

49. Hollien, H.F., *Forensic voice identification*. 2002, Academic Press.

50. Hollien, H., J. Saletto, and S. Miller, Psychological stress in voice: A new approach. *Studia Phonetica Posnaniensia*, 1993. 4: pp. 5–17.

51. Cestaro, V.L., *A comparison of accuracy rates between detection of deception examinations using the polygraph and the Computer Voice Stress Analyzer in a mock crime scenario.* 1996, Department of Defense Polygraph Inst Fort Mcclellan AL.
52. Meyerhoff, J.L., et al., *Physiological and biochemical measures of stress compared to voice stress analysis using the Computer Voice Stress Analyzer (CVSA).* 2001, Department of Defense Polygraph Inst Fort Jackson SC.
53. Esteban, O., et al., fMRIPrep: A robust preprocessing pipeline for functional MRI. *Nature Methods,* 2019. 16(1): pp. 111–116.
54. Arbabshirani, M.R., et al., Single subject prediction of brain disorders in neuroimaging: Promises and pitfalls. *Neuroimage,* 2017. 145: pp. 137–165.
55. Cearns, M., T. Hahn, and B.T. Baune, Recommendations and future directions for supervised machine learning in psychiatry. *Translational Psychiatry,* 2019. 9(1): pp. 1–12.
56. Poldrack, R.A., G. Huckins, and G. Varoquaux, Establishment of best practices for evidence for prediction: a review. *JAMA Psychiatry,* 2020. 77(5): pp. 534–540.
57. Hahn, T., A.A. Nierenberg, and S. Whitfield-Gabrieli, Predictive analytics in mental health: Applications, guidelines, challenges and perspectives. *Molecular Psychiatry,* 2017. 22(1): pp. 37–43.
58. Varoquaux, G., Cross-validation failure: Small sample sizes lead to large error bars. *Neuroimage,* 2018. 180: pp. 68–77.
59. Kappelmann, N., B. Müller-Myhsok, and J. Kopf-Beck, Adapting the randomised controlled trial (RCT) for precision medicine: Introducing the nested-precision RCT (npRCT). *Trials,* 2021. 22(1): pp. 1–5.

10

AI in Data Recovery and Data Analysis

Anubhav Singh, Ananta Joshi, Mahipal Singh Sankhla,
Kavita Saini, and Sumit Kumar Choudhary

INTRODUCTION

The exponential growth of data in the contemporary digital era has given businesses and organizations new opportunities as well as obstacles. Data has become a vital part of our lives in the modern world. It is more crucial than ever to be able to recover and analyze data effectively. Unfortunately, when dealing with huge datasets or challenging recovery scenarios, typical solutions frequently fall short. Thankfully, artificial intelligence (AI) has become a potent tool that can overcome these obstacles and completely transform the data recovery and analysis industry. This chapter explores how AI is being used for data analysis and recovery. It focuses especially on the interactions between cutting-edge AI methods and the extraction of useful insights from massive amounts of data. Businesses may improve their data recovery procedures, focus their research efforts, and find patterns and trends that might have otherwise gone undetected by employing AI [1].

Data recovery with AI has completely changed the industry by utilizing cutting-edge machine learning (ML) algorithms, deep learning models, and natural language processing (NLP) methodologies. AI enables independent

DOI: 10.4324/9781003287810-10

data recovery that can adapt to different types and sources of data by recognizing patterns and examples, unlike traditional methods that rely on user intervention or predefined criteria, which can be time consuming and unsuccessful. The speed and accuracy of data recovery procedures have significantly increased as a result of this paradigm change. AI also ushers in a new era of data analysis by enabling businesses to make sense of the enormous volumes of data they already have. Advanced data exploration and the extraction of insightful information are made possible by the use of AI techniques including sentiment analysis, text mining, anomaly detection, clustering, classification, and anomaly detection. Organizations can use these strategies to classify data, find anomalies, find hidden patterns, and extract actionable knowledge from their datasets [2].

While AI has a lot to offer in terms of data analysis and recovery, there are also disadvantages. Data quality, moral dilemmas, and outcomes that are simple to understand are the primary problems that need to be resolved. However, the continual developments in hardware, software, and infrastructure capabilities offer encouraging solutions to these issues, paving the way for additional study and invention in the area.

Throughout this chapter, we will examine the various ways that AI is used to recover and analyze data. We will look at the many methodologies and approaches employed, illustrate how they are implemented with examples from the real world, discuss the benefits and drawbacks of AI, and provide some insights into possible future directions and developing trends in this dynamic field [3].

Objective

We explore how AI can be used to enhance data analysis and recovery in this section. Our goal is to thoroughly explain to readers how AI techniques can improve the accuracy and speed of data recovery procedures while also making it easier to conduct intelligent analysis on huge datasets. To show the actual uses of AI in different disciplines, we emphasize the benefits, disadvantages, and real-world use cases throughout this chapter.

Scope

AI is used in data analysis and restoration:

1. *Data recovery*
   - The limitations of current methods for recovering damaged or destroyed data.

- ML techniques such as supervised, unsupervised, reinforcement, generative adversarial networks (GANs), recurrent neural networks (RNNs), and convolutional neural networks (CNNs) can be used to recover data.
- NLP is used to recover data from text-based sources.
- Presentation of relevant case studies showing how AI is applied to data recovery.

2. *Data analysis*
   - Overview of traditional methods and their drawbacks when applied to the analysis of large datasets.
   - A discussion of AI methods for data analysis, such as text mining, sentiment analysis, anomaly detection, clustering, and classification.
   - Analyzing case studies that demonstrate the application of AI to data processing tasks.

3. *Benefits and challenges*
   - We explore the benefits of incorporating AI techniques into data recovery and analysis processes, including improved automation, effectiveness, and precision.
   - A consideration of the challenges and constraints faced by AI in data recovery and analysis, such as data quality, ethical concerns, and interpretability.

INTRODUCTION TO DATA RECOVERY AND DATA ANALYSIS

Data recovery and analysis are essential elements of many industries' operations, including business, science, healthcare, and finance. Data recovery is the process of regaining access to lost, broken, or inaccessible data from storage systems or devices to guarantee its integrity and availability for use in the future. Data analysis, on the other hand, is focused on drawing important conclusions, spotting patterns, and noticing trends from data to assist decision-making procedures, encourage innovation, and improve overall effectiveness [4].

Data Recovery

Data preservation and loss prevention are essential for enterprises to ensure ongoing operations. Data loss can be brought on by several things, including hardware or software bugs, inclement weather, cyberattacks, and accidental deletion. Such occurrences may severely harm a business' operations. Data recovery procedures are used to recover lost data and make it usable once more to solve this problem. Traditional data recovery techniques frequently rely on established rules and heuristics or demand human involvement. These techniques might not work well with large datasets or complex situations, though. AI can help in this situation by automating and streamlining the recovery process with the help of ML algorithms, deep learning models, and pattern recognition techniques [5].

Effective data recovery solutions are more necessary than ever in the modern world. AI-powered systems have become a crucial resource for restoring corrupted or deleted data. These systems have greatly increased their accuracy and success rates in extracting useful information by examining past data patterns and situations. They can manage many sorts of data from numerous sources, such as databases, file systems, and storage devices, thanks to their amazing versatility. Businesses may reduce downtime while protecting their important information assets by incorporating AI into their data recovery processes. Additionally, this technology can greatly improve their overall strategy for managing data resources [6].

Data Analysis

Data analysis is becoming a crucial tool for drawing out important patterns and insights from a variety of data sources. Businesses must traverse a vast amount of information to stay ahead in today's competitive environment due to the growth of structured databases, unstructured text documents, sensor data, and social media platforms. Making educated decisions and fostering innovation depend on having the ability to glean useful intelligence from these various sources [7].

AI techniques are crucial in the field of data analysis because they enable businesses to fully utilize the power of sophisticated algorithms and computational models for the interpretation and processing of complex datasets. A wide range of approaches, including sentiment analysis, clustering, regression, classification, NLP, anomaly detection, and many others, are included in these techniques.

Organizations might utilize a variety of algorithms when it comes to data analysis. By combining related data points, clustering algorithms make it possible to spot patterns and dataset segments. Automated decision-making and predictive analytics are made possible by classification algorithms, which group data into specified classes or labels. Another

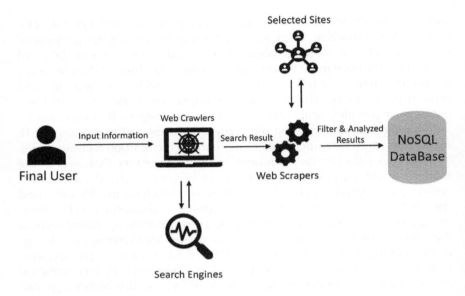

Figure 10.1   Schema of proposed system.

algorithm that finds connections between variables and forecasts future results is regression analysis. Additionally, text data can be analyzed using NLP methods that extract attitudes and comprehend linguistic context. As a final point, anomaly detection algorithms help spot outliers or unusual behavior in datasets, which might draw attention to possible fraud or inaccuracies in the data [8].

Businesses may enhance processes, personalize experiences, uncover hidden insights, identify patterns, forecast future outcomes, and gain a deeper understanding of their data with the help of AI. AI enables data analysts and specialists in a variety of industries to wring useful information from complex and varied datasets. This enhances corporate outcomes by enabling data-driven, well-informed decision-making [9].

TECHNIQUES USING AI TO RECOVER DATA

AI approaches have revolutionized the field of data recovery. These innovative techniques have provided a multitude of cutting-edge options for recovering lost, damaged, or inaccessible data. The effectiveness and

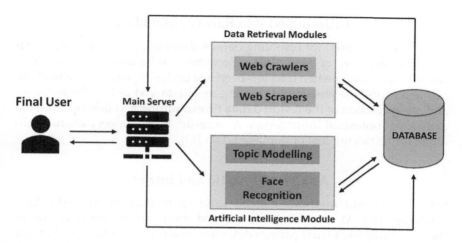

Figure 10.2   The architecture of the proposed system.

efficiency of the data recovery process have substantially increased thanks to the application of ML algorithms, deep learning models, and data analysis [10].

Let's examine some important AI methods applied to data recovery.

Recovery Using Machine Learning

By automating and improving the process of data recovery, ML algorithms have completely changed it. These algorithms can precisely locate and restore lost or damaged information by examining patterns and instances from previous data. ML algorithms can accurately predict missing or corrupted data by examining elements including file structures, data formats, and metadata [11].

Recovery Using Deep Learning

Multi-layer neural networks are used in deep learning, a type of ML, to analyze complex data. These models are tremendously helpful for data retrieval jobs since they are adept at seeing patterns and extracting characteristics. They can also create hierarchical representations of the data, which gives them the ability to restore broken or missing bits with astounding precision [12].

147

Utilizing NLP to Recover Metadata

Metadata is essential for revealing details about the properties, organization, and structure of data. NLP approaches can be used to recover this crucial information when data has been lost or destroyed. NLP algorithms can determine the absence of missing metadata and aid in the recovery and interpretation of the restored data by examining text descriptions, file names, or contextual information. As a result, NLP is a very useful technique for retrieving lost or damaged data [13].

Analysis of Audio and Image

Several different methods can be used to recover multimedia data. Implementing AI to analyze image and audio information is one of these techniques. Visual pattern detection, feature extraction, and image reconstruction can all be accomplished by training deep-learning models on large datasets. Additionally, audio analysis algorithms can recover audio data from files that have been corrupted or distorted. This strategy is quite successful and improves the overall recovery process for multimedia data [14].

Advanced File Carving

File carving is a technique used to extract files from a storage medium without using the architecture of a file system. ML algorithms are used by AI-enabled file carving techniques to recognize file headers, footers, and signatures. These algorithms can efficiently extract files from raw data even in the absence or degradation of file system information because they learn from existing file formats and structures [15, 16].

Intelligent Data Recovery

By analyzing historical trends and system performance, AI can be used to foresee potential data loss or corruption in the context of data management. Predictive models can identify potential threats and take preventative measures to prevent data loss or create quick recovery methods by thoroughly analyzing system logs, error codes, and other relevant information. This type of proactive data recovery provides confidence that efficient proactive data management practices are in place, protecting against the detrimental effects of data loss situations [17].

Recoverable Adaptive Algorithms

AI-enabled adaptive recovery methods can dynamically modify their plans in response to the particular properties of the data or underlying storage systems. These algorithms improve the recovery procedure and increase the possibility of successfully restoring data by learning from previous recovery attempts [18].

Utilizing AI techniques for data recovery may be very advantageous for businesses as it can considerably increase the reliability, speed, and accuracy of recovering lost or damaged data. These cutting-edge techniques enable the analysis of complex data patterns, delivering prescient insights and adaptable recovery solutions that ultimately improve overall data management practices while minimizing the consequences of any future data loss incidents [19, 20].

CONVOLUTIONAL NEURAL NETWORKS

Convolutional neural networks (CNNs) have had a significant impact in a variety of domains, including image processing and computer vision. Even the world of data recovery has adopted these complex models, particularly when the data incorporates images or spatial information. In this section, we'll look into how CNNs can be used for data recovery [21].

Reconstruction and Restoration of Images

CNNs outperform all other image analysis algorithms. They are therefore perfect for rebuilding and recovering images in cases of data recovery. These networks can extract intricate patterns and features from a large database of photos. A special method enables the astonishing ability to repair missing or damaged portions of an image. The ability of a CNN to accurately fill in data gaps is improved by exposing the network to a wide variety of images and their unaffected equivalents during training. The quality and importance of the restored data are ultimately improved by using this method to recover photos from files that are only partially corrupted [22].

Data Repair and Error Correction

CNNs have been demonstrated to be a successful method for repairing mistakes and retrieving corrupted data from a variety of file formats.

CNN can recognize patterns of corruption and correctly forecast missing or inaccurate values when exposed to a dataset that includes both uncorrupted and corrupted data samples. This method gives a precise way to correct mistakes and retrieve lost data. It is especially useful when data corruption exhibits distinct patterns or happens in particular areas. The qualified CNN can examine the damaged data, make the appropriate adjustments, and recover accurate and reliable information [23].

Data Representation and Feature Extraction

The ability of CNNs to extract important features from input data is well known. CNNs are capable of extracting important features from incomplete or corrupted data in the context of data retrieval, which can subsequently be expressed in a condensed fashion. For further research, reconstruction, or integration with other data sources, this feature representation might be used. Intricate relationships within the data can be recorded and analyzed more effectively for better recovery outcomes by utilizing the hierarchical structure included in CNNs [24].

Data Augmentation and the Creation of Synthetic Data

By generating synthetic data or augmenting existing datasets, CNNs can help with data recovery. A CNN can learn the essential patterns and structures of the original dataset by being trained on a dataset with complete data samples. Then, using this newly discovered information, synthetic data that closely resembles the characteristics of the initial dataset can be produced. When some of the original data is lost or out of reach, synthetic data may prove to be helpful. CNNs offer an advantage in bridging gaps in datasets and simplifying the recovery process due to their capacity to synthesize false samples [25].

Learning Transfer for Data Recovery

Transfer learning has the potential to revolutionize data recovery. Using pre-trained CNN models, which have already acquired broad picture representations from huge datasets, is the method. They can successfully recover missing or corrupted data by tweaking or adjusting these models to the particular data recovery task at hand. This expedites the training process while simultaneously enhancing CNN performance in data recovery circumstances. Transfer learning takes previously acquired knowledge and applies it to fresh circumstances to provide the best outcomes [25].

The use of CNNs in data recovery opens up the possibility of recovering and reconstructing crucial data from incomplete or defective datasets. CNNs are especially skilled in examining images, correcting mistakes, removing features, and representing data. Companies can improve the accuracy and effectiveness of their data recovery efforts, leading to more trustworthy and comprehensive information restoration, by utilizing the potential of deep learning and the skill of CNNs in understanding complex patterns.

GENERATIVE ADVERSARIAL NETWORKS (GANs) AND RECURRENT NEURAL NETWORKS (RNNs)

There are a few AI methods that have shown to be very successful when it comes to data retrieval. Recurrent neural networks (RNNs) and generative adversarial networks (GANs) are two techniques that stand out in addition to CNNs, which are frequently employed. These potent techniques have demonstrated astounding efficacy in data recovery. We will examine the use of RNNs and GANs explicitly in the context of data retrieval in this section [26].

Sequential Data Recovery Using RNNs

RNNs are the preferred option for processing sequential data because they were created with this need in mind. They are excellent at retrieving text, time series data, or any other type of data with a temporal component. Based on the context and information provided, RNNs can leverage patterns and dependencies within sequential data to forecast missing or corrupted values. An RNN can learn how to fill in the gaps and recover missing data by being trained on a dataset that includes both complete and damaged or partial sequences. They are therefore a priceless resource for recovering corrupted or lost sequential data of any kind [27].

Data Generation and Completion Using GANs

There is an effective class of neural networks called GANs. These networks are made up of a generator and a discriminator, and their main job is to produce fake data that closely resembles the real input data. As GANs may be trained to produce missing or corrupted data samples, this is very helpful when it comes to data recovery. The generator creates synthetic data to fill in any gaps or faulty sections after learning the underlying distribution of intact data samples. The discriminator then evaluates the reliability and caliber of this created content, offering commentary for upcoming performance enhancements. In circumstances where loss or corruption has occurred, GANs offer enormous value due to their capacity to fill or replace missing data [26, 27].

Hybrid Strategies

Data recovery tasks can benefit greatly from the use of hybrid techniques that mix RNNs and GANs. These methods can recover sequential data while also producing realistic and comprehensive data samples by combining the advantages of both models. This is accomplished by using the generated sequences from the GAN as inputs and training an RNN on entire sequences, enabling more precise reconstructions. Additionally, when working with complicated and sequential data types, this synergy between RNNs and GANs is especially helpful. Overall, this integration provides a strong foundation for data recovery tasks that can generate synthetic data that is more coherent and realistic due to the RNN's capability to capture temporal connections while utilizing GAN-generated sequences [8, 28].

Pre-trained Models and Transfer Learning

RNNs, GANs, and CNNs are all capable of utilizing transfer learning and pre-trained models. The training process can be sped up and the quality of the data recovery output improved by using pre-trained RNN or GAN models that have already been learned from large datasets. These pre-trained models capture the underlying structures and patterns in the data, which can be adjusted or customized to meet particular data recovery needs. Transfer learning allows for more effective information retrieval by utilizing expertise from earlier activities [6, 28].

In terms of data recovery, RNNs and GANs work best together. While GANs can produce comprehensive and accurate data samples, RNNs excel at capturing temporal dependencies and filling in the gaps. Organizations can considerably enhance their data recovery skills by utilizing these AI approaches. This guarantees the recovery of important information, enabling informed decision-making based on trustworthy and complete datasets.

AI DATA ANALYSIS TECHNIQUES

The use of AI approaches has changed the field of data analysis. In ways that were previously unimaginable, these tools have enabled organizations to get insights, make educated decisions, and acquire a competitive edge. AI approaches make it possible to quickly and effectively handle and analyze enormous amounts of data, revealing patterns, trends, and important information that could otherwise go unnoticed. We'll look into some of the AI methods used for data analysis in this section [29].

Machine Learning Techniques

ML techniques are heavily used in data analysis driven by AI. These algorithms operate without explicit programming, learning from data patterns to make predictions or judgments. For instance, supervised learning techniques for classification and regression problems include support vector machines, decision trees, random forests, and linear regression. On the other hand, unsupervised learning algorithms can find patterns and structures in data without labeled training material. Examples include clustering methods like k-means and hierarchical clustering, as well as dimensionality reduction techniques like principal component analysis (PCA). ML algorithms can be used to classify data points, predict outcomes with high accuracy, uncover correlations between variables, and extract useful insights from enormous datasets [11, 29].

Deep Learning

Deep learning is a strong subset of ML and shines out when it comes to sophisticated AI approaches. Deep neural networks, which have several layers of connected neurons and closely mirror the structure of the human brain, are trained using enormous datasets. CNNs and RNNs, two of the methods utilized in this method, have demonstrated extraordinary performance in tasks like time series analysis, NLP, and picture recognition. RNNs are excellent at identifying sequential patterns in data, while CNNs are particularly good at extracting features from images. Organizations may achieve cutting-edge performance across diverse data analysis activities by utilizing the capabilities of deep learning algorithms to acquire insights into complicated data representations and identify hidden patterns [15, 29].

153

NLP

NLP, an area of AI, is concerned with how computers and human language interact. NLP methods make it possible to analyze, comprehend, and create data in human language, such as text, social media posts, customer reviews, and more. NLP algorithms are capable of carrying out tasks like language translation, topic modeling, named entity recognition, sentiment analysis, and summary. Organizations can analyze customer feedback, automatically segment documents, and extract valuable information from text using NLP techniques [30].

Analysing Data and Identifying Patterns

Finding patterns, connections, and anomalies in large amounts of data is the goal of data mining. Data mining is made easier by AI techniques like association rule mining, grouping, and anomaly detection. While clustering algorithms organize similar data points based on their properties, association rule mining identifies undiscovered links and relationships between variables. If a data pattern deviates from the expected pattern, anomaly detection algorithms can detect it. These methods are useful in many different industries for market basket analysis, customer segmentation, fraud detection, and anomaly detection [30].

Reward-Based Learning

Reinforcement learning, an AI approach, trains employers to make decisions repeatedly in a situation to maximize reward signals. In fields like robotics, gaming, and autonomous programming, it has built a reputation. Reinforcement learning algorithms pick up knowledge by making mistakes, observing different behaviors, and gathering information from the environment. Reinforcement learning can be applied to improve decision-making, dynamic pricing, and other data analytic tasks [30].

Automated Machine Learning (AutoML)

The phrase "automatic machine learning" (AutoML) refers to the use of AI techniques in the development of ML models and the execution of programs. Model building operations are streamlined and accelerated by autoML tools and platforms by automating procedures including data pretreatment, feature selection, hyperparameter tuning, and model selection. AutoML only offers a few features to data analysts and domain specialists [30].

AI ADVANTAGES IN DATA ANALYSIS
AND DATA RECOVERY

- *Improvements in data processing*: Organizations are now able to analyze enormous amounts of data in real time while also processing data more rapidly and effectively thanks to AI technologies. This ability is especially important in data recovery situations where time is of the essence.
- *Enhanced precision and accuracy*: AI techniques like ML and deep learning can examine data with astonishing precision and accuracy. Businesses can obtain meaningful information as a result, and they can confidently make data-driven decisions.
- *Finding hidden trends and insights*: AI techniques can uncover complex relationships, connections, and insights that human analysts would not immediately notice. Through the use of AI, businesses can acquire a competitive edge by locating crucial information that may inspire innovation and improve product quality.
- *Data analysis tasks that can be automated*: AI enables the processing of time-consuming, repetitive data analysis tasks. Enabling human researchers to focus on more complex and strategic research boosts productivity.
- *Real-time surveillance and warning*: AI-powered systems can search databases continually, identify anomalies and patterns, and send out immediate notifications. Different types of companies can use this proactive strategy to help them respond quickly to significant events, lower risks, and make defensible decisions.

AI CHALLENGES FOR DATA ANALYSIS
AND RECOVERY

- *Data integrity and quality*: AI techniques heavily rely on accurate and reliable data to produce the best outcomes. It can be challenging to deal with incomplete, inconsistent, or erroneous data, which could jeopardize the dependability and correctness of the analysis.
- *Concerns about ethics and privacy*: Data collection and analysis using AI present ethical and privacy concerns. It is essential to ensure that AI technology is used responsibly and in compliance with privacy laws to process sensitive personal data.
- *Explainability and interpretability*: Some AI techniques, such as deep learning, are known for making it difficult to understand

and explain the reasoning behind their predictions or judgments because of their "black-box" nature. This lack of data could be problematic in sensitive applications when translation capabilities are weak. It will be important.

- *Requirements for scalability and resources*: Particularly deep learning approaches need a lot of computing power and training data. Businesses must spend money on infrastructure and processing power to support AI-powered data analysis because big data can be challenging to scale.
- *Knowledge and skill gap*: Even though skilled individuals with knowledge of AI, ML, and data analytics are difficult to find for organization types that have successfully applied AI to their data analytics efforts, using AI techniques for data mining and analytics still require their use as a problem develops.
- *Adoption and integration*: Integrating AI methods into existing data collection and analytics platforms can be challenging and time consuming. In addition to ensuring simple integration with their existing systems and operating procedures, organizations must protect the user.

Best practices for data governance must be employed, and AI systems must be regularly monitored and assessed to ensure they are of high quality and respect moral values, to overcome these challenges and maximize the benefits of AI recovery and analysis.

FUTURE DIRECTIONS AND EMERGING TRENDS IN ARTIFICIAL INTELLIGENCE FOR DATA ANALYSIS AND RECOVERY

- *Reasonable AI*: The need for translational AI is increasing as AI techniques become more sophisticated and potent. To provide approaches that can give explicit reasons for the decisions made by AI models, researchers and experts are working incredibly hard. This will improve understanding of the data gathering and analysis process and boost trust in AI systems [31].
- *Federated education*: As the demand for data security and privacy increases, blended learning is becoming more and more common. Federated learning enables AI models to be trained locally on user devices or decentralized data sources without transferring the raw data to a central server. This tactic improves data privacy

while enabling cooperative data analysis among networks in a distributed network.

- *Integrated models*: Combining AI models and methodologies is another emerging trend in data retrieval and analysis. Hybrid models can combine ML, deep learning, and other AI methods to benefit from each approach's advantages and generate more extensive and precise analytical results.
- *Utilizing the edge*: Edge computing includes data processing and analysis at the network's edge. This characteristic is crucial when data recovery calls for real-time examination. Business organizations can lower latency, improve data security, and hasten data recovery thanks to edge computing and AI technologies.
- *Processing natural language for unstructured data*: Unstructured data sources, including text files, emails, and social media posts, are examples of those that could provide insightful data when relevant data is retrieved using AI-powered NLP techniques. This enables firms to perform advanced data analytics and to gain more insightful information from data systems.
- *Internet of Things (IoT) with AI integration*: The incorporation of AI into IoT devices has the potential to completely transform data collecting and processing. IoT devices produce additional data that can be combined with AI methods to swiftly elucidate insightful data. Forecasting, anomaly identification, and edge decision-making are made feasible by this connectedness's data pretreatment and analytics [32].
- *Enhanced analytics*: Augmented analytics refers to the use of AI to automate and enhance data generation, data visualization, and data analysis operations.
- *Adaptive systems and continuous learning*: The value of AI systems that can adapt to shifting data patterns and trends is growing. Thanks to continuous learning processes, AI models may update their skills from scratch and react to new data, which eliminates the need for retraining. This enables the collection and analysis of more precise and dynamic data in ever-changing conditions.
- *Dependable AI*: As AI technology advances, it is more crucial than ever to ensure that it is used correctly and morally. Making rules and regulations for AI that collects and analyzes data ethically is one of the future directions. This entails addressing bias and ensuring that AI initiatives are just, open, and responsible [33, 38].

- *Data visualization with AI*: Data visualization is a crucial part of data analysis. AI approaches can enhance data visualization by automatically finding patterns, trends, and anomalies in data and displaying them in user-friendly interactive visual representations. Users may more fully examine and understand data as a result, which improves decision-making [34, 38].

As AI develops and new technologies are created, these upcoming directions and trends have the potential to alter the data restoration and data assessment environment, allowing organizations to gain deeper insights and fostering innovation in a range of industries.

FUTURE DIRECTIONS AND EMERGING TRENDS IN ARTIFICIAL INTELLIGENCE FOR DATA ANALYSIS AND RECOVERY

Improved Data Recovery Methods

It is anticipated that AI will greatly advance data restoration techniques. Future suggestions include the creation of AI systems that may successfully enhance and rebuild data from multiple sources, including tainted or incomplete data. To increase the accuracy and effectiveness of facts recovery tactics, this may entail the use of complex system learning approaches, such as deep learning [35].

Analyzing Data with Intelligence

As the amount and complexity of data continue to increase, more sophisticated information analysis skills are required. One of the major areas in AI for information evaluation is the development of better algorithms that can automatically find patterns, developments, and anomalies in large datasets. To create more accurate and insightful evaluation outcomes, this integrates ML, deep learning, and other AI techniques [35, 38].

Analysis of Real-time and Streaming Data

As real-time data streams from diverse sources become more widespread, there is a need for AI algorithms that could evaluate records in real time. Future suggestions include the development of AI systems that could filter and analyze streaming data, allowing firms to quickly decide based on the most recent facts. The use of techniques like online learning and adaptive models, which can continuously replace evaluation results as new data becomes available, is included in this [36].

Edge Computing and AI Integration

Edge computing, which places processing and analysis on the edge of the network, is gaining popularity. In the future, it may be possible to combine AI methods with regional computer systems to speed up and improve data analysis and restoration. To do this, AI models may need to be installed directly on peripheral devices or local servers may need to be used to do AI-based analysis on the data generated at the threshold [36, 38].

Data Analysis that Respects Privacy

Data privacy is a crucial concern in the assessment of facts. One of the potential possibilities for AI in the future is the creation of techniques that could analyze information while preserving the confidentiality of private data. This covers the use of federated learning, robust multi-birthday party computation, and differential privacy techniques that enable collaborative analysis without leaking character data.

Data Preparation via Automation

Data preparation is an important and time-consuming step in the analysis of facts. One of the future approaches is the development of AI-based tools and techniques that can automate the processes of data cleansing, transformation, and feature engineering. NLP, device learning, and automatic feature selection approaches may be used to automate records training chores and enhance the overall review process [37].

Combining Domain Knowledge

Domain-specific expertise and understanding could improve AI systems for data analysis and recovery. The creation of AI models that can effectively use location data to direct the evaluation process and produce more illuminating and intelligible outcomes will be the main goal of future research. Ontologies, expert systems, and information graphs may need to be integrated into AI-based frameworks for data evaluation to achieve this [38].

AI and Human Collaboration

The future of AI in record restoration and analysis will depend on how well humans and machines can work together. Future requirements include creating AI systems that could collaborate with human analysts, taking advantage of their subject-matter expertise, and producing understandable and practical results. This encompasses the development of interactive visualization tools, decision-guiding systems, and interfaces for NLP [38].

Responsible and Ethical AI

As AI technology develops, there may be an increasing focus on assuring the moral and proper use of AI in fact recovery and evaluation. Future guidelines must establish frameworks, suggestions, and rules that enable AI system accountability, justice, and openness. This requires eliminating biases, guaranteeing the confidentiality and security of data, and establishing rules for the development and application of AI models [38].

AI and Emerging Technologies Integration

The future of AI in data recovery and analysis will undoubtedly include integration with other cutting-edge technologies. This includes integrating AI with blockchain, quantum computing, IoT, and augmented reality (AR) to enable more complex and thorough statistics recovery [38].

CONCLUSION

Using AI, information restoration, and record assessment have lastly emerged as a revolutionary and promising topic. The effectiveness and insights derived from the processes of fact restoration and evaluation have been demonstrated to be improved by AI approaches. CNNs, RNNs, GANs, and other AI techniques have all been discussed in this chapter, along with their applications to the recovery and analysis of statistical data. In image and signal processing, AI techniques and CNNs have proven effective, assisting in the recovery of priceless information from a range of data. On the other hand, RNNs are great at assessing sequential information and can support the discovery of styles and historical trends. The ability of GANs to generate synthetic data that can be used to improve both existing datasets and the analysis system as a whole is promising.

We have also discussed the advantages and challenges of applying AI to information evaluation and recovery. The benefits include the potential to unearth hidden patterns and insights from huge datasets as well as improved records restoration techniques in terms of accuracy, performance, and scalability. But issues like fact privacy, moral quandaries, and the need for domain expertise force a cautious interest in the use of AI frameworks. When looking into the future, many fresh patterns and guidelines were seen. Improved data restoration techniques, sensible data analysis, real-time and streaming data analysis, integration with component computing, privacy-preserving data evaluation, automatic information instruction, integration of domain knowledge, human–AI collaboration, and the moral and responsible use of AI are a few of these. These hypothetical future instructions can enhance the field of AI in data evaluation and recovery, breaking through existing barriers and creating entirely new opportunities for knowledge extraction and judgment.

In conclusion, fusing AI methodologies with data analysis and restoration opens up new possibilities for organizations to mine their records for useful information. Decision-makers are given timely and trustworthy statistics, allowing them to make wise choices and spur innovation. To properly employ AI's capability for information retrieval and analysis, it is necessary to resolve ethical concerns, secure data privacy, and foster human–AI collaboration as the technology develops. This chapter has provided an overview of AI techniques for data recovery and evaluation, covered their advantages and disadvantages, looked at potential future directions and emerging trends, and emphasized how AI may alter data-driven decision-making techniques. By adopting and employing AI in data restoration and analysis, businesses can reveal hidden patterns, improve their knowledge of complex statistics, and produce significant effects across a range of industries.

REFERENCES

[1] Ali, Nouman, Khalid Bashir Bajwa, Robert Sablatnig, and Zahid Mehmood. "Image retrieval by addition of spatial information based on histograms of triangular regions." *Computers & Electrical Engineering* 54 (2016): 539–550.
[2] Ali, S., A. Rauf, N. Islam, H. Farman, and S. Khan. "User profiling: a privacy issue in online public network." *Sindh University Research Journal-SURJ (Science Series)* 49, no. 1 (2017).

[3] Allahyari, Mehdi, Seyedamin Pouriyeh, Mehdi Assefi, Saied Safaei, Elizabeth D. Trippe, Juan B. Gutierrez, and Krys Kochut. "A brief survey of text mining: Classification, clustering and extraction techniques." *arXiv preprint arXiv:1707.02919* (2017).

[4] Amos, Brandon, Bartosz Ludwiczuk, and Mahadev Satyanarayanan. "Openface: A general-purpose face recognition library with mobile applications." *CMU School of Computer Science* 6, no. 2 (2016): 20.

[5] Bahrami, Mehdi, Mukesh Singhal, and Zixuan Zhuang. "A cloud-based web crawler architecture." In *2015 18th International Conference on Intelligence in Next Generation Networks*, pp. 216–223. IEEE, 2015.

[6] Balduzzi, Marco, Christian Platzer, Thorsten Holz, Engin Kirda, Davide Balzarotti, and Christopher Kruegel. "Abusing social networks for automated user profiling." In *International Workshop on Recent Advances in Intrusion Detection*, pp. 422–441. Springer, Berlin, Heidelberg, 2010.

[7] Barbosa, Luciano, and Juliana Freire. "Siphoning hidden-web data through keyword-based interfaces." *Journal of Information and Data Management* 1, no. 1 (2010): 133–133.

[8] Dalal, Navneet, and Bill Triggs. "Histograms of oriented gradients for human detection." In *2005 IEEE Computer Society Conference on Computer Vision and Pattern Recognition (CVPR'05)*, vol. 1, pp. 886–893. IEEE, 2005.

[9] Dang, Nhan Cach, Fernando De la Prieta, Juan Manuel Corchado, and María N. Moreno. "Framework for retrieving relevant contents related to fashion from online social network data." In *International Conference on Practical Applications of Agents and Multi-Agent Systems*, pp. 335–347. Springer, Cham, 2016.

[10] Davoodi, Elnaz, Mohsen Afsharchi, and Keivan Kianmehr. "A social network-based approach to expert recommendation system." In *International Conference on Hybrid Artificial Intelligence Systems*, pp. 91–102. Springer, Berlin, Heidelberg, 2012.

[11] Drucker, Peter. *Innovation and entrepreneurship*. Routledge, 2014.

[12] Falahrastegar, Marjan, Hamed Haddadi, Steve Uhlig, and Richard Mortier. "Tracking personal identifiers across the web." In *International Conference on Passive and Active Network Measurement*, pp. 30–41. Springer, Cham, 2016.

[13] Jayaram, Dureen, Ajay K. Manrai, and Lalita A. Manrai. "Effective use of marketing technology in Eastern Europe: Web analytics, social media, customer analytics, digital campaigns and mobile applications." *Journal of Economics, Finance and Administrative Science* 20, no. 39 (2015): 118–132.

[14] Jose, Benymol, and Sajimon Abraham. "Exploring the merits of nosql: A study based on mongodb." In *2017 International Conference on Networks & Advances in Computational Technologies (NetACT)*, pp. 266–271. IEEE, 2017.

[15] Kandias, Miltiadis, Lilian Mitrou, Vasilis Stavrou, and Dimitris Gritzalis. "Profiling online social networks users: an omniopticon tool." *International Journal of Social Network Mining* 2, no. 4 (2017): 293–313.

[16] Pla Karidi, Danae, Yannis Stavrakas, and Yannis Vassiliou. "Tweet and followee personalized recommendations based on knowledge graphs." *Journal of Ambient Intelligence and Humanized Computing* 9, no. 6 (2018): 2035–2049.

[17] Kasar, Manisha M., Debnath Bhattacharyya, and T. H. Kim. "Face recognition using neural network: a review." *International Journal of Security and Its Applications* 10, no. 3 (2016): 81–100.

[18] Kazemi, Vahid, and Josephine Sullivan. "One millisecond face alignment with an ensemble of regression trees." In *Proceedings of the IEEE Conference on Computer Vision and Pattern Recognition*, pp. 1867–1874. 2014.

[19] Liyew, Mr Binyam Tesfahun. "Applying a deep learning convolutional neural network (CNN) approach for building a face recognition system: a review." *Journal of Emerging Technological Innovation Research* 4, no. 12 (2017): 1104–1110.

[20] Marx, Matthew. "The extension and customization of Maltego data mining environment into anti-phishing system." *South Africa* (2014).

[21] Moreno, Antonio, and Teófilo Redondo. "Text analytics: the convergence of big data and artificial intelligence." *IJIMAI* 3, no. 6 (2016): 57–64.

[22] Mori, Katsuhiko, Masakazu Matsugu, and Takashi Suzuki. "Face recognition using SVM fed with intermediate output of CNN for face detection." In *MVA*, pp. 410–413. 2005.

[23] Nguyen, Thu-Hien Thi, Duy-Tai Dinh, Songsak Sriboonchitta, and Van-Nam Huynh. "A method for k-means-like clustering of categorical data." *Journal of Ambient Intelligence and Humanized Computing* (2019): 1–11.

[24] Chuang, Hsiu-Min, Chia-Hui Chang, and Ting-Yao Kao. "Effective web crawling for Chinese addresses and associated information." In *International Conference on Electronic Commerce and Web Technologies*, pp. 13–25. Springer, Cham, 2014.

[25] Perisetla, Kartik Kumar. "Mutual exclusion principle for multithreaded web crawlers." *Edit Preface* 3, no. 9 (2012).

[26] Perkins, Jacob. *Python text processing with NLTK 2.0 cookbook*. PACKT Publishing, 2010.

[27] Ramos, Juan. "Using tf-idf to determine word relevance in document queries." In *Proceedings of the First Instructional Conference on Machine Learning*, 242, no. 1, pp. 29–48. 2003.

[28] Rivas, Alberto, Lucía Martín, Inés Sittón, Pablo Chamoso, Javier J. Martín-Limorti, Javier Prieto, and Alfonso González-Briones. "Semantic analysis system for Industry 4.0." In *International Conference on Knowledge Management in Organizations*, pp. 537–548. Springer, Cham, 2018.

[29] Roy, Dwaipayan, Debasis Ganguly, Mandar Mitra, and Gareth JF Jones. "Representing documents and queries as sets of word embedded vectors for information retrieval." *arXiv preprint arXiv:1606.07869* (2016).

[30] Shah, Jamal Hussain, Muhammad Sharif, Mussarat Yasmin, and Steven Lawrence Fernandes. "Facial expressions classification and false label reduction using LDA and threefold SVM." *Pattern Recognition Letters* 139 (2020): 166–173.

[31] Singh, Vivek Kumar, Nisha Tiwari, and Shekhar Garg. "Document clustering using k-means, heuristic k-means and fuzzy c-means." In *2011 International Conference on Computational Intelligence and Communication Networks*, pp. 297–301. IEEE, 2011.

[32] Soentpiet, Rosanna. *Advances in kernel methods: support vector learning.* MIT Press, 1999.

[33] Spiekermann, Sarah, Alessandro Acquisti, Rainer Böhme, and Kai-Lung Hui. "The challenges of personal data markets and privacy." *Electronic Markets* 25, no. 2 (2015): 161–167.

[34] Sun, Shengtao, Jibing Gong, Albert Y. Zomaya, and Aizhi Wu. "A distributed incremental information acquisition model for large-scale text data." *Cluster Computing* 22, no. 1 (2019): 2383–2394.

[35] Vasanthakumar, G. U., P. Deepa Shenoy, and K. R. Venugopal. "Ptib: profiling top influential blogger in online social networks." *International Journal of Information Processing* 10, no. 1 (2016): 77–91.

[36] VenkateswarLal, Pallavaram, Gnaneswarar Rao Nitta, and Ande Prasad. "Ensemble of texture and shape descriptors using support vector machine classification for face recognition." *Journal of Ambient Intelligence and Humanized Computing* (2019): 1–8.

[37] Zhao, Xu, Wenju Zhang, Weijun He, and Chuanchao Huang. "Research on customer purchase behaviors in online take-out platforms based on semantic fuzziness and deep web crawler." *Journal of Ambient Intelligence and Humanized Computing* 11, no. 8 (2020): 3371–3385.

[38] Singh, Anubhav, Kavita Saini, Varad Nagar, Vinay Aseri, Mahipal Singh Sankhla, Pritam P. Pandit, and Rushikesh L. Chopade. "Artificial intelligence on edge devices." In Pethuru Raj, Kavita Saini, and Chellammal Surianarayanan (Eds.), *Edge/fog computing paradigm: the concept platforms and applications*, pp. 437–484. Elsevier, 2022.

11

Artificial Intelligence in Forensic Anthropology and Odontology

Abraham Johnson

INTRODUCTION

Forensic science is a diverse discipline that brings together forensic scientists and investigators, research scientists and the criminal justice system. It is referred to as criminalistics wherein the knowledge of science is applied to the enforcement of laws (Morgan, 2017). It is an essential component of any criminal investigation since it helps investigators to identify a suspect in a crime and precisely determine how and when the crime occurred. Forensic science is a vast discipline with six major branches: forensic anthropology, forensic engineering, forensic odontology, forensic pathology, forensic entomology, and toxicology (Morgan, 2017).

Forensic Anthropology

Forensic anthropology is a subdomain of physical anthropology that involves the study of applying skeletal analysis and techniques for solving criminal cases. It deals with the examination of the remains of deceased persons to determine their identity and the cause of death. The routine scope of forensic anthropology is the identification of badly decomposed, skeletonised or unidentified human remains. A forensic anthropologist works with enforcement agencies to create a profile of unidentified human remains, which involves age, gender, ancestry, time since death, stature and an assessment of any trauma found on the bones (Ubelaker, 2018). Forensic anthropologists are highly skilled at analysing bones (hard tissues) as they have specialised knowledge about buried remains. Forensic anthropology centres the assessment of every aspect of human remains from the medico legal perspective for the purpose of the establishment of identity and the cause of death with other circumstances that are associated with the event. Forensic anthropologists collaborate with forensic odontologists and forensic pathologists to authenticate and investigate human remains in prehistoric and historic times (Wescott, 2018).

In the practice of forensic anthropology, quite often forensic anthropologists receive skeletal remains or other body parts in a highly fragmented and disintegrated state. It is quite difficult to work out whether the bone remains belong to humans or other animals as they look similar, such as in the case of subadults. Initially, to assess the individuality, skeletal parts are checked to see whether they belong to the same individual or not based on criteria such as joint articulation, fracture edges, muscle size and attachments, and appearance (Ubelaker, 2018). Additionally, molecular polymorphisms are conducted in special cases and for confirming results and cross-checking. Skeletal muscles are also examined for any signs of disease that might have affected the morphology and growth of the bones that could be used for the morphological diagnosis of age and sex. Forensic anthropologists employ a two-step procedure for identifying individuals. Initially, they evaluate general characteristics such as height, body build, age, and gender to narrow down potential matches. Subsequently, they ascertain the person's ancestry, offering valuable clues for legal authorities to concentrate their search. These steps aid in streamlining the investigative process, enhancing efficiency in locating and identifying individuals based on distinct characteristics and background information (Wescott, 2018).

Fragmented or altered materials may confuse forensic anthropologists. Detailed knowledge of the skeletal anatomy of humans and its supplementary collection helps in the rejection of non-human remains. Specific tests are performed on fragmented materials, such as stereomicroscopic analysis of the surface and of thin sections to enable detailed microscopic study. For a DNA analysis, proteins are more resistant as compared with DNA due to many environmental factors and the detection of species-specific protein in bone samples and, hence, morphological evaluation by forensic anthropologists is important (Ubelaker & Wu, 2020).

Many traditional methods are employed in the field of forensic anthropology such as molecular analysis, commingling analysis, facial imaging and biomechanics of bone trauma. Techniques for measuring DNA variation extracted from tooth and bone fragments have shifted from restriction fragment length polymorphism (RFLP) to short tandem repeat (STR) derived from human remains. RFLP analysis uses radiolabelled human-specific probes to discover polymorphisms in the variable number of tandem repeats (VNTR) within the human genome in specific regions (Ubelaker & Wu, 2020). The most prevalent forensic markers are STRs, which can be found in low-quality DNA templates and fragmented DNA samples. These are polymorphic in nature, which means that the number of times the tandemly repeated DNA sequences are replicated changes between individuals, which aids in distinguishing between closely related individuals (Ubelaker & Wu, 2020).

Another technique, commingling analysis, is also used for the analysis and interpretation of remains and obtaining data. Secondary human deposit remains or samples that have been subjected to sustained disruption result in the loss of normal bone articulation patterns (Palmiotto, Brown & LeGarde, 2019). When multiple individuals are concerned, commingling analysis presents challenges with the determination of the number of persons and the assembling of individuals for identification, analysis and return to the families. Commingling concerns have developed in traditional procedures, which require sorting by bone side and type (right or left), bone size, age of death, bone maturation, gender and pathological diseases. Taphonomic markers may be useful in the case of particular skeletal assemblages. Commingling analysis addresses the issue of bone morphology associated with humans. Can a robust femur, for example, be associated to a robust humerus representing the same individual as resolved by this technique? Computerised tools and new databases have proved that various bones can be linked to the same person (Palmiotto, Brown & LeGarde, 2019).

Biomechanics of bone trauma is one of the primary functions of anthropological analysis. Anthropologists must distinguish skeletal abnormalities caused by peri-mortem trauma from those caused by ante-mortem injury, post-mortem or developmental traits, and taphonomic variables. Biomechanical factors are assessed which play a key role in such interpretations. Knowledge of biomechanical principles explains fracture patterns and other modifications caused by peri-mortem trauma. Analysis of biomechanics of bone injuries is difficult for forensic anthropologists since it requires a deeper understanding of forensic principles as well as experimental work aimed at enhancing interpretations (Ubelaker, 2018).

Decomposition research is another form of analysis in forensic anthropology that is related to decomposition research. The process and variations in hard tissue alteration and soft tissue decomposition have been revealed greatly by the experiments that involve non-human animals and humans (Wescott, 2018). These investigations demonstrated that numerous factors influence the timing and type of the breakdown process. Location and temperature, such as aquatic, in-ground and surface temperatures, are important elements, as are moisture, soil conditions, body condition, body composition, the existence of enclosures or clothes and any other factors such as funerary treatment. Time since death (interval of post-mortem) and post-mortem events related with the criminal behaviour are required (Wescott, 2018).

Forensic anthropology practice also encompasses facial image analysis that supports investigations dealing with living individuals. This includes the identification of living individuals involved in immigration problems, robbery, human trafficking, theft or burglary, reported by occasional witnesses or shown by surveillance cameras. Forensic anthropologists deal with challenges linked to facial imaging in craniofacial photographic superimposition, facial approximation, and interpretations of surveillance camera images. The method of determining an individual's living facial image from evidence obtained from the recovered skull is referred to as facial approximation. It is used to solicit information from the public in cases of missing persons in order to aid in their identification (Baryah, Krishan & Kanchan, 2019). Craniofacial photographic superimposition is the comparison of a missing person's facial image with a recovered skull. This imaging approach is primarily employed to rule out cases where images of a missing individual, presumed to be represented by the found remains, are available.

One of the greatest challenges faced by forensic anthropologists is that they have to keep themselves updated with the demographic structure of the populations with which they deal, as the forensic cases and samples are drawn from the population.

Forensic Odontology

Forensic odontology is the examination, handling and evaluation of the dental evidence that has been obtained from criminal justice cases (Manica & Forgie, 2017). This field of forensic sciences uses the dentist's skill in the personal identification of an individual in cases of sexual assault, mass calamity and so on. In other words, forensic odontology ensures the accuracy of dental records and offers necessary information to assist legal authorities in recognising malpractice, carelessness, abuse or fraud, and in identifying individuals. The evidence is gathered from teeth to determine the age and owner of the teeth. Dental records are gathered that identify the individual or offer the necessary information for authorities to establish case identification (Manica & Forgie, 2017).

Forensic odontologists take photographs by attending autopsies, making cranial measurements, and taking X-rays and dental impressions from the remains. They determine the source of bite marks in case of assault or suspected abuse, estimate the age of the skeletal remains and identify individuals who are not identified through fingerprints, facial recognition or by other means. Forensic odontologists can determine species, as evidence is obtained from crime scenes in the forms of mandible pieces or a single tooth of a few millimetres. Species are also determined using dental tissues because dentinal fluids contain unique information that may be compared and analysed using counter current electrophoresis and artificial antisera (Rathod et al., 2017).

DNA analysis is performed in forensic dentistry on biofluids such as blood, hair roots, sperm, teeth, bone, tissue and saliva. Teeth are a good source for forensic DNA analysis as they are the only sample in which DNA is available in fragmented forms and have a unique location and composition adding protection to the DNA. As teeth are seated in the jawbone, they are insulated from the degradation that usually occurs in bones (Corradi et al., 2017).

DNA fragmentation occurs in post-mortem degraded tissue due to bacterial and autolytic enzymes; nonetheless, the sequence information in the DNA fragment remains intact. As a result, the information from the sample in the decomposed body is not fully lost. Furthermore, unclotted blood in a fresh cadaver could be a useful source of DNA. First, the specimen is frozen and kept in a cool environment. Desiccation or airdrying could be used for storing the bloodstains and bone. For PCR-DNA testing, the tissue is stored in a formalin solution. Second, for the collection of the specimen, forensic dentists are very careful about contamination and, thus, use pristine equipment and gloves (Chaudhary et al., 2020). Fresh specimens are collected using incisional biopsy. When there is little information regarding the ante-mortem, specimens are gathered from the children and spouse for DNA testing as a reference sample. As previously stated, saliva and teeth are good sources of DNA. Saliva is a source of DNA because it contains sloughed epithelial cells from the inner surface of the lip and oral mucosa. Enzymes found on teeth and in saliva, such as *Streptococcus mutans* and *Streptococcus salivarius,* are used in PCR technology because the DNA sequence in streptococcus provides good evidence for the identification of bacterial composition obtained from bite marks and could be matched with the teeth that are solely responsible (Chaudhary et al., 2020).

Similarly, because teeth can endure alterations, they are a substantial source of DNA, much better than skeleton bones. DNA is found in the odontoblastic process, vascular pulp, cellular cementum and accessory canals in forensic odontology. Dental pulp is an excellent source of DNA analysis as well as blood group testing. The presence of ABO blood group-ing antigens in hard and soft tissues allows for the detection of blood types in highly degraded remains. DNA extracted from teeth not only serves as a foundation for primary identification, but also as a reference sample related to other tissue components (Shanbhag, 2017).

Dental ageing, which estimates age using dental data, is divided into two categories: developmental changes and degenerative changes. The changes that have occurred in human dentition during growth in the oral cavity are referred to as developmental alterations (Marroquin et al., 2017). Degenerative alterations are those that occur after teeth have erupted and begin to wear down. To estimate age based on developmental changes, each tooth is rated according to developmental stage, and scores are then assigned that are compared with values corresponding to the specific age. For assessing the age of an unknown individual in case of dental eruption, post-mortem radiographs are compared with eruption standards. Third molar eruption is also measured using radiographs. Length of tooth is also measured. This is known as dental measurement, which is an alternative to qualitative assessment. For measuring degenerative changes, volume of pulp cavity is used because it reduces secondary dentine deposition due to ageing (Marroquin et al., 2017). In forensic odontology, age estimation is an important aspect as human dentition has a developmental sequence which is predictable and reliable.

Sex determination is a vital subdivision of forensic odontology wherein unknown individuals are identified in scenarios of bomb explosion or natu-ral disasters. It is determined by four methods (Bansod & Pisulkar, 2021): first, craniofacial dimension and morphology in which the morphology of the mandible, skull and its patterns are taken into consideration; second, gender variations in tooth dimensions, measured by buccolingual and mesiodistal dimensions, which are the most reliable and simple approach, and these dimensions are greater in males than in females; third, tooth morphology wherein distal accessory ridges present in canines are more prominent in males than in females as females have a smaller number of cusps in the distal or distal buccal cavity (mandibular first molar). Finally, DNA analysis for sex determination can be acquired up to four weeks after death by analysing the X and Y chromosomes (Bansod & Pisulkar, 2021).

Bite mark is a physical alteration on a medium through teeth contact as in some criminal cases wherein the victim or suspect has left teeth marks on objects or on another person (Nagi et al., 2019). The outside edge of arches with abrasion and/or laceration indicates the shape, size and arrangement of occlusal or incisal surface characteristics in teeth. In the case of aggressive bite marks, the soft tissues are drawn into the mouth, resulting in representations of the incisal and palatal tooth surfaces. In the wound's centre, bites also show tissue laceration and petechial haemorrhage. In the case of less aggressive bites, skin is not completely penetrated and oval marks may be seen on the anterior teeth. Images are taken if the bite marks are found on a dead person using standardised techniques. Good bite mark impressions are created on objects, and swabs taken from them may identify the assailant's blood group through DNA analysis (Nagi et al., 2019).

Identification of unknown individuals based on lip traces or cheiloscopy is also a part of investigation in forensic odontology. Wrinkle pattern in lip print is unique and varies from one individual to another as do fingerprints. Lip prints are distinctive grooves and wrinkles on the labial mucosa that can be used to identify unknown individuals since they are consistent throughout life (Nalliapan et al., 2018). Lip grooves are classified into straight, curved, angled and sine-shaped lines. Palatal rugoscopy in forensic odontology is the study of palatal rugae and its uniqueness provides a reliable source of identification. These rugae are asymmetric, irregular ridges of mucous membrane that extend laterally from the incisive papilla and the median palatal raphe's anterior part. Palatal rugae are well protected by the cheeks, lips and tongue and are also immune from trauma as they do not undergo change with age and they reappear after surgical procedures or trauma. It has been postulated that palatal rugae could be used for soft-tissue oral casts and impressions in forensic identification (Gupta & Kaur, 2021).

ARTIFICIAL INTELLIGENCE

Artificial intelligence (AI) encompasses emerging technologies that influence every sphere of life including clinical dentistry. AI in clinical dentistry assists practitioners by simplifying intricate processes and offering predictable outcomes while providing high-quality patient care. Artificial Neural Networks (ANNs) have immense applications in forensic sciences that help to reveal information from the crime scene so that clear judgments can be made. This means the guilty are charged with the crime and criminal investigation becomes smoother, faster and error-free. AI is providing new algorithms for narrative-based communication and supporting augmentation with statistical evidence that is building justice and probabilistic reasoning. AI is providing useful tools for dealing with big datasets and assisting forensic specialists in the field of forensic anthropology, forensic odontology and also in the field of forensic medicine, as illustrated in the subsequent subsections.

Forensic Anthropology and AI

Three-dimensional convolutional neural networks (3D CNNs) are powerful in deep learning recognition and image processing for descriptive and generative applications. 3D CNN is employed in forensic anthropology in five ways: biological age estimation, sex determination, 3D cephalometric landmark annotation, face soft-tissue estimation from the skull, and growth vector prediction.

In a study, deep CNN was used for age estimation using orthopantomography images obtained from archaeological skull remains. The skulls were scanned using X-ray scanners, and the images obtained were utilised as a testing dataset, with 73 per cent accuracy in classifying the orthopantomography images. Transfer learning method in deep learning was used, which utilised pre-trained layer weights on the gigantic ImageNet dataset. The main reason for using layer weights was that these weights determine the strength of the connections between neurons and play a crucial role in the network's ability to learn from data obtained from a general-purpose dataset, which is divided into three parts: train set, test set and validation set. Train set trains the network, validation set is used during training and test datasets evaluate the model at each step, and this neural net determines the age using panoramic images obtained from dental x-rays (Banjšak, Milošević & Subašić, 2020).

AI techniques are also used for human identification using biomedical images. This is important in medico-legal contexts based on forensic anthropology (FA). Forensic facial reconstruction is one of the most contentious processes in the field of FA, in which the face of a person whose identity is unknown is reconstructed from his or her skeletal remains using CT (computed tomography) images as training sets. Facial approximation software with a craniofacial template containing skull, soft tissue and face information acquired from a head database is employed. An acceptable geometric transformation that is similar to the craniofacial template is applied to the unknown skull, and then the template face is deformed onto the predicted face using information from the unknown skull and database, and finally, hairiness and skin texture are added. A 3D generative model is also used for the reconstruction process using a CT scan of the head as a database for a given skull. Active Shape Models are associated with 3D points, having landmark detection and reconstruction (Mesejo et al., 2020).

Blockchain technology provides a safe, reliable and holistic system with a forensic interface in the electronic health record (EHR) that professionals may access for the purpose of identifying human remains and retrieving data from compatible missing persons. The software component employs input and output gateways, as well as data mining blocks, for the human identification process, which is accessed by forensic professionals. A blockchain-based architecture for patient EHRs linked with an interoperable and structured design would aid in the identification of unknown humans. Through a lawful blockchain, forensic chains will assist forensic experts in reviewing post-mortem and ante-mortem data of missing persons and unidentifiable human remains (Nuzzolese, 2020).

Machine learning algorithms such as support vector machines (SVMs), ANNs and penalised multinomial logistic regression (pMLR) help in the estimation of skeletal sex or ancestry estimation. SVMs are algorithms that generate hyperplanes which separate data into categories based on classification problems. ANNs comprise interconnected neurons that are organised into layers and have a hidden layer in between outer and inner layers. Statistical analyses were then carried out using two packages in R. The inputs written as ancestry or sex estimation were run at constant seed value having main output as portion p having correct classification (Nikita & Nikitas, 2020).

Deep learning ANN helps in the sex determination of skeletal remains. Using CT scans, a neural network (NN) was trained onto those unseen images obtained from the skulls and it was found that ANN showed 95 per cent accuracy for sex determination. Pre-existing CNN known as GoogLeNet was utilised for the optimisation of image classification. Modification of the NN for a new task is called transfer learning and MATLAB has in-built NNs that classify an input image into many object categories, and in this way it is classified as male or female. For GoogLeNet neural network, skull images were resized and the dataset was divided into testing and training subsets. After training, NN was evaluated and sex was determined for the skull documented on medical record (Bewes et al., 2019).

Forensic Odontology and AI

In forensic odontology, AI is used for multiple applications, and identification of bite marks, prediction of mandibular morphology, gender and age estimation are widely studied. CNNs and ANNs, along with Bayesian convolutional neural networks (BCNNs), are also designed for the assessment of digital photographs, panoramic radiographs and lateral cephalometric radiographs. AI-based models are used for the prediction of mandibular morphology having craniomaxillary variables on the radiographs using ANN and SVM (Khanagar et al., 2021a).

AI improves the image interpretation in the field of dental radiology, and in 2D radiographs digital radiographs consist of up to thousands of pixels representing different brightness levels within the grid. This pixel exhibits radiopacity, which is associated with a greater density structure or metal (Chen, Stanley & Att, 2020). AI programs "learn" to analyse digital images such as digital radiographs, which can be calculated utilising algorithms via input layers, output layers and hidden layers for caries detection. The clinical expert analyses a large number of dental radiographs and

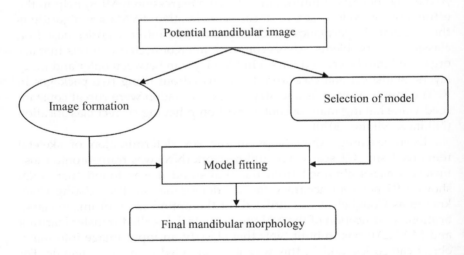

Figure 11.1 Mandibular morphology prediction using CNN (AI).

chooses a certain number as a training set. The skilled doctor manually annotates anatomical landmarks, while the software engineer uses these training sets and architects' learning models to teach AI how to forecast the remaining information as an adaptive set. Both software engineers and clinicians verify the accuracy of adapting sets. Coordination between the AI trainers expands the software capacity (Chen, Stanley & Att, 2020).

ANNs and CNNs in AI models are also being used in clinical dentistry for the diagnosis and detection of dental caries, apical lesions, vertical root fractures, prediction of orthodontic extractions, treatments, gender and age determination, etc. AI-based models are also used for the diagnosis of proximal dental caries, and to decide on extractions prior to treatment and on permanent tooth extraction. Other examples include the use of various techniques in dental applications, such as CNNs for the staging of lower third molars and the detection of oral squamous cell carcinoma, ANNs for studying mandibular morphology and aiding in surgery for determining extractions, deep-CNN based systems for the detection of periodontal bone loss, as well as AI-based models for root caries prediction, gender determination, and skeletal diagnostic systems (Khanagar et al., 2021b).

In a study conducted by Yoon et al. (2018) interproximal caries were identified using a series of bitewing radiographs. Deep learning technology has also been applied to the technology of image analysis. A pre-trained deep learning network (GoogLeNet Inception v3) was employed for the diagnosis of dental caries, with 88 per cent, 89 per cent and 82 per cent accuracy in identifying dental caries in molars and premolars, and between molars and premolars, respectively, by Lee et al. (2018). In the field of orthodontics, decision-making is assisted using AI as a clinical decision support system (CDSS) established through the Bayesian network model. The Artificial Neural Network (ANN) was developed for the diagnosis of the extraction process in orthodontic patients, with a 93 per cent success rate; however, it exhibited a lower success rate in terms of thorough examination of the extraction patterns (Thanathornwong, 2018). A study conducted by Jung and Kim (2016) showed that before and after orthodontic treatments, facial photos could be investigated using convolutional NN models (pre-trained). Dental Monitoring is an AI-based monitoring system in orthodontics that allows patients to scan their teeth using a unique tool on their phones, and the scans obtained may be analysed and monitored by orthodontists to check treatment status (Patcas et al., 2019). Genetic algorithms are used to optimise dental implant systems, reducing mechanical fracture and imparting long-term strength to the implant (Tandon, Rajawat & Banerjee, 2020). A genetic algorithm combined with a back propagation neural network aids in improving tooth colour matching, which is regarded as one of the most difficult tasks in the field of prosthodontic dentistry. Dental and oral diseases are quite common, affecting every age, however, they are much ignored. In a study conducted by Ambara, Putra and Rusjayanthi (2017), a time-efficient and cost-effective fuzzy logic-based expert system was built that provides advice without the use of any tools, thus decreasing patient worry. Herrera et al. (2010) built a fuzzy logic-based system that predicted the change in colour following tooth bleaching based on the baseline chrome values of the tooth. This system provides a set of principles that correspond to pre-bleaching teeth shades from the commercial shade guide, Vita.

Forensic Medicine and AI

The assessment of time since death utilises AI during forensic examination by using blood markers such as lipid, cholesterol, proteins and pH levels, which are supplied to a gadget that, after examining the information, estimates time of death. The cause of death and the prediction of post-mortem interval are also determined using machine learning (Pathak & Narang, 2021). 3D-CNNs are also used for image recognition and processing utilising deep learning methods.

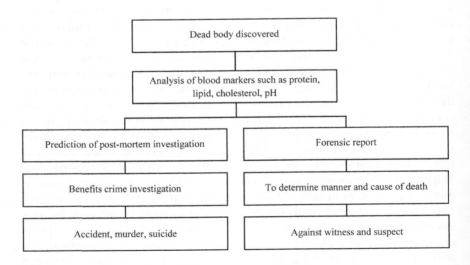

Figure 11.2   Application of AI in forensic science.

Thurzo et al. (2021) did research to identify forensic sex and age determination using machine learning models that resemble neurons in the brain and can learn from experiences to tackle complex problems. Post-mortem skeletal remains and living people are studied for age and sex determination in order to identify victims and suspects, determine criminal culpability or identify individuals who lack sufficient legal paperwork. To teach AI to determine an individual's gender or age, MRI images, X-rays, or CT scans of the skull or bones are investigated. A whole 3D CT scan image can be utilised to estimate a person's approximate age, with the current state of the art functioning as the backbone being a regression model represented by a 3D deep neural network. Because sex classification from human remains is a difficult task in the field of forensic and physical anthropology, 3D Deep Neural Networks are being used. The deep learning approach is eliminating human bias and time consumption leading to sex determination using reliable software applications. The computation is the same as in the age estimation approach; however, the final output from the NN is divided into two classes of gender. The SoftMax activation function for NN computation uses fully connected and convolutional blocks to acquire class probabilities (Thurzo et al., 2021).

The estimation of wound age is now making progress in forensic medicine by using AI models. Multiple datasets are being used in combination with AI algorithms which are based on transcriptomics data. Omics technologies, which include mass data creation in the dimensions of protein measurement, gene expression, metabolite levels and microbial interrelationships have revolutionised forensic medical research. Mathematical tools have been established using AI algorithms for wound age estimation based on quantitative analysis of time-related data of gene expression from transcriptomes. In a study be Ren et al. (2020), after regular standardisation and analysis using bioinformatics, second-generation sequencing was employed, and time-related analysis utilising maSigPro and STEM integrated the data and gave time-related genes. Machine learning was used to pick features, and the top gene indicators were found. The Python platform was then utilised to construct machine learning models for the expression level of gene indicators, which were then compared and analysed for the accuracy of wound age assessment using mathematical models in machine learning. SVM and logistic regression (LR) showed better results in the estimation of wound age, with Random Forest (RF) having higher stability, accuracy and generalisability among the five modules in machine learning used in the study (Ren et al., 2020).

CHALLENGES AND FUTURE PROSPECTS

Although much progress has been made in the field of forensics, this field is still motivated by problems and issues discovered during investigations at crime scenes or other locations. Typically, the unique data given in forensic investigations necessitates the best scientific approach, and certain concerns are not always appropriately addressed by existing tools and approaches. Such cases in forensic anthropology and odontology necessitate unique solutions based on thorough and specialised investigation. Although AI has numerous applications in forensic disciplines such as odontology, anthropology and medicine, the algorithm must be more complete in order to solve forensic challenges. AI programs must be designed in partnership with expert engineers and doctors to ensure appropriate interpretation, as misinterpretation may result in misconduct. The use of AI in forensics is still in its early stages and requires significant improvement. Machine learning models require training and the clinicians need to be cautious and aware while interpreting data using AI to minimise its potential risks. In deep learning technology, additional future studies are required for better analysis of the tools. Although AI is being applied in the field of forensic odontology suggesting treatment plans, such procedures are still traditional and require further research. Most importantly, it is too early for a complete application of AI in forensic sciences as development in this field is still in its infancy.

CONCLUSION

It is evident that AI systems have revolutionised the fields of forensic anthropology and forensic odontology, including forensic medicine, in the last few years. AI-driven automated systems have been observed to have performed well in many scenarios. AI-based models have provided tremendous value to the profession by improving diagnosis accuracy, predicting treatment prognosis, and improving clinical decision-making so that doctors may provide the best quality of care to patients under their care provision. The use of AI models such as CNN, BCNN and ANN has demonstrated, as in the documented studies, age and sex determination from skeletons collected from unknown human remains, and facial reconstruction in forensic anthropology. Similarly, AI has made inroads into the fields of forensic dentistry and forensic medicine, where it can estimate a person's age using panoramic radiographs, digital pictures and lateral cephalometric radiographs. AI-based algorithms are also used for the prediction of mandibular morphology with 3D Deep Neural Networks for image recognition and processing utilising deep learning methods in forensic examinations. Although AI is a helpful tool for clinicians in the early diagnosis and treatment of diseases, many domains in dentistry and anthropology, such as oral pathology, pedodontics and so on, have yet to develop and apply AI-based technology.

REFERENCES

Ambara, B., Putra, D., & Rusjayanthi, D. (2017). Fuzzy expert system of dental and oral disease with certainty factor. *International Journal of Computer Science Issues (IJCSI)*, *14*(3), 22. https://translateyar.ir/wp-content/uploads/2019/12/Fuzzy-Expert-System-of-Dental-and-Oral-Disease-with-Certainty.pdf

Banjšak, L., Milošević, D., & Subašić, M. (2020). Implementation of artificial intelligence in chronological age estimation from orthopantomographic X-ray images of archaeological skull remains. *Bulletin of the International Association for Paleodontology*, *14*(2), 122–129. https://hrcak.srce.hr/file/361703

Bansod, A. V., & Pisulkar, S. K. (2021). Artificial intelligence & its contemporary applications in dentistry. *Turkish Journal of Computer and Mathematics Education* (TURCOMAT), *12*(6), 4192–4196. https://www.turcomat.org/index.php/turkbilmat/article/download/8389/6565

Baryah, N., Krishan, K., & Kanchan, T. (2019). The development and status of forensic anthropology in India: A review of the literature and future directions. *Medicine, Science and the Law*, *59*(1), 61–69. https://journals.sagepub.com/doi/pdf/10.1177/0025802418824834

Bewes, J., Low, A., Morphett, A., Pate, F. D., & Henneberg, M. (2019). Artificial intelligence for sex determination of skeletal remains: Application of a deep learning artificial neural network to human skulls. *Journal of Forensic and Legal Medicine*, *62*, 40–43. https://www.academia.edu/download/64244025/Bewes%20et%20al.%202019.pdf

Chaudhary, R. B., Shylaja, M. D., Patel, A., & Patel, A. (2020). DNA in forensic odontology: New phase in dental analysis. *International Journal of Forensic Odontology*, *5*(1), 43. https://www.ijofo.org/article.asp?issn=2542-5013;year=2020;volume=5;issue=1;spage=43;epage=47;aulast=Chaudhary

Chen, Y. W., Stanley, K., & Att, W. (2020). Artificial intelligence in dentistry: Current applications and future perspectives. *Quintessence International*, *51*(3), 248–257. https://cephx.com/wp-content/uploads/2020/03/qi_2020_03_s0248.pdf

Corradi, L. M., Travassos, D. V., Coste, S. C., Moura, R. N. V. D., & Ferreira, E. F. (2017). Identifying missing people: The contribution of forensic dentistry and DNA. *Revista de Odontologia da UNESP*, *46*, 313–318. https://www.scielo.br/j/rounesp/a/cXNGyg6CZzz9HxLNKfs3zmF/?lang=en

179

Gupta, V., & Kaur, A. (2021). Palatal rugoscopy as an adjunct for sex determination in forensic odontology (Sri Ganganagar population): A cross-sectional study of 100 subjects. *Journal of Oral and Maxillofacial Pathology, 25*(3), 556. https://www.jomfp.in/article.asp?issn=0973-029X;year=2021;volume=25;issue=3; spage=556;epage=556;aulast=Gupta

Herrera, L. J., Pulgar, R., Santana, J., Cardona, J. C., Guillén, A., Rojas, I., & del Mar Pérez, M. (2010). Prediction of color change after tooth bleaching using fuzzy logic for Vita Classical shades identification. *Applied Optics, 49*(3), 422–429. https://www.academia.edu/download/56893302/Prediction_of_color_ change_after_tooth_b20180629-15045-1wiw14s.pdf

Jung, S. K., & Kim, T. W. (2016). New approach for the diagnosis of extractions with neural network machine learning. *American Journal of Orthodontics and Dentofacial Orthopedics, 149*(1), 127–133. https://www.researchgate.net/ profile/Seok-Ki-Jung/publication/287797054_New_approach_for_the_ diagnosis_of_extractions_with_neural_network_machine_learning/ links/60910e89a6fdccaebd078d10/New-approach-for-the-diagnosis-of-extractions-with-neural-network-machine-learning.pdf

Khanagar, S. B., Al-Ehaideb, A., Maganur, P. C., Vishwanathaiah, S., Patil, S., Baeshen, H. A., … & Bhandi, S. (2021a). Developments, application, and performance of artificial intelligence in dentistry – A systematic review. *Journal of Dental Sciences, 16*(1), 508–522. https://www.sciencedirect.com/science/ article/pii/S1991790220301434

Khanagar, S. B., Vishwanathaiah, S., Naik, S., Al-Kheraif, A. A., Divakar, D. D., Sarode, S. C., … & Patil, S. (2021b). Application and performance of artificial intelligence technology in forensic odontology – A systematic review. *Legal Medicine, 48*, 101826. https://www.researchgate.net/profile/Sanjeev-Khanagar/ publication/347068383_Application_and_performance_of_artificial_intel-ligence_technology_in_forensic_odontology_-_A_systematic_review/links/ 6146496ba3df59440b97e3f9/Application-and-performance-of-artificial-intelligence-technology-in-forensic-odontology-A-systematic-review.pdf

Lee, J. H., Kim, D. H., Jeong, S. N., & Choi, S. H. (2018). Detection and diagnosis of dental caries using a deep learning-based convolutional neural network algorithm. *Journal of Dentistry, 77*, 106–111. https://www.sciencedirect.com/ science/article/pii/S0300571218302252

Manica, S., & Forgie, A. (2017). Forensic dentistry now and in the future. *Dental Update, 44*(6), 522–530. https://discovery.dundee.ac.uk/ws/files/17087126/ Dent_Update_2017_44_522_530_3_.pdf

Marroquin, T. Y., Karkhanis, S., Kvaal, S. I., Vasudavan, S., Kruger, E., & Tennant, M. (2017). Age estimation in adults by dental imaging assessment systematic review. *Forensic Science International, 275*, 203–211. http://www.smilewith confidence.com.au/wp-content/uploads/2016/11/Age-estimation-in-adults-by-dental-imaging-assessment_systematic-review.pdf

Mesejo, P., Martos, R., Ibáñez, Ó., Novo, J., & Ortega, M. (2020). A survey on artificial intelligence techniques for biomedical image analysis in skeleton-based forensic human identification. *Applied Sciences, 10*(14), 4703. https://www. mdpi.com/2076-3417/10/14/4703/pdf

Morgan, R. M. (2017). Conceptualising forensic science and forensic reconstruction. Part I: A conceptual model. *Science & Justice, 57*(6), 455–459. https://www.sciencedirect.com/science/article/pii/S1355030617300813

Nagi, R., Aravinda, K., Rakesh, N., Jain, S., Kaur, N., & Mann, A. K. (2019). Digitization in forensic odontology: A paradigm shift in forensic investigations. *Journal of Forensic Dental Sciences, 11*(1), 5. https://www.ncbi.nlm.nih.gov/pmc/articles/PMC6822309/

Nalliapan, G., Ulaganathan, M., Andamuthu, Y., Thangadurai, M., Vadivel, I., & Periyasamy, T. T. (2018). Cheiloscopy: An evolving tool in forensic identification. *Journal of Indian Academy of Dental Specialist Researchers Volume, 5*(2). http://jiadsr.org/images/book-pdf/2018/JIndianAcadDentSpecRes_2018_5_2_37_255624.pdf

Nikita, E., & Nikitas, P. (2020). On the use of machine learning algorithms in forensic anthropology. *Legal Medicine, 47*, 101771. https://www.academia.edu/download/65555791/Nikita_Nikitas_2020_Legal_Med.pdf

Nuzzolese, E. (2020). Electronic health record and blockchain architecture: Forensic chain hypothesis for human identification. *Egyptian Journal of Forensic Sciences, 10*(1), 1–5. https://ejfs.springeropen.com/articles/10.1186/s41935-020-00209-z

Palmiotto, A., Brown, C. A., & LeGarde, C. B. (2019). Estimating the number of individuals in a large commingled assemblage. *Forensic Anthropology, 2*(2), 129–138. http://journals.upress.ufl.edu/fa/article/download/814/895

Patcas, R., Bernini, D. A., Volokitin, A., Agustsson, E., Rothe, R., & Timofte, R. (2019). Applying artificial intelligence to assess the impact of orthognathic treatment on facial attractiveness and estimated age. *International Journal of Oral and Maxillofacial Surgery, 48*(1), 77–83. https://www.zora.uzh.ch/id/eprint/169362/1/Patcas_et_al_Applying_artificial_intelligence_INT_J_ORAL_MAXFAC_SURG.pdf

Pathak, M., & Narang, H. (2021). Application of Artificial Intelligence in the Field of Forensic Medicine. *Medico-legal Update, 21*(4). https://www.researchgate.net/profile/Himanshi-Narang-3/publication/354424013_Application_of_Artificial_Intelligence_in_the_Field_of_Forensic_Medicine/links/6137e083cf1e892b691a22f6/Application-of-Artificial-Intelligence-in-the-Field-of-Forensic-Medicine.pdf

Rathod, V., Desai, V., Pundir, S., Dixit, S., & Chandraker, R. (2017). Role of forensic dentistry for dental practitioners: A comprehensive study. *Journal of Forensic Dental Sciences, 9*(2), 108. https://www.ncbi.nlm.nih.gov/pmc/articles/PMC5717769/

Ren, K., Li, N., Liang, X., Wang, L., Li, J., & Sun, J. (2020, October). Investigating the new orientation of wound age estimation in forensic medicine based on biological omics data combined with artificial intelligence algorithms. In *Proceedings of the 2020 Conference on Artificial Intelligence and Healthcare* (pp. 54–59). https://dl.acm.org/doi/pdf/10.1145/3433996.3434007?casa_token=rMCLmNmCnlAAAAAA:9dtMEHxFHbTzLolBCVoqdQBX0wd39X3qrP-hBvj86FKhqie94fsUy1gT7FR7MBjwiWpNfmcOklM

181

Shanbhag, V. K. L. (2017). Teeth as a Source of DNA to identify mass disaster victims. *International Journal of Forensic Odontology*, 2(1), 43. https://www.ijofo.org/article.asp?issn=2542-5013;year=2017;volume=2;issue=1;spage=43;epage=44;aulast=Shanbhag

Tandon, D., Rajawat, J., & Banerjee, M. (2020). Present and future of artificial intelligence in dentistry. *Journal of Oral Biology and Craniofacial Research*, 10(4), 391–396. https://www.ncbi.nlm.nih.gov/pmc/articles/pmc7394756/

Thanathornwong, B. (2018). Bayesian-based decision support system for assessing the needs for orthodontic treatment. *Healthcare Informatics Research*, 24(1), 22–28. https://synapse.koreamed.org/articles/1075886

Thurzo, A., Kosnáčová, H. S., Kurilová, V., Kosmeľ, S., Beňuš, R., Moravanský, N., ... & Varga, I. (2021, November). Use of Advanced Artificial Intelligence in Forensic Medicine, Forensic Anthropology and Clinical Anatomy. In *Healthcare* (Vol. 9, No. 11, p. 1545). Multidisciplinary Digital Publishing Institute. https://www.mdpi.com/2227-9032/9/11/1545/pdf

Ubelaker, D. H. (2018). A history of forensic anthropology. *American Journal of Physical Anthropology*, 165(4), 915–923. https://onlinelibrary.wiley.com/doi/pdfdirect/10.1002/ajpa.23306

Ubelaker, D. H., & Wu, Y. (2020). Fragment analysis in forensic anthropology. *Forensic Sciences Research*, 5(4), 260–265. https://www.tandfonline.com/doi/pdf/10.1080/20961790.2020.1811513

Wescott, D. J. (2018). Recent advances in forensic anthropology: decomposition research. *Forensic Sciences Research*, 3(4), 278–293. https://www.tandfonline.com/doi/pdf/10.1080/20961790.2018.1488571

Yoon, D. C., Mol, A., Benn, D. K., & Benavides, E. (2018). Digital radiographic image processing and analysis. *Dental Clinics*, 62(3), 341–359. https://www.dental.theclinics.com/article/S0011-8532(18)30016-8/abstract

INDEX

For Product Safety Concerns and Information please contact our EU
representative GPSR@taylorandfrancis.com Taylor & Francis Verlag GmbH,
Kaufingerstraße 24, 80331 München, Germany

Printed and bound by CPI Group (UK) Ltd, Croydon, CR0 4YY
08/06/2025
01897009-0006